CONSISE CLOUD COMPUTE

IT Professionals' Handbook

VIJAY

PARTRIDGE

To order additional copies of this book, contact
Partridge India
000 800 10062 62
orders.india@partridgepublishing.com

www.partridgepublishing.com/india

CONTENTS

BASIC TENETS

http://www.opengroup.org/cloud/cloud_sme/p3.htm

Cloud is basically for enhancing business functions, deliver services, efficiently, securely, increase productivity and all this with lower cost. Below listed are the value proposition, cloud delivers to an organization. High levels agility supports business with rapid time to market, that leads to increasing customer footfall, on time, creates a highly competitive environment, often leading to customers being retained and increased market share. Cloud especially, helps in start-ups and SMEs proactively that services can be delivered in timely and with high quality outputs, reduced time and cost, not without having to plan for capacity. Cloud has since its inception, cloud platforms have demonstrated the stated objectives can be met, truly, in multiple instances; outputs have been proven to deliver multi-dimensional benefits. With cloud, core business can witness tectonic shift, by moving away from traditional Capex - Capital Expenditure to Opex Operational Expenses model, which implies, companies need not spend on traditional monolithic IT equipments, subscribe to of many platforms that are in offer, and go through due process, and design host applications, at this model drastically reduces manpower and cost. Plethora of platform, software and datacenter providers offer combo offers and what a customer needs to do is, finalize the requirements, arrive at the maximum cost that can be spent, and approach any service provider, who will take care of the rest. And the best part of cloud is it reduces acquisition periods, drastically from months for hardware to weeks, software to days and to summarize, Cloud helps in, a. business staying relevant; focus on business development rather on investing time on development and design

Essentials of cloud

http://www.opengroup.org/cloud/cloud_sme/p3.htm

Because traditionally IT organizations have planned, built, and operated IT reactive mode, and traditionally and typically, business functions has to wait multiple capabilities, that are primarily drive by business requirements and traditional activities of building solution, requirement gathering needs, building services based on agreed specifications, and then operating as per defined SLAs (Service Level Agreements) was discussed, the thinking amongst IT heads was of waiting for the business to request something, gathering detailed requirements, and building the corresponding IT capabilities is performed, many times, in reactive, but what a customer needs to do is, finalize the requirements, arrive at the maximum cost that can be spent, and approach any service provider, who will take care of the rest. And the best part of cloud is it reduces the acquisition time drastically from months for hardware to weeks, software to days and to summarize, Cloud helps in, a. business staying relevant, focus on business development rather on investing time on development and design. Cloud has introduced concept of service catalog, where products and services are enlisted, and delivered by reasonable time, and in includes list of services that can be delivered immediately or on designated dates, it could be hours or days which implies that the developers need not have to submit procurement request, once subscription is confirmed, the only Acton to be taken is provision the requested instances, and which gives the users origination, can deploy the services once requested from the consumers

CONSISE CLOUD COMPUTE

http://www.opengroup.org/cloud/cloud_sme/p3.htm

Cloud computing is becoming a game changer for business of all types and size, by of. Offering scalable IT infrastructure components, enabling business of sizes, all categories like retail, finance, even aerospace, to minimize on capital IT spends, increase speed of service delivery, enhance employee productivity. Compute resources are billed, on pre-determined period, depending on actual consumption .Basic tenet of cloud is resources sharing, the primary concept, which helps in driving costs down. Service can purchased d on the fly, with subscribed resources billed on actual utilization, as is being followed in case of, power, water, with services can be to subscribe to cloud is with desktop of standard configuration, internet browser, high speed broadband connection, subscription to required service platform like AWS, MS Azure, user account with respective service provider, credit cards are accepted. Whenever user wants to develop application or deploy service, he can sign up for suitable platform, by creating user credentials, select services, viz, software, compute, database, make payments, and post confirmation, platform is for use, that can be used for any purposes, vast quantity of services, software bits, utilities, are available to chose. Cloud helps in minimizing complexities of managing resources, effectively, The cloud concept represents a shift in the consumption and delivery of IT with the goal of simplifying to manage complexity more effectively Besides represents the industrialization of delivery for IT-supported services, different models facilitates, business turn smart by way of offering durable, highly available, flexible, cost-effective access to technology and information. Users can swiftly provision resources, release with minimal management effort, or service provider interactions, which implies IT managers have more control over resources, an organization can more or fewer servers, stores, applications, or services, configure specific instances for hosting services, in order to meet needs, whoever is needed, with minimal management effort. Essential characteristics are-

- Pay per use
- On-demand self-service
- Broad network access
- Resource pooling
- Rapid elasticity
- Measured service

Cloud presents new business paradigm for resources which empowers organizations to create and use IT and business services on-demand from optimal sources to maximize utilization and cost-effectiveness, which can be within the organization or extending to multiple entities.

Service Management

Besides the security-related concerns, service management is, is a key factor, in process o evaluation, selection. Key risk assessment factors:

- What are the provider's service management principles and does the strategy integrate with SME policies and principles?
- How do Cloud service providers provide back-up and recovery services?
- Are there specific Recovery Time Objectives (RTOs) and Recovery Point Objectives (RPOs)?
- Are Service-Level Agreements (SLAs) and Service-Level Objectives (SLOs) acceptable? Maturity of Cloud services that are offered by providers
- The ability to implement Cloud solutions with existing software stacks (in-house)
- The viability of selected Cloud providers

<u>Applicable workload</u>

http://www.opengroup.org/cloud/cloud_sme/p4.htm

<u>Infrastructure</u>

- Desktops/laptops/printers
- Servers
- Storage
- Application servers
- Business continuity/disaster recovery
- Data archiving
- Data back-up
- Data center network capacity
- Security
- Training infrastructure

<u>Office applications</u>

- Email, calendar, and contacts solution
- Collaboration, sharing, and document editing service
- Communications features including presence information, instant messaging
- Audio/video calling and online meetings
- Web conferencing with application sharing, whiteboards
- Applications required to do work with office documents, spreadsheets, presentation

<u>Business services</u>

- Finance & Accounting
- Customer Relationship Management (CRM)
- Human Resource (HR) Management
- Payroll
- Project Management System

Industry vertical applications

- ERP solutions specific to the domain – for example, material, sales, stock, and production management solutions for manufacturing, point-of-sale solutions for the retail industry, etc.
- Data warehouse/data mining
- Web-hosted custom applications

Cloud computing challenges

http://www.opengroup.org/cloud/gov_snapshot/p4.htm#X_Cloud_Computing_Challeng

Challenges in cloud is galore, every component, service exposes its own, making the task of planners more difficult and as the concept as vast, challenges that will be encountered will equally be vast, and only expert teams can find solution to the issues and address. Listed below are few: Cloud has forced tectonic shift, from earlier scene of isolated dedicated IT scenarios to far more inclusive scenario, where collaboration, is the pole and all services revolve around this, also entailing, robust and cooperation among an assembled set of components and services, potentially provided by multiple internal and external cloud service providers. Distributed across multiple domains delineated by boundaries including architectural, design, geographical, cross-organizational, corporate, and governmental, a resulting in, governance aspects of a cloud topology are also more distributed. Such concentration often needs proactive and well stargazed steps to be taken to understand, delegate, and govern the associated authority, responsibility, and accountability. The success facto of such large scale distribution largely related to how well a Greenfield connections that are created to support seamless coexistence, integration, and operation of cloud computing across these boundaries capabilities and These trusted relationships are essential to establish, maintain, and verify the underlying shared policies and standards which becomes mandatory to power a seamless operation of on-premise and off-premise enterprise and cloud technology and services. Generally, a cloud service consumer or enterprise may not be aware of the physical location, of the IT infrastructure, from where services are offered, how data is stored, or how network and data security is established, besides most instances, the physical location is opaque to the consumers, the details of the hardware, make, model who is manning those. Regardless of whether data is in flight or at rest, physical location and transit between locations could potentially have an impact on the ability to meet enterprise policies and requirements, which in turn could be influenced by other spheres of governance including governmental statutes and regulations. Since these policies and requirements could vary from location to location and are established and applied by multiple entities, a critical issue for data governance, and as a result also for cloud governance, is addressing the question of how to ensure at least a minimal but sufficient level of consistency across this dramatically expanding landscape. One of major application area is automation and can drive changes in organization structure ex, recruitment of Cloud architects, security specialists. Compliance is major work area, refers to companies adherence to established regulations that govern cloud. One of them, is ability to secure data, applications, in multiple locations, compliance often means, ability of company to ensure adherence of established practices standards ex, HIPPA, A major compliance issue might location of data and ensures compliance in that particular region.

http://www.opengroup.org/cloud/wp_cloud_roi/p2.htm

Capacity utilization curve

Famed graph adopted by Amazon Web Services (shown below) describing capacity utilization as a graph has become iconic which illustrates central theme, associating cloud characteristics with utilization, Surrounding Cloud-based services enabled through an on-demand business provisioning model to meet actual usage an example graph has been shown

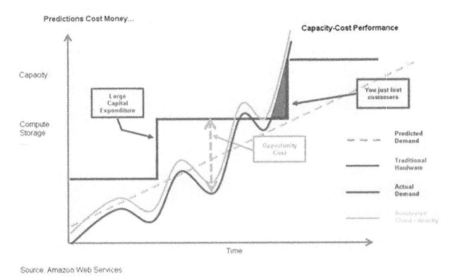

Source: Amazon Web Services

Source http://www.opengroup.org/cloud/wp_cloud_roi/p2.htm

Why usage is of concern is one of fundamental characteristic is to minimize cost impact Of over-provisioning and under-provisioning, which opens door for improving for cost, revenue, and margin advantages of business services in order to enhance revenue, and margin advantages of business services which powers rapid deployment for enhancing cost,revenue-margins, to business advantage when deploying services, with minimal entry costs, which gives opportunity to deploy services with better agility, with low entry cost, and the potential to enter and exploit new markets.

Examples to cite are:

- The Moore's Law model that establishes the concept of exponential growth in computational power but has subsequently been seen in other technology areas, including storage and network

- The technology hype cycle that established the emergence of innovation lifecycles
- The Boston Consulting Group Growth-Share Matrix that can be used to show how key industrial markets and products and services undergo transitions as the maturity lifecycles emerge, grow, and recede

Matching capacity and actual utilization on demand accelerates operational efficiency; Capacity and utilization are Key Performance Indicators (KPIs). They measure how much or how little something is being used. But is this aligned and being used to generate Return on Investment (ROI) and it is measured on below parameters

- Pricing and costing of Cloud services
- Funding approaches to Cloud services
- Return on Investment (ROI)
- Key Performance Indicators (KPIs)
- Total cost of ownership (TCO)
- Risk management
- Decisions and choices evaluation processes for Cloud service

Below describes a comparison between two models

Traditional model

- Hardware is hosted on the premises of the organization and/or manage hosted.
- Hardware and software is provisioned for peak demand.
- Service management monitoring is used to generate forecasts of demand usage and current SLA performance.
- Chargeback's and compensations are used to adjust usage and payments.
- Under-provisioning and over-provisioning of capacity can result from unforeseen demand changes.

- Business invests in ownership of assets that can be enhanced and extended through IT programs and development.
- Changes to IT involve migration and divestment/investment issues and programs

Cloud

- Hardware and/or software is hosted off-premise (public or hybrid) or on-premise as a private Cloud service.
- Services are provisioned and used based on actual demand, providing this elasticity as a managed service.
- Services are typically focused on short-term "burst" demand to gain cost savings over provisioning and owning the assets.
- Statistical automated scaling is used to optimize the shared virtual assets.
- Risk is transferred from the buyer to the seller/provider of the Cloud service.
- Cloud sellers and providers seek to grow amortized economies of scale through increasing the numbers of users of the shared resources.
- The IT infrastructure and operation is masked from the service user. Cloud is more than just SaaS.

http://www.opengroup.org/cloud/wp_cloud_roi/p6.htm#discuss_busperspective

Building return on investments

It is of foremost important and from business perspective to differentiating business processes and their Quality of Service (QoS) that could lead to success. Top managers need to Identifying competitive business processes, besides standard commodity operations, that has potential to identify, enhance focus on innovative market growth and cost of service optimization activities which made feasible with business models based on Cloud Computing opportunities, focusing on QoS, but can miss the impact and value of applications and business processes to the end users. QoS is a significant component, in the process of evaluating the business effectiveness. The elements of QoS consist of infrastructure, resources, activities, and services spanning the whole lifecycle of business.

Costs

To a large extent, solutions can be found, for operational challenges that faces customers, and each of them are bound to be different which can be in proactive approach, fixed for all the other customers of the Cloud service by means of establishing a shared platform. And, Amortization is basically single illustration or the manner, by which cloud solution can achieve favorable QoS levels, so that tangible financial benefits of scale, across platform can be achieved, which generally includes economy of scale cutting across ecosystem From a business perspective, manner an enterprise conducts variety of business process, and QoS, leads to favorable business results Success of cloud majorly depends on designing competitive business processes and as standard commodity operations will lead to enhance focus on innovative market growth and cost of service optimization activities made possible by business models based on Cloud Computing opportunities. Simply concentrating on infrastructure enhancements, optimization, to a large extent deliver cost benefits, but may fail to bring forth the impact and value of applications and business processes to clients, and in this backdrop. QoS is an essential component in the process of evaluating the business effectiveness. The elements of QoS comprises of infrastructure, resources, activities, which engulf entire services spanning the whole lifecycle of business.

Business focus

Eventually, what does it mean defining values? It can be defined in multiple ways and it always represent financial values of Total Cost of Ownership (TCO) and Return on Investment (ROI),it also defines client values, besides seller provider value, broker value, market brand value, corporate value, as well as technical value of the investment. Typically, business is considered a portfolio of business processes, and it is always prudent to adopt portfolio management techniques, collate business processes into three domains where the processes in each domain possess a common IT enablement solution selection criteria (for example, differentiating based on IT, differentiating not based on IT, and not differentiating), and apply the solution selection criteria. Business perspective includes consideration should consider questions viz adopting cloud can assist in interactions with business partners or partner organizations −and to cite an example, Deploying g SOA or EDI through the Cloud − and whether using Cloud services may disrupt any existing interactions, where suppliers of data impose particular conditions for handling confidential data.

http://www.opengroup.org/cloud/wp_cloud_roi/p4.htm

Key aspects for consideration are:

Cloud computing ushered in new model of cash flow for business. Sources of revenue and outgoing cash expenditure are deduced on actual a usage basis which is based parameters viz. unit such as time, volume, or component Cash flow − Cash Flow post Taxes are a financial measure of a business's capacity to create cash flow mechanisms, through its operations, Switching to OPEX model, for financial calculations, adopt model where of operational expenses rather than capital assets and the treatment of operating statements rather than balance sheet management Cash flow describes revenue, cash, and working capital changes which flow within part of the operating expenses liquidity and available usage of funds. One of the reason for cloud adoption, is to enhance avenues of revenue avenues, simultaneously, reducing Capex, by improving efficiency of OPEX variations Recalibration of Net Present Value (NPV) of investments, which are some items needs detailed consideration, on discounted cash flows of the cost of capital,

Cost of Capital

Moving from CAPEX to OPEX is financially a structural change, in the basis of capital investment usage as upfront and ongoing costs are changed by the Cloud Computing business model, and enormous effort has to be invested, The focus is on the ability to maximize the leverage of that capital to acquire IT and business services, simultaneously while minimizing the risk to the business in capital used for initial investment and ongoing maintenance charges and in an event of moving away While moving away from investments in long-term assets may be seen as context of Cloud Computing, action towards long-term OPEX-style service, in situation, where QoS and costs are still equally relevant regardless of asset ownership and the binding factor is the business performance and SLA requirements, An enterprise incurring high cost of capital (WACC) and which would benefit from bringing in their tax shield (high CFAT), is a candidate for shifting CAPEX to OPEX – but other aspects of the business context may contradict that candidacy such as availability of appropriate solutions and security constraints on using shared services and in a situation, where, If CAPEX to OPEX is desired, then the company should be considering and evaluating outsourcing solutions, including public Cloud solutions, hybrid Cloud, and Private Cloud solutions.

OPEX Adopting this model has ability to remove and release capital, that in some other circumstances, be used for initial investment and ownership of IT assets. Cloud is capital intensive, many a times require Capital infusement t and changes to the payment and funding of the service as it is amortized over a wider shared service model for economies of scale. If over-arching goal is to maximize the utilization of capital by best use of the debt and equity funds in such cases, in Cloud Computing the use of OPEX moves the funding towards optimizing capital investment leverage and risk management of those sources of funds.

Portability

http://www.opengroup.org/cloud/cloud_iop/p4.htm

Portability and interoperability relate to the ability to build systems from re-usable components that will work together "out of the box". Specific concern which has given architects, have been facing in on-boarding, which is process of the deployment or migration of systems to a cloud service or set of cloud services. Considering complexity, vast options, mobility of components to be migrated to cloud, for instance, when an enterprise, looking to exercise absolute control, over personal data, and in absence of ability of portability, not even single component can be migrated to cloud, and in such scenario, theory remains, within confines of the organizations network

Categories

System that involves cloud computing typically includes data, application, platform, and infrastructure components, are:

- Data is the machine-process able representation of information, held in computer storage.
- *Applications* are software programs that perform functions related to business problems.
- Platforms are programs that support the applications and perform generic functions that are not business-related.
- *Infrastructure* is a collection of physical computation, storage, and communication resources.

The application, platform, and infrastructure components can be as in traditional enterprise computing, or they can be cloud resources that are (respectively) software application programs (SaaS), software application platforms (PaaS), and virtual processors and data stores (IaaS).Non-cloud systems include mainframes, minicomputers, personal computers, and mobile devices owned and used by enterprises and individuals. Portability, interoperability of infrastructure components are achieved through hardware and virtualization architectures, mostly internal to IaaS, component interfaces exposed by such components are internal to the IaaS and infrastructure component interface which is s exposed by these components are physical communications interfaces, while these are significant, but similar as traditional one. Applications shall include programs which is concerned with concerned with the deployment, configuration, provisioning, and operation of cloud resources, besides, Interoperability between these programs and the cloud resource environments is essential, and termed as management interoperability. Applications can include programs viz as app stores (for applications), data markets (for, e.g., openly available data) and cloud catalogues (e.g., reserved capacity exchanges, cloud service catalogs), by accessing such catalogues users can procure software products, data and cloud services, on to which developers are allowed to publish their applications, data, services

Cloud computing portability and interoperability categories are:

- Data Portability
- Application Portability
- Platform Portability
- Application Interoperability
- Platform Interoperability
- Management Interoperability
- Publication and Acquisition Interoperability and few are described

Two kinds of platform portability are:

- Re-use of platform components across cloud IaaS services and non-cloud infrastructure — *platform source portability*
- Re-use of bundles containing applications and data with their supporting platforms — *machine image portability*

Architecture of Unix is example of source platform portability and is compiled in C programming language that can be deployed on multiple hardware independent selections which are basically did not get coded in C. Few other operating systems can be ported in a similar fashion. Few OS allows themselves to be ported in the above manner.

Why is it difficult to achieve?

http://www.opengroup.org/cloud/cloud_iop/p2.htm#pgfIdX2d1011151

Portability and interoperability between system components calls for defining standards that describes how the components behave.

Creation of standards

Creation of standards is set of complicated tasks. Vendors may see their immediate commercial advantage in discouraging their customers from using products supplied by other vendors, which could lead them to not to support applicable standards. Authoring, a comprehensive definition of effectiveness of standards call for agreement between producers on specific details of the interfaces which in all probability difficult to adhere in-spite of, producers have the desire to achieve. Besides, the identification and description of the requirements that the standards place on products or services again calls for involvement of SME. inferior quality standards, defined without bringing such qualities to fore r, imposes burden on technicians and users, without even guaranteeing actual advantages, besides cases of designing poor standards aren't common Technical parameters which needs to be defining reasonable standards are complex, includes other fields of IT, include functional aspects, besides, quality of delivery of that functionality such as portability and interoperability: security and performance, equally important is quality of delivery of that functionality

Architecture domains

- Business Architecture: Description of the structure and interaction between the business strategy, organization, functions, business processes, and information requirements.

Information system architecture

Cloud ushers new dimensions to Data Architecture, in form of initiating, processing of "big data. Data storage services include services based on new storage innovations, which includes those of, including those characterized as "NoSQL", particularly the simple key-value pair paradigm. *Big data* indicates collection of data sets so large and complex that it turns out difficult to process using existing DB management tools. Social networking and other cloud services in likes of important source of such data, and cloud resources give themselves for bursts of computationally-intense processing to obtain results from it, and it is based on loosely-coupled services, not on information silo applications with tightly-coupled components.

Technology Architecture

Describes the structure and interactions between platform services, logical, physical technology components.

Performance, security

Components apart from perform equally well, with equally good execution and response times, and they must be as secure in the cloud as they are in-house, they should exhibit same characteristic even in cloud systems.

Legal jurisdiction

Large service providers operate multi-nationally. An organization utilizing their services is likely to have processing performed in, and data moved between, different regions or zones, which has the ability to place restrictions on processing which can be performed, on the transit of the data, and on the degree of control that the enterprise has. and cloud certainly can be seen an opportunity For example, the growth of cloud computing could contribute to achieving the objectives of the European Union for improved interoperability of IT systems across national borders.

http://www.opengroup.org/cloud/wp_cloud_roi/p2.htm

Capacity utilization curve

Famed graph adopted by Amazon Web Services (shown below) describing capacity utilization as a graph has become iconic which illustrates central theme, associating cloud characteristics with utilization, Surrounding Cloud-based services enabled through an on-demand business provisioning model to meet actual usage an example graph has been shown.

Why usage is of concern is one of fundamental characteristic is to minimize cost impact Of over-provisioning and under-provisioning, which opens door for improving for cost, revenue, and margin advantages of business services in order to enhance revenue, and margin advantages of business services which powers rapid deployment for enhancing cost,revenue-margins, to business advantage when deploying services, with minimal entry costs, which gives opportunity to deploy services with better agility, with low entry cost, and the potential to enter and exploit new markets.

Examples to cite are:

- The Moore's Law model that establishes the concept of exponential growth in computational power but has subsequently been seen in other technology areas, including storage and network
- The technology hype cycle that established the emergence of innovation lifecycles,

- The Boston Consulting Group Growth–Share Matrix that can be used to show how key industrial markets and products and services undergo transitions as the maturity lifecycles emerge, grow, and recede

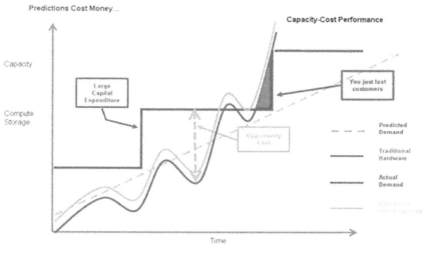

Source: Amazon Web Services

Source http://www.opengroup.org/cloud/wp_cloud_roi/p2.htm

Matching capacity and actual utilization on demand accelerates operational efficiency; Capacity and utilization are Key Performance Indicators (KPIs). They measure how much or how little something is being used. But is this aligned and being used to generate Return on Investment (ROI) and it is measured on below parameters

- Pricing and costing of Cloud services
- Funding approaches to Cloud services
- Return on Investment (ROI)
- Key Performance Indicators (KPIs)
- Total cost of ownership (TCO)
- Risk management
- Decisions and choices evaluation processes for Cloud service

Below describes a comparison between two models

Traditional model

- Hardware is hosted on the premises of the organization and/ or manage hosted.
- Hardware and software is provisioned for peak demand.
- Service management monitoring is used to generate forecasts of demand usage and current SLA performance.
- Chargeback's and compensations are used to adjust usage and payments.
- Under-provisioning and over-provisioning of capacity can result from unforeseen demand changes.
- Business invests in ownership of assets that can be enhanced and extended through IT programs and development.
- Changes to IT involve migration and divestment/investment issues and programs

Cloud

- Hardware and/or software is hosted off-premise (public or hybrid) or on-premise as a private Cloud service.
- Services are provisioned and used based on actual demand, providing this elasticity as a managed service.
- Services are typically focused on short-term "burst" demand to gain cost savings over provisioning and owning the assets.
- Statistical automated scaling is used to optimize the shared virtual assets.
- Risk is transferred from the buyer to the seller/provider of the Cloud service.
- Cloud sellers and providers seek to grow amortized economies of scale through increasing the numbers of users of the shared resources.
- The IT infrastructure and operation is masked from the service user. Cloud is more than just SaaS.

http://www.opengroup.org/cloud/wp_cloud_roi/p6.htm#discuss_busperspective

Building return on investments

It is of foremost important and from business perspective to differentiating business processes and their Quality of Service (QoS) that could lead to success. Top managers need to Identifying competitive business processes, besides standard commodity operations, that has potential to identify, enhance focus on innovative market growth and cost of service optimization activities which made feasible with business models based on Cloud Computing opportunities, focusing on QoS, but can miss the impact and value of applications and business processes to the end users. QoS is a significant component, in the process of evaluating the business effectiveness. The elements of QoS consist of infrastructure, resources, activities, and services spanning the whole lifecycle of business Cost

To a large extent, solutions can be found, for operational challenges that faces customers, and each of them are bound to be different which can be in proactive approach, fixed for all the other customers of the Cloud service by means of establishing a shared platform. And, Amortization is basically single illustration or the manner, by which cloud solution can achieve favorable QoS levels, so that tangible financial benefits of scale, across platform can be achieved, which generally includes economy of scale cutting across ecosystem From a business perspective, manner an enterprise conducts variety of business process, and QoS, leads to favorable business results Success of cloud majorly depends on designing competitive business processes and as standard commodity operations will lead to enhance focus on innovative market growth and cost of service optimization activities made possible by business models based on Cloud Computing opportunities. Simply concentrating on infrastructure enhancements, optimization, to a large extent deliver cost benefits, but may fail to bring forth the impact and value of applications and business processes to clients, and in this backdrop. QoS is an essential component in the process of evaluating the business effectiveness. The elements of QoS comprises of infrastructure, resources, activities, which engulf entire services spanning the whole lifecycle of business.

Business focus

Eventually, what does it mean defining values? It can be defined in multiple ways and it always represent financial values of Total Cost of Ownership (TCO) and Return on Investment (ROI),it also defines client values, besides seller provider value, broker value, market brand value, corporate value, as well as technical value of the investment. Typically, business sis considered a portfolio of business processes, and it is always prudent to adopt portfolio management techniques, collate business processes into three domains where the processes in each domain possess a common IT enablement solution selection criteria (for example, differentiating based on IT, differentiating not based on IT, and not differentiating), and apply the solution selection criteria. Business perspective includes consideration should consider questions viz adopting cloud can assist in interactions with business partners or partner organizations —and to cite an example, Deploying g SOA or EDI through the Cloud — and whether using Cloud services may disrupt any existing interactions, where suppliers of data impose particular conditions for handling confidential data.

http://www.opengroup.org/cloud/wp_cloud_roi/p4.htm

Key aspects for consideration are:

Cloud computing ushered in new model of cash flow for business. Sources of revenue and outgoing cash expenditure are deduced on actual a usage basis which is based parameters viz. unit such as time, volume, or component Cash flow — Cash Flow post Taxes are a financial measure of a business's capacity to create cash flow mechanisms, through its operations, Switching to OPEX model, for financial calculations, adopt model where of operational expenses rather than capital assets and the treatment of operating statements rather than balance sheet management Cash flow describes revenue, cash, and working capital changes which flow within part of the operating expenses liquidity and available usage of funds. One of the reason for cloud adoption, is to enhance avenues of revenue avenues, simultaneously reducing Capex, by by improving efficiency of OPEX variations Recalibration of Net Present Value (NPV) of investments, which are some items needs detailed consideration, on discounted cash flows of the cost of capital,

Cost of Capital

Moving from CAPEX to OPEX is financially a structural change, in the basis of capital investment usage as upfront and ongoing costs are changed by the Cloud Computing business model, and enormous effort has to be invested, The focus is on the ability to maximize the leverage of that capital to acquire IT and business services, simultaneously while minimizing the risk to the business in capital used for initial investment and ongoing maintenance charges and in an event of moving away While moving away from investments in long-term assets may be seen as context of Cloud Computing, action towards long-term OPEX-style service, in situation, where QoS and costs are still equally relevant regardless of asset ownership and the binding factor is the business performance and SLA requirements. An enterprise incurring high cost of capital (WACC) and which would benefit from bringing in their tax shield (high CFAT), is a candidate for shifting CAPEX to OPEX – but other aspects of the business context may contradict that candidacy such as availability of appropriate solutions and security constraints on using shared services and in a situation, where, If CAPEX to OPEX is desired, then the company should be considering and evaluating outsourcing solutions, including public Cloud solutions, hybrid Cloud, and Private Cloud solutions.

OPEX

Adopting this model has ability to remove and release capital, that in some other circumstances, be used for initial investment and ownership of IT assets. Cloud is capital intensive, many a times require capital investments, and changes to the payment and funding of the service as it is amortized over a wider shared service model for economies of scale. If over-arching goal is to maximize the utilization of capital by best use of the debt and equity funds in such cases, in Cloud Computing the use of OPEX moves the funding towards optimizing capital investment leverage and risk management of those sources of funds.

Ecosystem reference model

http://www.opengroup.org/cloud/cloud_ecosystem_rm/p3.htm

It is compulsory to develop a reference model for all architectures, irrespective of the services that are being proposed, and the primary reason to create an abstract foundation for the instantiations of architectures and business solutions of an enterprise, which represents, an re-usable, re-sizable, flexible and agile collaborative designs, that can be deployed to offer, the most efficient means for sharing business information securely regardless of its underlying data location and the term itself indicates, it one of the best practices to adopt in its entirety. The primary aim to develop such a model is to ensure consistency and applicability of Cloud Services within a wide variety of Enterprise Architecture management frameworks. Below diagram, explains, relation-ships, dependencies that are is to be existing amongst different enterprise frameworks, in order to manage life cycle of Cloud Services utilizing the Architecture Building Blocks (ABBs), as defined in Cloud Ecosystem Reference Model for the purpose of delivering an high-performance, high–availability cloud services to the customers. One of the primarily objective for developing such a model is to define and explain to the clients, details of all the stake-holders, their relationships, besides defining minimum set of ABBs. The diagram below explains architectural capabilities which can be realized, enabled by at least one of the new or existing stake-holders of enterprise Cloud Ecosystem. Models are also designed to baseline a common language for the various stake-holders of an enterprise Cloud Ecosystem, which supports the validations of Cloud Service Providers' solutions in order to deliver high levels of integrity for business solutions. And it is always necessary, that The Cloud Ecosystem Reference Model, always treated as an extension of an Enterprise Architecture Model and it should be practice that any such modes that are used to describe architecture designs for any specific environment or any specific c environment or any specific application, for any company that, utilizes enterprise utilizing Solution Building Blocks (SBBs) which has already been impended by any new entrant or existing participants of an enterprise Cloud Ecosystem. The visibility of these capabilities will vary according to the role(s) of the participants. A few important taxonomies are described:

Auditing & reporting

Audit & Reporting Service enables, administrators to record activities (including exceptions, events which is eventually archived for specific time duration, in order to assist in further investigations, as and when such a need arises. However, it is essential to plan for all measures to minimize the performance degradation, risk of disruption to business processes. And it is highly necessary for the concerned teams, to in a periodic basis, monitor reports that is being generated in a periodical basis, to pre-empt any un-desired events occur.

Designing a governance model

An illustration is shown below, that explains relation of ABBs, SBBs for the tasks of swift provisioning, data protection in an enterprise

Cloud Ecosystem an SBB for rapid provisioning, shall be offered by the individual participants of an enterprise Cloud Ecosystem delivering the Cloud Service (e.g., Cloud Service Provider, Cloud Service Broker, etc.). An ABB for such capabilities, viz. Cloud Service Provider, Cloud Service Broker, etc. However, an ABB that has been specifically developed for offering these capabilities are also a part of the architecture of the consuming enterprise, since requirement for rapid provisioning will remain even if another participating entity in the enterprise Cloud Ecosystem provides the SBB, It is mandatory that data protection ABB, should be made visible in each and every applicable participant's architecture and from the end-user's stand-point, is each instantiation (SBB) of that concerned building block is treated as another participant with which there is a relevant relationship as part of the customer's Cloud Ecosystem and the reason for this is being, security policies applicable to the customer's data, warrants to be performed in a consistent fashion, across all parties managing the data, irrespective of how ABBS are designed, implemented. Irrespective of the type of organization, it is highly recommended to interact with diverse external Cloud Service Providers for soliciting support, recommendations from external technology providers for providing an integrated support for designed cloud platform, besides the software and application support. It is highl necessary to adopt any suitable standards viz. TOGAF, COBIT. Cloud EcoSource exhibits, has currently three distinct cloud-specific initiatives which have the characteristics of IaaS, PaaS, and SaaS for cloud.

Designing a governance model

An illustration is shown below, that explains relation of ABBs, SBBs for the tasks of swift provisioning, data protection in an enterprise Cloud Ecosystem an SBB for rapid provisioning, shall be offered by the individual participants of an enterprise Cloud Ecosystem delivering the Cloud Service (e.g., Cloud Service Provider, Cloud Service Broker, etc.). An ABB for such capabilities, viz. Cloud Service Provider, Cloud Service Broker, etc. However, an ABB that has been specifically developed for offering these capabilities are also a part of the architecture of the consuming enterprise, since requirement for rapid provisioning will remain even if another participating entity in the enterprise Cloud Ecosystem provides the SBB, It is mandatory that data protection ABB, should be made visible in each and every applicable participant's architecture and from the end–user's stand–point, is each instantiation (SBB) of that concerned building block is treated as another participant with which there is a relevant relationship as part of the customer's Cloud Ecosystem and the reason for this is being, security policies applicable to the customer's data, warrants to be performed in a consistent fashion, across all parties managing the data, irrespective of how ABBS are designed, implemented. Irrespective of the type of organization, it is highly recommended to interact with diverse external Cloud Service Providers for soliciting support, recommendations from external technology providers for providing an integrated support for designed cloud platform, besides the software and application support. It is highl necessary to adopt any suitable standards viz. TOGAF, COBIT. Cloud EcoSource exhibits, has currently three distinct cloud–specific initiatives which have the characteristics of IaaS, PaaS, and SaaS for cloud.

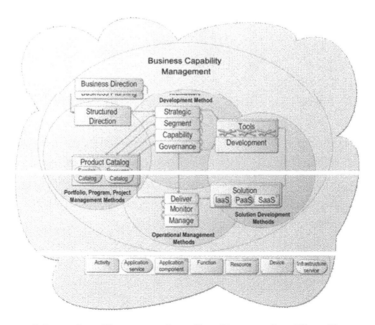

Managing Frameworks of an Enterprise Cloud1

http://www.opengroup.org/cloud/cloud_ecosystem_rm/p3.htm

Governance concepts

http://www.opengroup.org/cloud/gov_snapshot/p10.htm

Cloud governance is as important as any other tasks or operations, since, eventually, defines, implementing practices, in a manner that aligns with the design and makes sure that, all the policies have been implemented. Doing it right should be the motto, rather than what should be done. Factoring, that governance directs the company to channelize the efforts in the right direction and ensuring, organization is performing "the right thing" and at the same time, it is also imperative to conclude on the aspect of deciding on appropriate stake-holders, making, executing decisions, which experts term as "right thing" is. Also, it becomes much vivid, in case clear that if we expect to have things done the right way, we cannot keep what a "right thing" is secret – it needs to be communicated. And communications can happen in multiple ways, and while doing so, it has to be strategized and ensured it reaches, the appropriate audience and at the intended time, and it should be in a form which is easily recognizable, to be trusted as accurate, current and authoritative. Communication steps assumes significance, as it is the responsibility of the concerned to ensure that critical details emanating from source has possess the right authority, to take decisions reflected in a manner, that information is made and seemed to accessible to the consumers of such details made available to consumers of that information in an pre-planned manner, and contained in an agreed location for storing and archiving data for this particular type It is important to include all factors in developing the process, with inclusion of, both governance processes and governed processes produces outcomes, which in certain cases, be made to be visible to other parties. Communication strategy is of most importance, that has to designed to make sure that process is aware of its operations, what kind of information needs to be processed, which is responsible for communicating, in fashion where is is known that what kind of information should be allowed in, and where the permitted information, would be placed. Described are few guidelines that can be followed while designing the principles. A decision on what could be the correct thing necessarily has to be taken only by those concerned about the need to make decisions, and it is needed to record the description of a right thing and in authoritative manner, which needs to be circulated to relevant parties. And it is must that, process designed needs to be tested and validated in an relevant environment, to ensure process compliance and the rules are followed. And by adherence, should ensure information flow is streamlined, and methods designed has to ensure, the concerned teams, are in-time informed in a precise and timely manner, that they are able to perform naturally and with consistency, that an external consultant, can assist in the process that has the higher probability of turning successful, by the way of ensuring performing tasks in right manner, leading to ticking many check-boxes, as possible, which is made possible by negating uncertainty that surrounds the process of how to manage new or unexpected circumstances

http://www.opengroup.org/cloud/gov_snapshot/p1.htm#X_ Introduction

Some of the traditional non-cloud computing governance frameworks viz. ITIL® v3, COBIT® 5, the TOGAF® 9.1 standard, and the SOA Governance Framework are mostly generic, which doesn't present governance framework around the environment, which supports cloud characteristics, viz. elasticity. Besides they in majority of use-cases, adequately factor in the aspect of division of responsibilities between user and suppliers, turn significantly different, important. With Cloud, IT managers these days are able to make distinctions between WHAT and HOW regarding dual functionality and infrastructure and with its ubiquitous property, makes it as a reality for architects to design an efficient systems .It isn't un-common that an environment be defined and designed by users n the basis of a script, executed by the cloud service provider's end. End-users, as always possess the freedom of choice of selecting

a. Platform,
b. OS,
c. Applications
d. Service provider.

Different levels of controls are recommended to be combined, within a single landscape, and in many cases such of type of variability doesn't gets supported by existing languages, frameworks. Multiple governance frameworks are in vogue, from which an organization can select; a few of them also address overlapping domains. These Snapshots possess capabilities to recognize their differences and importance, and is holistic and vendor-neutral..

- Shift from CapEx to OpEx investment models
- Need for additional management controls to address anticipated changes in delivery model(s)
- New business and IT roles required to manage risk
- Transparent consumer-provider interactions
- Gaps in coverage of architectural and technology decisions
- Inadequate support for making decisions around multi-tenancy and resource virtualization
- Standards listed contain options which through references, in the snapshots constitute provisions of the Cloud Computing Governance Framework. Registered standards are listed:
- ISO/IEC 17788:2014: Information Technology – Cloud Computing – Overview and Vocabulary; refer to: www.iso.org/iso/catalogue_detail?csnumber=605455.
- ISO/IEC 17789:2014: Information Technology – Cloud Computing – Reference Architecture; refer to: www.iso.org/iso/catalogue_detail?csnumber=60545.

And these standards are updated periodically.

Definitions

And for the standards, below definitions apply

Can	Describes a possible feature or behavior available to the user or application.
May	Describes a feature or behavior that is optional. To avoid ambiguity, the opposite of "may" is expressed as "need not", instead of "may not".
Shall	Describes a feature or behavior that is a requirement. To avoid ambiguity, do not use "must" as an alternative to "shall".
Shall not	Describes a feature or behavior that is an absolute prohibition.
Should	Describes a feature or behavior that is recommended but not required.
Will	Same meaning as "shall"; "shall" is the preferred term.

http://www.opengroup.org/cloud/gov_snapshot/p8.htm

Metrics

Metrics shall be made to record at frequent intervals, and can be configured to be made to tracked across the various process pairs for governance, and these metrics are designed by rationale which needs to be tracked which contains the same parameters ex. descriptions of the process pairs reference these metrics and listed below are the metrics that can be tracked:

Level of Cloud Adoption

The following metrics can be tracked to determine the extent to which cloud computing has been adopted across the enterprise:

- % of existing projects that are not part of cloud transformation
- % of enterprise cloud services subscribed
- Average # of subscribers per service
- Actual against expected consumption
- Percentage of consumption patterns (IaaS, SaaS, PaaS)
- Rate of change to subscriber count

Level of Cloud Computing Governance

The metrics below help establish the extent to which cloud computing governance is in place across the enterprise:

- % of cloud-ability reviews exercised
- % of service compatibility reviews exercised
- % of service provider usage reviews exercised
- Ratio of planned *versus* actual cloud services
- Frequency of exceptions

Operational Efficiency

These metrics can be used to track the parameters that drive the operational efficiency for the ongoing sustenance of application and infrastructure components in the cloud:

- % of incidents reported
- Average time to deploy
- Average time to onboard

Cost Reduction

This metric can be used to drive the funding of cloud computing transformations across the enterprise:

- % of budget allocated to IT

Business Value Alignment

These metrics can be used to drive the extent to which cloud computing adoption is in alignment with the overall business objectives for the enterprise:

- % of idle services decreased
- % of business service-level requirements met
- Ratio of # of subscriptions/# of unsubscriptions
- Number of consumer/provider combinations impacted by exceptions

Service-Driven Integration

These metrics can be used to track the extent to which the cloud computing deployment is building upon the existing services-based ecosystem within the enterprise:

- % of service provider exceptions/service provider integrations
- % of enterprise services subscribed
- Number of SLAs impacted by exceptions

Risk Mitigation

These metrics can be used to drive preventive measures that can be taken to avoid potential risks generated from cloud computing adoption:

- % of compliance with security policies

- % variance in schedule
- Number of incidents related to unsubscribe
- Severity of exceptions

What is Cloud computing?

https://www.redhat.com/en/topics/cloud

Cloud computing, is a combination of set of principles, approaches, designed to deliver compute services,platforms,applications—sourced from clouds—to cloud subscribers, in an on-demand basis, across environment using internet. A Cloud can be described pools of virtual resources viz.CPU, storage, databases, cloud based applications, that are orchestrated by management, automation software, facilitating access for users to access resources, in an on-demand means, using self-service portals supported by automatic scaling and dynamic resource allocation .Primary reason of Cloud deployments, deployed is to minimize spending on voluminous hardware, highly-priced software, and focus on developing business applications, services. And for purpose of developing applications, companies need to subscribe to any of the cloud platforms like Amazon web services, IBM Softlayer, Redhat, and use resources from those platforms to design, deploy commercial applications, services. In reality, Cloud computing doesn't represent any technologies themselves and to make operational, administrators needs to install operating systems, virtualization software, besides deploying automation, management tools OS establishes networks host user interfaces; virtualization abstracts resources and pools them into clouds; automation software allocates resources, while management tools provision new environments. Platforms viz. OpenStack, packages majority of above mentioned technologies, into simple to deploy systems, thus creating an integrated, unique, and easy to deploy systems—a one-stop shop for developing and orchestrating clouds.

Virtualization, basis of cloud

https://www.redhat.com/en/topics/virtualization

    Virtualization is technology that which lets users to create multiple simulated environments or dedicated resources from a single, physical hardware system, and to make hardware operational, a software which is termed as "hypervisor" is deployed on the hardware for purpose of splitting a monolithic hardware into multiple, distinct secure, trusted environment which is termed as Virtual machines (VMs), which in turn depend on the capability of hypervisor to separate the machine's resources from the hardware and distribute them in manner which designed to suit the compute needs and in turn distribute them in an appropriate fashion. By deploying virtualization IT team achieves optimization of resources, utilize existing hardware and make plans for making all hardware resource including storage devices which can be virtualized. Physical hardware which is equipped with Hypervisor, is termed as Host, while multiple VMs which utilize its resources are called Guests, which regards physical hardware, equipped with a hypervisor, is called the host, while the many VMs that use its resources are guests and such guests can easily be relocated, which means a pool of compute resources comprising of CPU, memory, storage can be easily relocated to any other similar hypervisor, from where users can be configured for access. Users have compete control over the resources, viz instances of CPU, memory, storage, and other resource, hence guests are configured to gain access to appropriate resources. viz. Compute instance, storage, CPU, memory By design, all VMs are managed using a single window based virtualization management console, which, accelerates actions. Virtualizations software allows users to slice each hardwarein order to decide, how much processing power, storage, and memory to give VMs, and environments are better protected since VMs are separated from their supporting hardware and each other. Considering an hypothetical situation, where an environment with physical servers with individual dedicated purposes, email server, web–servers, application servers, where legacy applications are hosted, and hypothetically individual servers, operate 35% capacity which runs legacy applications, and assume each server operates at 35% capacity, which is considered as underutilized by cloud standard, but as legacy application is still running, internal operations, it is necessary that, third server is always active, it was traditionally simpler, trust-worthy to execute individual tasks on individual servers, but with virtualization it is possible to partition servers, into multiple independent environments, made to handle independent tasks so that legacy applications can get migrated, and it is same underlying hardware, atop which opera ions occur which implies, this method can lead to higher efficiencies. Taking into account, that security, partitions can be created in first server again, enabling it to handle another task, enhancing its usage from 30 to 60, once you are able to achieve this, now empty servers could be reused for other tasks or retired altogether to reduce cooling and maintenance costs.

Types of virtualization

https://access.redhat.com/documentation/en-us/red_hat_enterprise_linux/7/html/virtualization_getting_started_guide/chap-virtualization_getting_started-what_is_it

- Full virtualization uses an unmodified version of the guest operating system. The guest addresses the host's CPU via a channel created by the hypervisor. Because the guest communicates directly with the CPU, this is the fastest virtualization method.
- Para virtualization uses a modified guest operating system. The guest communicates with the hypervisor. The hypervisor passes the unmodified calls from the guest to the CPU and other interfaces, both real and virtual. Because the calls are routed through the hypervisor, this method is slower than full virtualization.
- Software virtualization (or emulation)

- Software virtualization (emulation) uses binary translation and other emulation techniques to run unmodified operating systems. The hypervisor translates the guest calls to a format that can be used by the host system. Because all calls are translated, this method is slower than virtualization. Note that Red Hat does not support software virtualization on Red Hat Enterprise Linux.

Containerization

While KVM virtualization creates a separate instance of OS kernel, operating-system-level virtualization, also known as containerization, operates on top of an existing OS kernel and creates isolated instances of the host OS, known as containers, which doesn't exhibit versatility of KVM virtualization are comparatively lightweight, flexible to manage.

https://access.redhat.com/documentation/en-us/red_hat_enterprise_linux/7/html/virtualization_getting_started_guide/chap-virtualization_getting_started-advantages

What is the need for virtualization?

Virtualization technology shall be used for server deployments, stand-alone desktops, that delivers advantage of deploying a cost-efficient centralized management, an enhance disaster recovery methods. Utilities viz. SSH, makes it feasible to get connected to a desktop remotely access services that has been hosted on that desktop. In an event of adopting for servers, it delivers double benefit which is virtualzing networks and also deployments with more than a single server. Virtualization offers live migration, high availability, fault tolerance, and streamlined backups.

Virtualization costs

At the beginning, Virtualization will need additional investments, and would give an impression that is is expensive, which is is true in initial stages, but it delivers long term benefits, reduces spend over a period of time. Cuts down on any additional hardware purchase, reduces power consumption, and virtualzing leads to reduction in the number of servers and associated devices, resulting in reduction in maintenance costs, and minimizes manpower. It delivers the following advantages.

Reduced power consumption

Basic premise is that, virtualization minimizes the requirement for multiple physical platforms, which directly translates to significantly reduced power consumption, which is associated with machine operations, cooling systems, and when combined with the machines' power consumption and required cooling, gets significantly reduced by configuring virtualization.

Extended life for installed software

Many a times, older versions of the software may not be compatible to be executed directly on baremetal machines, however by deploying outdated software virtually on a larger, faster system, the life of the software may be extended by utilizing the properties that delivers an enhanced performance that is offered by new systems, configurations.

Optimizes on physical space

Consolidating servers onto fewer machines leads to reduction in the quantity of physical systems, which leads to reduction in number of physical servers, server racks, power connections, lesser physical space being utilized, and lesser manpower.

Cloud types

Public cloud

https://www.redhat.com/en/topics/cloud-computing/what-is-public-cloud

Public clouds are architected as a collection of virtual resources, which has been exclusively designed for hosting hardware, typically hosted in third-party premises, where resources are automaticity provisiononed between multiple clients with the help of self-service portal. Public clouds are suited for environments, host scale out workloads that are susceptible to undergo unexpected demand fluctuations. Majority of cloud installations aren't usually deployed as a standalone infrastructure setup, instead is is created as part of a heterogeneous mix of environments, which promises to deliver enhanced levels of security, performance, optimizing expenses, exposes to larger canvas offering available, scalable enhanced security levels, increased performance, lower cost, high availability of compute components, services, applications.

How does it work?

Public cloud is regarded as simplest amongst all deployments. A company which looks for expanding the resources, platform or in constant lookout for adding resources, or services can get hooked to any desired public cloud vendor, by the hour or byte, gain access to quantity of resources that is is actually needed. Infrastructure, raw processing power, storage, or cloud-based applications are delivered as virtualized resources, carved out individually for specific needs, by service provider's who have created large size pooled into data lakes, orchestrated by management and automation software, which is transmitted either through internet or dedicated VPN to company's datacenter. Company's don't invest in acquiring gigabytes of storage where it is stores nor manages operations, of server farms where hardware is located, besides not making determination of strategy regarding aspects of how cloud-based platforms, applications, or services are secured or maintained. All that a subscriber needs to do is, enter into agreement with the chosen provider, utilize resources, and make payments as per quantity consumed within a certain amount of time.

Advantages

- private clouds, are treated as part virtualization platform, which abstracts range of computing resources, offering a environment of controlled self-service access to resources, and extending away of the advantages of traditional virtualization by offering:
- Higher quantity of infrastructure capacity, which is capable of addressing the needs of large compute, storage demands.
- Provides On-demand services, with help of self-service user interfaces, policy-based management
- Efficient resource allocation,which commensurate with IT department requirements
- This type minimizes instances of underused capacity, giving the necessary freedom to automatically configure reconfigure resources in the manner that suits the architecture, as access to such resources aren't restricted by installations, which is made possible by virtualization. The USP is, the manner it offers highest levels of security, which can also be customized to specific needs and also aligning with prescribe security policies.

Private cloud

https://www.redhat.com/en/topics/cloud-computing/what-is-private-cloud

As the terminology indicates, they are pools of virtual resources in isolated environments, carved out of dedicate systems, managed by dedicated teams, enabling users to perform automatic provisioning, allocation of resources, with assistance of self-service interface. Private configurations are characterized by privacy settings, management responsibilities—not location or ownership, creating a situation where, resources are dedicated to a single customer with isolated access, on–site or off–site infrastructure can power private clouds. In order to conceptualize,administrators needs to think as if an traditional resource allocation system is being run and when necessary for development of custom deployment, it is simple to pull resources from their physical systems, virtualizes them, locks them down as part of a virtual machine (VM).Process of implementing an on–demand, scalable private cloud involves consolidating such virtual resources into shared pools, defining requisite self-service parameters through management software which is binded to automation tools. And when resources requirements are raised, IT management has 2 choices -purchase new hardware that needs to be installed in the site, or rent from capacity as per requirements from, appropriate vendors, and since it is independently deployed, maintained, it is still considered as private cloud, inspite of resources being hosted elsewhere, as long as hardware is environments managed by the company's staff, it still can be termed as private. And, in both instances, the costs will directly enter in company's book of accounts, besides having to take responsibility of expenses.. It is the responsibility of the company to, manage, maintain underlying cloud infrastructure. Contracting services of a vendor, means that, IT team strategy is not to purchase any new hardware, instead rent them. Decision regarding the choice of Cloud, deployments solely depends on the nature of workloads that needs to be supported. It has been determined that, state-full workloads are perfectly supported by enterprise virtualization solutions, however, stateless, loosely coupled workloads, that are traditionally deployed in development, research,telecom, specifically those connected with network functions virtualization)—are better supported by private clouds. Once the upper-limit capacity of hard-wired infrastructure, is breached, it is recommended to switch-over to virtualization services, and once breached limits of virtualization, it is the time to design private cloud and offers benefits:

- Provides, enhanced capacity to meet large compute, storage requirements. Facilitates, on-demand self-service, with assistance of self-service user interfaces, policy-based management. Strives to increase efficiency by performing resource allocation, based on demands. Offers, enhanced resources visibility of resources across infrastructure, environments.
- Provides, high available On-demand services, through self-service user interfaces, policy-based management
- Programmatically performs resources allocation, as per user requirements, which results in delivering increased efficiency
- Users, administrators has can experience enhanced visibility into resources across the infrastructure
- Private clouds are universally recognized to offer highest levels of protection, compared to other options. Besides it can be customized to address the company's security standards

Hybrid

https://www.redhat.com/en/topics/cloud-computing/what-is-hybrid-cloud

Hybrids are suitable for very complex, distributed architectures, hosting diverse applications. This model is combination of 1 or more public and private cloud environments. Designed as centralized pool of virtual resources—developed partially from hardware owned and managed by a third-party entity, with hardware typically owned, managed by a third-party, besides hardware is owned by company, utilizing orchestrated by management, automation software, which assists users to gain access to resources, in on-demand, by making use of elf-service portals supported by automatic scaling, dynamic resource allocation. While public, private cloud environments, which constitute a hybrid cloud, remain as unique, independent entity, migration steps between them, is facilitated by encrypted application programming interfaces (APIs) that assists transmitting resources, workloads. This separate—yet connected—architecture is what facilitates, execution of critical workloads within private cloud, relatively less sensitive workloads in public cloud, pull resources from either environment when required and this stratagem minimizes data exposure, lets architects undertake customization of scalable, flexible, and secure portfolio of IT resources and services. It is technically feasible that hybrid cloud environments can include on-premise infrastructure, traditional virtualization, bare-metal servers, and containers, which well designed, implemented has the potential to increase performance. And technically feasible is the idea of commissioning hybrid's that constitutes multiple public clouds, which are being hosted in multiple providers' locations.

Interoperability

Interoperability is the essence of hybrid clouds, while private, public cloud configurations, in cases can exist with this property, independent of each other, however, might not be treated as hybrid inspite of such configurations are being deployed, along with the existing configurations. In an event of an environment hosting all customer-centric applications in public cloud, and with entire set of applications in private cloud, pulling resources only from the cloud it's stored on with no infrastructure between them it can't be treated as hybrid. One of essential property is the ability to include multiple touch points, which encapsulates multiple touch points, comprises of shared core software services, which facilitates seamless migration of workloads, resources, platforms, applications across environments. Exhibits highest scalability, capable of offering on demand access to resources beyond, even beyond what virtualization can provide. Makes scaling simple, by providing access to unlimited pool of resources.

Cloud-native application development

Hybrid cloud, DevOps, cloud-native applications bridges gap between monolithic and current day's modern application development approaches. Functionality of hybrid is to connect private, public, which traditionally utilized independently by development, operations teams, for porting applications back, forth between environments, teams as an when needed. It creates a stable compute foundation for purpose of design, install, deploy, and manage developed applications.

Scalability

Private configuration, exhibits highest levels of scalability offering on demand access to resources, beyond the capabilities offered by virtualization. Public model enhances scaling by way of opening access to theoretically unlimited pool of resources.

Secure

While it is secure, there exists some unique challenges viz. Data migration, increased complexity, higher levels of complexity, desert of attack surface, availability of multiple environments, provide a sturdy defense mechanism against any sort of security risks.

Cloud computing models

https://aws.amazon.com/types-of-cloud-computing/

Listed below are the predominant models, which are widely adopted by companies, want to install cloud platform.

Infrastructure as a Service (IaaS)

IaaS, houses, fundamental building-blocks, giving access to services viz. Networking computers (virtual or on dedicated hardware), data storage space and is characterized by maximum level of flexibility, management control of resources, which is similar to existing IT resources.

Platform as a Service (PaaS)

Deploying this model, eliminates responsibility of companies to manage the core infrastructure layer which is constituted of Hardware, OS, thereby giving more time to developers, administrators to concentrate more on deployments, rather than managing the environment, including hardware, OS. Beneficial, in a situation, where managers doesn't need to concentrate on resource planning, procurement, maintenance, environment maintenance, lift-shift tasks, instead on deploying business services.

Software as a Service (SaaS):

This model, frees companies to out rightly purchase software products, licenses, rather rent. This service gives access to third-party entity, which runs, manages the environment, where necessary products are hosted, managed, and offered as-as-service, on pay-per-user model. Typically environments are hosted in service provider's premises. Advantage this model offers is, end-users needn't think about how services are provided, maintained or which hardware systems are powering them, or the location, type of infrastructure, how are they managed, users need to only focus on how to use this service. Prominent use-case of this model is any web-based e-mail service.

Portability

http://www.opengroup.org/cloud/cloud_iop/p4.htm

Portability and interoperability relate to the ability to build systems from re-usable components that will work together "out of the box".

Specific concern which has given architects, have been facing in on-boarding, which is process of the deployment or migration of systems to a cloud service or set of cloud services. Considering complexity, vast options, mobility of components to be migrated to cloud, for instance, when an enterprise, looking to exercise absolute control, over personal data, and in absence of ability of portability, not even single component can be migrated to cloud, and in such scenario, theory remains, within confines of the organizations network

Categories

System that involves cloud computing typically includes data, application, platform, and infrastructure components, where:

- Data is the machine-process able representation of information, held in computer storage.
- Applications are software programs that perform functions related to business problems.
- Platforms are programs that support the applications and perform generic functions that are not business-related.
- Infrastructure is a collection of physical computation, storage, and communication resources.

The application, platform, and infrastructure components can be as in traditional enterprise computing, or they can be cloud resources that are (respectively) software application programs (SaaS), software application platforms (PaaS), and virtual processors and data stores (IaaS).

Non-cloud systems include mainframes, minicomputers, personal computers, and mobile devices owned and used by enterprises and individuals. Portability, interoperability of infrastructure components are achieved through hardware and virtualization architectures, mostly internal to IaaS, component interfaces exposed by such components are internal to the IaaS and infrastructure component interface which is s exposed by these components are physical communications interfaces, while these are significant, but similar as traditional one. Applications shall include programs which is concerned with concerned with the deployment, configuration, provisioning, and operation of cloud resources, besides, Interoperability between these programs and the cloud resource environments is essential, and termed as management interoperability. Applications can include programs viz as app stores (for applications), data markets (for, e.g., openly available data) and cloud catalogues (e.g., reserved capacity exchanges, cloud service catalogs), by accessing such catalogues users can procure software products, data and cloud services, on to which developers are allowed to publish their applications, data, services

Cloud computing portability and interoperability categories are:

- Data Portability
- Application Portability
- Platform Portability
- Application Interoperability
- Platform Interoperability
- Management Interoperability
- Publication and Acquisition Interoperability and few are described

Two kinds of platform portability are:

- Re-use of platform components across cloud IaaS services and non-cloud infrastructure – *platform source portability*
- Re-use of bundles containing applications and data with their supporting platforms – *machine image portability*

Architecture of Unix is example of source platform portability and is compiled in C programming language that can be deployed on multiple hardware independent selections which are basically did not get coded in C. Few other operating systems can be ported in a similar fashion. Few OS allows themselves to be ported in the above manner.

Why is difficult to achieve?

http://www.opengroup.org/cloud/cloud_iop/p2.htm#pgfIdX
2d1011151

Designing portability and interoperability between system components calls for defining standards that describes how the components behave.

Creation of standards

Creation of standards is considered as complicated tasks. First, vendors may see their immediate commercial advantage in discouraging their customers from using products supplied by other vendors, which could lead them to not to support applicable standards. A comprehensive definition of effectiveness of standards call for agreement between producers on specific details of the interfaces which in all probability difficult to adhere, inspite of producers have the desire to achieve. Besides, the identification and description of the requirements that the standards place on products or services again calls for involvement of SME. inferior quality standards, defined without bringing such qualities to fore r, imposes burden on technicians and users, without even guaranteeing actual advantages, besides cases of designing poor standards aren't common Technical parameters which needs to be defining reasonable standards are complex, includes other fields of IT, include functional aspects, besides, quality of delivery of that functionality such as portability and interoperability: security and performance, equally important is quality of delivery of that functionality

Architecture domains

- Business Architecture: Description of the structure and interaction between the business strategy, organization, functions, business processes, and information requirements

Information system architecture

Cloud ushers new dimensions to Data Architecture, in form of initiating, processing of "big data. Data storage services include, services based on new storage innovations, characterized as "NoSQL", particularly the simple key-value pair paradigm. Big data indicates collection of data sets so large and complex that it turns out difficult to process using existing DB management tools. Social networking and other cloud services in likes of important source of such data, and cloud resources give themselves for bursts of computationally-intense processing to obtain results from it. Architecture based on loosely-coupled services, not on information silo applications with tightly-coupled components.

Technology Architecture: description of the structure and interaction of the platform services, and logical and physical technology components.

Performance, security

Components apart from perform equally well, with equally good execution and response times, and they must be as secure in the cloud as they are in-house, they should exhibit same characteristic even in cloud systems.

Legal jurisdiction

Large service providers operate multi-nationally. An organization utilizing their services is likely to have processing performed in, and data moved between, different regions or zones, which has the ability to place restrictions on processing which can be performed, on the transit of the data, and on the degree of control that the enterprise has certainly and can be seen an opportunity For example, the growth of cloud computing could contribute to achieving the objectives of the European Union for improved interoperability of IT systems across national borders.

Cloud management

https://www.redhat.com/en/topics/cloud-computing/what-is-cloud-management

Cloud management is a concept, that defines, how much an user can exercise control over environment, resources, and virtually that resides, operates within cloud-data, infrastructure, services. Managememem utilities which are typically executed as platforms are software's, which was deployed for managing those components, application, data, and services. Primary objective of such management platform, to monitor, guarantee that services are being executed in an efficient, secure manner, while also made accessible to users, companies, which require them. Primary objective is to ensure that, anything executed in cloud platform, functions, delivers services that have been designed for. Core of the management, is lies a strategy, which incorporates, multiple fundamentals of management platform. Similar to the diversity of cloud, such strategies, utilities, are designed to server different use-cases that serve multiple cloud types, the utility vary from cloud architects deploy cloud resources, tracking, optimizing performance. Services viz. Disaster recovery, data-retention, however, motive is to offer administrative controls over the infrastructure, platforms, applications, data which are supposed to operate all the time.

Basic functionalities

Though public clouds are generally hosted, managed in within the service providers premises, it is feasible for users to deploy the own cloud management platform to integrate management across public and private clouds. In an ideal scenario, in an event of new capability is introduced to management platform, it will begin operations as an independent, self-sufficient entity, which requires minimal supervision. And to operate this platform to full efficiency, professionals with the abilities to design efficient workflows within the management tools, which has been designed for specific platforms, which has been designed, and irrespective of performance, in monitoring data, it is mandatory for the administrators to still manage utilities, which are being executed in cloud, which displays symbiotic relationship.

Outcomes

Integrates with existing environment

In order to achieve better productivity, it is mandatory, that management platform, needs to be customized to fit into the environments needs of OS, applications, storage frameworks, besides, whatever is being executed from cloud.

Should be accessible

Similar to compute resources, management systems needs to be configured that management tools, are accessible by administrator's through internet, irrespective of physical location.

Support for multi-clouds

Technology, Should be capable of supporting multi-cloud environments By default, chosen management system, should be able to work, support all types of cloud deployment, service models, seamlessly, securely

Manage anything, everything

Self-service capability is the core of cloud management platform, that is capable of exercising control over everything, and policies should be drafted to guide user access to resources, configurations, and capacity.

https://www.redhat.com/en/topics/cloud-computing/public-cloud-vs-private-cloud-and-hybrid-cloud

Choice of cloud

Selection of cloud is akin to customizing for particular needs. Following criteria's needs to be considered:

- Types of applications and their current and predicted use
- Compliance and regulations that affect your workloads
- Technical knowledge of your staff
- Business goals
- Budget
- Legacy workload interoperability
- Disaster recovery plans
- Integration strategies
- Compliance

Public clouds are good choice for

- Workloads with high volumes or has to meet fluctuating demands.
- Operate for supporting Non-sensitive data, minimal-security workloads
- Certain public-facing operations
- Meet to satisfy Long-term storage or data archives
- Supporting Collaborative projects.

Private clouds are good choice for

- Hosting, Workloads for predictable usage patterns.
- For, Sensitive workloads which demands high levels of security, privacy regulations.
- Suitable for Mid to large-sized, companies, which has where-withal to establish enhance controls

- Purpose of hosting legacy applications, which is not compatible in public clouds

Hybrid configuration will suit:

- Hosting, Workloads, with predictable usage patterns.
- Sensitive workloads, that calls for high levels of security, privacy regulations.
- Good choice for,mid to large-sized workloads, which has the heft to establish enhance controls
- Platform of choice for hosting legacy applications, that may not be compatible with public clouds

Cloud security

https://www.redhat.com/en/topics/security/cloud-security

Cloud security is method of safeguarding data, application, environment, which involved in cloud. Several features of cloud security for all environments are similar, as applicable for any on-premise Cloud, IT architecture. High-level security concerns—viz. Unauthorized data exposures, leaks, ill-designed access controls, levels impact of susceptibility to intrusions, availability disruptions, create an impact on traditional, cloud systems are alike. Basis tenet of security must incorporated strategies which involves maintaining adequate preventative protections so that, users are guaranteed that data is secure. Security principles needs to be designed to ensure users are satisfied that data, systems are fully secured .Administrators must be in position to view current status live, to be alerted instantaneously of any un-usual occurrences, and must be able to trace, respond to un-expected events.

It is different

Security is highly inter-twined with access. Generally, traditional environments configure perimeter security. As clouds are highly interconnected, it simpler for traffic to be bypassed away from traditional perimeter defense systems. Weak APIs, insecure identity and credentials management, account hijacks, malicious insiders, can cause problems, which might jeopardize security of system, data Weak APIs, insecure identity and credentials management, account hijacks, malicious insiders, can cause problems that might jeopardize security of system, data.

- Actions, that are need to preventing unauthorized access in cloud, necessitates devising a data-centric Strong multi-level encryption for data
- Enhance authorization mechanism
- Mandatory to implement strong passwords, multi-factor authentication.
- Configure security in every level
- Strong multi-level encryption for data
- Enhance authorization mechanism
- Mandatory to implement strong passwords, multi-factor authentication.
- Configure security in every level

Impact of increased sophistication

Increasingly sophisticated malware, other attacks viz. Advanced Persistent Threats (APTs) are designed for purpose of by-passing defenses by targeting vulnerabilities in the compute stack. Data breaches can lead to dissemination of unauthorized information disclosures, besides tampering of data. All technologies provide their own protection systems. There are one-size-fit all approach to handle threats; it is the responsibility of the cloud management team to frame requisites policies.

Understanding compliance

It is mandatory, that Personal, financial, any sensitive information, needs to be scrutinized for compliance regulations. Such regulations differ depending on where the company is, or transacting with whom. Every country has its own regulations and it is mandatory for business to comply within Europe, European Union's General Data Protection Regulation (GDPR), is the governing body and all entities needs to abide by the guidelines laid out, ahead of preparing for cloud deployments.

Threats

Possess, has the capability of creating negative impact to cloud sophisticated malwares, other attacks viz. Advanced Persistent Threats (APTs) are created to subvert network protection, by targeting vulnerabilities in the stack. Data breaches, can lead to unauthorized information disclosure, data tampering, to prevent such threats, impacting cloud, architects must design state-of-art design, which will serve as first lineOracle cloud platform

https://docs.us-phoenix-1.oraclecloud.com/Content/home.htm

Oracle

O racle Cloud Infrastructure presents bouquet of services that assists developers to design, create, design, deploy HA applications which can be deployed both in on-premise and cloud, by default this platform exhibits capabilities viz. (as physical hardware instances) storage capacity in a flexible overlay virtual network which can be accessed by secure methods from the on-premise datacenter, which facilitates business users design, execute a extensive set of applications, services in a completely secure, HA, setup, beds offering igh-performance compute capabilities (as physical hardware instances) and storage capacity in a flexible overlay virtual network that is securely accessible from your on-premises network, offering following services, platform offers:

https://docs.us-phoenix-1.oraclecloud.com/Content/General/Reference/PaaSprereqs.htm

Accessing cloud infrastructure

For the fundamentals of cloud, even Oracle platform is modeled as like any other cloud solutions, however as technology differs, property of each service is modeled uniquely, Oracle has unique set of interfaces, credentials, users can gain access to the environment, Oracle creates a compartment in datacenter/hosting facility terned as tenancy for Oracle Platform Service, this compartment is specially configured by Oracle for the Oracle Cloud Infrastructure resources which users can create platform services, once a compartment is selected Oracle denies permission for second compartment, Along with this compartment, Oracle creates the IAM policies to allow Oracle Platform Services, and rest follows standard cloud principle, and all customized to suit and to be deployed on Oracle technology

The compartment that Oracle creates for Oracle Platform Services is named as ManagedCompartmentForPaaS

Policies, that Oracle creates for Oracle Platform Services are:

- PSM-root-policy

This policy is attached to the root compartment of your tenancy.

- PSM-mgd-comp-policy

This policy is attached to the ManagedCompartmentForPaaS compartment.

https://docs.us-phoenix-1.oraclecloud.com/Content/home.htm

Oracle Cloud Infrastructure presents bouquet of services that assists developers' to design, create, design, deploy HA applications which can be deployed both in on-premise and cloud, by default this platform exhibits capabilities viz. (as physical hardware instances) storage capacity in a flexible overlay virtual network which can be accessed by secure methods from the on-premise datacenter, which facilitates business users design, execute a extensive set of applications, services in a completely secure, HA, setup, beds offering high-performance compute capabilities (as physical hardware instances) and storage capacity in a flexible overlay virtual network that is securely accessible from your on-premises network, offering following services. platform offers:

Compute

https://docs.us-phoenix-1.oraclecloud.com/Content/Compute/Concepts/computeoverview.htm

Oracle offers two types of instances

- Bare Metal - bare metal compute instance gives you dedicated physical server access for highest performance and strong isolation.
- Virtual Machine - A Virtual Machine (VM) is an independent computing environment that runs on top of physical bare metal hardware. The virtualization makes it possible to run multiple VMs that are isolated from each other. VMs are ideal for running applications that do not require the performance and resources (CPU, memory, network bandwidth, storage) of an entire physical machine.

An Oracle Cloud Infrastructure VM compute instance runs on the same hardware as a Bare Metal instance, leveraging the same cloud-optimized hardware, firmware, software stack, and networking infrastructure.

Components for launching instances

cloud environment in each geographic region host all relevant resources, which includes instances, network devices, where users can deploy instances, either in the same region or different availably domains,which needs to be determined based on a. required performance, b. latency, c, availability, d, redundancy, e, application performance. A virtual version of a traditional network—including subnets, route tables, and gateways—on top of which users instances are executed, it is mandatory that a single cloud network has to be established ahead of launching instances, besides establishing a protected environment to configure cloud networks, besides setting up of security mechanism required for Secure Shell (SSH) access to an instance.

Tagging

Users can create, apply tags to individual resources, which will help in organizing them, which can suit the business needs. Tags can be applied at any points of times and can also be removed, for instance, users can apply tags at a time of creation, or can update the resource later with desired tags

Resource identifiers

Every oracle resources is assigned unique, Oracle-assigned identifier called an Oracle Cloud ID (OCID)Users can gain access to by connecting to console, or with REST APIs, with help any standard browser.

Authentication, Authorization

Every service integrates with IAM for authentication and authorization, for all interfaces (the Console, SDK or CLI, and REST API). It is necessary that groups, compartments, policies should be defined which controls users who needs to gain access to services, to which resources, and the type of access. It is the job of the administrator to configure groups, compartments, and policies which defines which user/ user groups can gain access to what set of services, which resources, and the type of access. In case of a one-off users, to gain access, one contact the administrator who will assist in setting up user ID, create, allocate the compartment(s) that an user needs to use

Metadata limits

Custom defined metadata keys which are not ssh_authorized_ keys or user data) have the following limits:
- Max number of metadata keys: 128
- Max size of key name: 255 characters
- Max size of key value: 255 characters

Archive storage:

https://docs.us-phoenix-1.oraclecloud.com/Content/Archive/ Concepts/archivestorageoverview.htm

Oracle Cloud presents two distinct storage class tiers to address requirements both perform ant, frequently accessed storage, leased frequently accessed "cold storage., oracle storage is designed for tiered operations, that helps to optimize wherever is needed, which also leads to cost optimization, wherever it is executed

Configure Archive Storage for data which experience in-frequent access, however must be preserved for long periods of time, ex historical data, but the flipside is economics achieved by cost optimization, offsets the protracted lead time that is actual needed to access data.

Object store_can be deployed for requirements that where instant access for data is needed, though it comes with relatively higher price tag, it satisfied requirement of performance, accessibility besides that of almost instant, fast ., frequent access, data to which you need fast, immediate, and frequent access.

Archive storage

Archive Storage is recommended for data which experience in-frequent access, long term retention, offers better cost economics over Object storage for archiving data, mainly for purpose of:

- Compliance and audit mandates

- Retroactively analyzing log data to determine usage pattern or debug problems
- Historical or infrequently accessed content repository data
- Application generated data that requires archival for future analysis or legal purposes
- Unlike Object Storage, Archive Storage data retrieval is not instantaneous.

User's can perform interaction with data store in archival is performed with the help of same resources and management interfaces which is being already being deployed for object storage

Method of archival

Archive Storage and Object Storage share the *same* management interfaces:

- The Console is an easy-to-use, browser-based interface.

After signing into the Console, click Storage, and then click Object Storage. A list of the buckets in the compartment you're viewing is displayed. If you don't see the one you're looking for, verify that you're viewing the correct compartment (select from the list on the left side of the page). Find the particular Archive Storage tier bucket you want to manage.

- The command line interface (CLI) provides both quick access and full functionality without the need for programming. For more information, see Command Line Interface (CLI).

The syntax for the CLI commands includes, specifying a service. You will use the Object Storage service designation: oci os to manage Archive Storage using the CLI.

- The REST API provides the most functionality, but requires programming expertise. API Reference and Endpoints provides endpoint details and links to the available API reference documents.. .

Managing buckets

https://docs.us-phoenix-1.oraclecloud.com/Content/Object/Tasks/managingbuckets.htm

In Oracle Cloud Object Storage service, a bucket is a container for storing objects in a compartment within an Object Storage namespace. typically A bucket is associated with a single compartment, is defined by rules, by which actions are completed, polities direct appropriate actions for which users are entitled to perform within a bucket. In order to access cloud environment, individuals need to be provided with suitable type of policy scripted by administrators, irrespective usage of console or REST API with an SDK, CLI, or other tool, in case of if users receive message that you don't have permission that that you don't have permission or are unauthorized, confirm with your administrator the type of access you've been granted and which compartment you should work in.

Pre-authenticated requests

Pre-authenticated requests provides methods to permit users gain access to a bucket or an object, even in absence of creating individual user credentials, for instance, an individual has privileges to create a request that lets a user upload backups to a bucket without owning API keys.

Tagging resources

Users can affix tags to resources, which will aid in organizing them, can apply tags at the time of creating requests, also can create resources, update same; update can also take place later in time, besides updating the resource later with the desired tags.

Bucket names

- Unlike other resources, buckets do not have assigned Oracle Cloud Identifiers (OCIDs). Instead, it is user's responsibility to create, name,configure and recognized as distinct entities with being tagged with any sort of oracle identifies, OCID, it is essential to use the following convention while creating one,
  a. Use from 1 to 256 characters.
  b. Valid characters are letters (upper or lower case), numbers, hyphens, underscores, and periods.
  c. Do not include confidential information.
  d. Make the name unique within the Object Storage namespace.

Users define a bucket name when they create a bucket.

Storage tiers

It is necessary to decide on the tier, that could suitable for object storage, generally, standard object storage tier is selected for swift, in-frequent access, and chose the standard Object Storage tier for data to which you need fast, immediate, and frequent access, besides opting for archive storage tier for data with in-frequent access, but is is need to be preserved for an elongated period of time, once configured, the storage tier configuration mustn't be changed where buckets are housed

Public buckets

When you create a bucket, the bucket is considered a private bucket and the access to the bucket and its contents requires authentication and authorization. However, Object Storage supports anonymous, unauthenticated access to a bucket. You make a bucket *public* by enabling read access to the bucket, following

Permissions

- To enable public access when creating a bucket, use permission BUCKET_CREATE.
- To enable public access for an existing bucket, use permission BUCKET_UPDATE.

Block volume

https://docs.us-phoenix-1.oraclecloud.com/Content/Block/Concepts/overview.htm

Cloud Infrastructure Block Volume service allows dynamic provisioning of resources, manage block storage volumes. Users can create, attach, connect, and migrate volumes at will, in order to satisfy storage, application needs. Once attached, connected, to an instance one can utilize the volume as a regular hard-disk. Volumes can be attached or detached at will to meet storage, application needs, once done, it can be used as volume like regular HDD volume can also be attached, detached to another instances without suffering data loss.Components needed for creation of of a volume and attach it to an instance are listed

- Instance: A bare metal or virtual machine (VM) host running in the cloud.
- Volume attachment: There are two types of volume attachments:
  o ISCSI: A TCP/IP-based standard used for communication between a volume and attached instance.
  o Para virtualized: A virtualized attachment available for VMs.
- Volume: There are two types of volumes:
  o Block volume: A detachable block storage device that allows you to dynamically expand the storage capacity of an instance.

a. Boot volume: A detachable boot volume device that contains the image used to boot a Compute instance instance. One such scenarios is explained individual Block Volume shall be removed from an instance, moved to a different instance without loss of data., data persistence lets users to effortlessly migrate data between instance, which guarantees data is secure albeit not attached to, even any instance, besides data will be intact unless volumes aren't deleted or reformatted. To migrate a volume to another instance, first un-mount the drive from existing instances, cut-off iscsi connection, attach it to the second instance. From there, you simply connect and mount the drive from that instance's guest OS to instantly have access to all of the data. In case of migration of volume to another instance, un-mount the drive from the initial instance, terminate the iscsi connection. block volumes provides higher levels of data durability in comparison to standard attached drives, this also offers more durability as by default, all volumes are automatically replicated, thus minimizing data loss Even if both instance failed, the boot volumes will be active, which can be used for launching new instances, using different instance types or shape, in case of an instance termination, users can keep then associated to boot volume, utilize for launching fresh instances using different instance type or shape which offers administrators flexibility of switching from a bare metal instance to a VM instance and vice versa, or scale up or down the number of cores for an instance.

Compute service

https://docs.us-phoenix-1.oraclecloud.com/Content/Compute/Concepts/computeoverview.htm

- Oracle technology permits users to and manage compute hosts termed as instances, which can be launched at any point of time, to satisfy the compute, application needs, once deployed, same can be accesses through secure connection, access them any time, any sort of applications / services can be hosted in such instances, instances can be attached, detached any time, as well as terminate, inherent flexibility offers attach / detach any time, however users need to be careful about the data, as whatever modification effected on instance's local drives are lost when you terminate it. Any saved changes to volumes attached to the instance are retained. Bare Metal – compute instance presents users with independent physical server instance, which facilitates higher performances, sturdy isolation access for highest performance and strong isolation.

- Virtual Machine – A Virtual Machine (VM) is an independent computing environment which is executed atop, a physical bare metal hardware, which is made possible by deploying virtualization technologies, which facilitates execution of multiple VMs simultaneously, run independently, each VM is a complete environment in itself, capable of operating independently, running all possible compute services.

- Independent operations are made possible by Virtualization which propels execution of multiple VMs simultaneously, which are isolated from each other. VMs are ideal for executing applications which doesn't demand higher the performance, (CPU, memory, network bandwidth, storage) of an entire physical machine. Instances can be placed in existing or different availability domains, depending on individual needs of performance, availability.

Methods to access

Standard method for accessing cloud, is through console – browser-based interface) or the REST API,the requirements for gaining access control is one must have standard desktop, high memory, high speed processor, any internet browser, higher memory capacity, higher CPU increases performance, access needs to be gained through console, connections can be made through Rest APIs, or scripts, SDKs, existing console can be used.

Authorization/authentication

Cloud architecture is such that, every service gets integrated with IAM for purpose of authorization, authentication, and is true for all all interfaces (the Console, SDK or CLI, and REST API), it is the responsibility of administrator, to configure groups, compartments, and policies that decides, which users can gain access to which resources, services, resources, besides type of access, cloud operation works based on policies, which drive major part of operations, single or multiple policies can be scripted, executed indecently or clubbed, for instance policies control who can create new users, create and manage the cloud network, launch instances, create buckets, download objects, etc, and in case of regular users it is must that admistrtator's create user credentials through which all tasks can be carried out.

Regions and availability zones

https://docs.us-phoenix-1.oraclecloud.com/Content/General/Concepts/regions.htm

Instances are hosted in localized availability domains which are called as region, which is complete private, localized geographic area, availability domain is individual or multiple virtual datacenters, houses within a region, region is comprised of multiple availability domains, majortity of them are either region specific viz virtual cloud network, or availability domain-specific, such as a compute instance, typically Availability domains are isolated from each other, fault tolerant, besides the chances of simultaneous failures happening being very less, besides availability domains doesn't share common facilities viz power or cooling, or the internal availability domain network, a failure at one availability domain is unlikely to impact the availability of the others. All the availability domains in a region are connected to each other by a low latency, high bandwidth network, that facilitates design high-availability connectivity to the Internet and customer premises, and to build replicated systems in multiple availability domains for both high-availability and disaster recovery. Regions are architected to be totally completely independent of other regions, which can operate harmoniously even separated by huge distances, across countries, continents and general practice being, Generally, you would deploying an application in the region where it is commonly used, and since using nearby resources enhances availability, performance, reduces latency, but with cloud, services can be delivered from any location, but, localized region offers better performance, a best practice to disperse applications, for two reasons:

- mitigate the risk of region-wide events, such as large weather systems or earthquakes
- meet varying requirements for legal jurisdictions, tax domains, and other business or social criteria

Global Resources

- API signing keys
- compartments
- dynamic groups
- federation resources
- groups
- policies
- tag namespaces
- tag keys
- users

Regional Resources

- Buckets: Although buckets are regional resources, they can be accessed from any location if you use the correct region-specific Object Storage URL for the API calls.
- customer-premises equipment (CPE)
- DHCP options sets
- dynamic routing gateways (DRGs)
- images
- internet gateways
- load balancers
- local peering gateways (LPGs)
- reserved public IPs
- route tables
- security lists
- virtual cloud networks (VCNs)
- Volume backups: They can be restored as new volumes to any availability domain within the same region in which they are stored.

Availability Domain-Specific Resources

- DB Systems
- ephemeral public IPs
- Instances: They can be attached only to volumes in the same availability domain.
- subnets
- Volumes: They can be attached only to an instance in the same availability domain.

Database service

https://docs.us-phoenix-1.oraclecloud.com/Content/Database/Concepts/databaseoverview.htm

DB service allows users to instantaneously launch an Oracle Database System (DB System) and create single or multiple DBs on it, over which users can exercise complete control, gain full access to every single feature, services which are avaiailble, but ownership rests with oracle who manages entire environment. Native DB service offers support to diverse set of DB Systems, ranging in size, price, and performance The Database service supports several types of DB Systems, ranging in size, price, and performance.

Exadata DB Systems

Exadata DB Systems permits to take advantage of capabilities of Exadata within the Oracle Cloud, which consist of An Exadata DB System consists of a quarter rack, half rack, or full rack of compute nodes and storage servers, integrated together with help of a high-speed, low-latency InfiniBand network and intelligent Exadata software, which also supports auto-backups, create scripts for optimization of multiple types of workloads, scale up or down, to address the fluctuating demands.

Supported versions

Exadata DB Systems demands Enterprise Edition - Extreme Performance. which features Database Enterprise Edition, entire along with entire the database enterprise management packs and all the Enterprise Edition options, such as Oracle Database In-Memory and Oracle Real Application Clusters (RAC).

Exadata DB Systems support the following software releases:

- Oracle Database 12c Release 2 (12.2)
- Oracle Database 12c Release 1 (12.1)
- Oracle Database 11g Release 2 (11.2)

Subscription types

- Non-metered Subscription: A non-metered subscription is an agreement to purchase a specific number of service units over a specific term. Consequently, the charge for a non-metered subscription is not related to actual service usage. Non-metered subscriptions are also referred to as standard subscriptions.
- Metered Subscription: With a metered subscription, you are charged based on your service usage. Two varieties exist:
  - Pre-Paid: With a pre-paid subscription you pay an up-front amount to establish an account that is consumed as you use a service.

Pay As You Go: With a pay as you go subscription you do not pay an up-front amount and are billed periodically for your actual service usage.

Scaling an Exadata DB System

Following methods are supported for an Exadata DB System:

- Scaling within an Exadata DB System lets you modify compute node processing power within the system.
- Scaling across Exadata DB System configurations lets you move to a different configuration, for example, from a quarter rack to a half rack.

System configuration

Exadata DB Systems are offered in quarter rack, half rack or full rack configurations, and each configuration consists of compute nodes and storage servers. Individual nodes are configured with a Virtual Machine (VM), with endowing of privilege for the compute node VMs, allowing to configure LBs, execute more software on them, but individuals are deprived of administrative access to the Exadata infrastructure components, which includes g physical compute node hardware, network switches, power distribution units (PDUs), integrated lights-out management (ILOM) interfaces, or the Exadata Storage Servers, which are all administered by Oracle. System Configuration Exadata DB systems are delivered as quarter rack, half rack or full rack configurations which compute nodes storage servers. Individual nodes are configured with a Virtual Machine, for which users has root-privileges, enabling users to launch, execute additional software, but hasn't been granted administrative privileges to Exadata components viz. Physical compute node hardware, network switches, power distribution units (PDUs), integrated lights-out management (ILOM) interfaces, or the Exadata Storage Servers, which are all administered by Oracle.

Compute

https://docs.us-phoenix-1.oraclecloud.com/Content/Compute/ Concepts/computeoverview.htm

Oracle follows standard compute technology, while the principle, operation procedures are similar, instances, types definitely differ, which is listed below. Oracle Linux 6 Unbreakable Enterprise Kernel Release 4 can host following

Centos 7
Centos 6
Ubuntu 16.04 LTS
Ubuntu 14.04 LTS
Windows Server 2016
Windows Server 2012 R2
Windows Server 2008 R2 - Virtual Machine (VM)

All Oracle-provided images include rules that allow only "root" on Linux instances or "Administrators" on Windows Server 2012 R2 and Windows Server 2016 instances to make outgoing connections to the iscsi network endpoints (169.254.0.2:3260, 169.254.2.0/24:3260) that serve the instance's boot and block volumes. Firewalls, in instances, for purpose of deleting the rules

- Individuals need to be forbidden to firewalls, in instances, for purpose of deleting the rules
- Do not create configurations in firewall in individual instances or delete rules, doing such facilitates, non-root users or non-administrators to access the instance's boot disk volume.
- Oracle recommends users need to exercise caution, while creating custom images, until a. requirements are fixed, b.ensure proper back systems in case of failure, c. don't have prior experience in, and have an expert by side, while operating.
- It is not advisable to create custom images, in absence of well designed rules, and understand security risks

Update for Linux images

For instances created using Oracle Linux and Centos images, the user name opc is generated automatically. The opc user has sudo privileges and is configured for remote access over the SSH v2 protocol using RSA keys. The SSH public keys that you specify while creating instances are added to the /home/opc/.ssh/authorized keys file, besides for instances which was created by deploying For instances created using the Ubuntu image, user name Ubuntu is created by default, The Ubuntu user has suedo privileges and is configured for remote access over the SSH v2 protocol using RSA keys. The SSH public keys that needs to be mentioned during creation of are added to the /home/Ubuntu/.ssh/authorized keys file.

Kernel updates

Oracle Linux images on Oracle Cloud include Oracle Linux Premier Support without any additional costs, offering an all-inclusive option, including option of Ksplice, which enables users to apply important security, kernel updates, without shutting down system,

Users

For instances created using the Ubuntu image, the user name Ubuntu is created automatically. The Ubuntu user has suede privileges and is configured for remote access over the SSH v2 protocol using RSA keys. The SSH public keys that you specify while creating instances are added to the /home/ubuntu/.ssh/ authorized keys file. Users shall gain access by using browser to connect to console, or REST APIs. Each service in Oracle Cloud get lightly integrated with IAM for authentication and authorization, for all interfaces (the Console, SDK or CLI, and REST API).Groups, policies compartments needs to be configured which manages groups, compartments, and policies that control which users can access which services, which resources, and the type of access., policies direct actions viz who is responsible for creating users, manages cloud, configure and launch instances, create buckets, download objects.

Bring your own image

https://docs.us-phoenix-1.oraclecloud.com/Content/Compute/References/bringyourownimage.htm

Oracle cloud facilitates users personalize by getting own version of OS, as long platform supports it, this is termed as BYOD, works well as long as underlying physical it platform supports it, this service is independent to hardware, OS, environment, which comes with following benefits

- Enables lift-and-shift cloud migration projects.
- Supports both older and cutting edge operating systems.
- Encourages experimentation.
- Increases infrastructure flexibility.

Building new OS Images

Oracle-provided images: Oracle provides several pre-built images for Oracle Linux, Microsoft Windows, Ubuntu and Centos, using which users can design new RHEL 7.4 images for bare metal and VM instances using a Terraform template

RHEL 7.4 images

Bringing existing operating system images

- Importing custom images for emulation mode: Developers can import current OS image utilizing VMDK or QCOW2 formats, to run in emulation mode VMs
- Bring own KVM – Users can get own operating system images or older operating systems such as Ubuntu 6.x, RHEL 3.x, CentOS 5.4 using KVM on bare metal instances

Bring Your Own OVM: One shall personalized Oracle VM workload to Oracle Cloud Infrastructure own Hyper : users shall get their our own operating system images or older operating systems such as Windows Server 2003, Windows Server 2008, as well as older Linux -based operating systems using Hyper-V on bare metal instances.

Deploy customized Own Hyper-V: Users are free to configure own customized OS images, older Windows OS versions, viz. Windows Server 2003, Windows Server 2008, along with older Linux -based OS, using Hyper-V on bare metal instances, latest configurations are available in the web-site.

Importing custom images for paravirtualized mode: Users shall, import Linux-based operating system images, which supports paravirtualized drivers, using either VMDK or QCOW2 formats, execute paravirtualized-mode VMs.

Importing custom images for emulation mode: Users, shall import Windows based OS images, retired Linux based OS images, which can be accomplished by utilizing VMDK or QCOW2 formats, to be executed in an emulation mode VM's. It is mandatory, that for Linux-based OS, it is must, images need to be executed, only in emulation mode, specially for systems that run kernel versions older than 3.4

Bring Own KVM's:

Oracle supports executing customized OS images or older OS images viz. Ubuntu 6.x, RHEL 3.x, Centos 5.4, using KVM on bare metal instances. Can customized OVM: Users are allowed to design, execute independent OVM, workloads on Oracle cloud.

Customized Hyper V

It is simpler to export, proprietary OS images, or older operating systems, viz.Windows Server 2003, Windows Server 2008,besides older Linux -based operating systems using Hyper-V on bare metal instances. For a full list of supported Hyper-V

https://docs.us–phoenix-1.oraclecloud.com/Content/Compute/ Tasks/launchinginstance.htm

Launching instances

Users can launch instances with help of console, API, scripts, once an instance is launched, automatically it gets attached to virtual network interface card, in cloud network subnet, assigns private IP from subnets CIDR, users can instances using console, APIS, scripts, once launched by default gets attached to a Virtual Network Interface Card (VNIC) in the cloud network's subnet and given a private IP address from the subnet's CIDR. users are provided with the choice regarding IP, which is users can allow auto allocation or enter specific address of the choice, private IP address permits instances within cloud network communicative with one and another, however they also have a choice which is use private network communicate between them, else utilize FQDNs, in case of establishing cloud network for DNS Users can assign instances, public IP address if the subnet is public, which is essential for communicating with instances through internet, besides creating Secure Shell (SSH) or RDP connection to the instance from outside the cloud network._steps are listed

- Create a cloud network and subnet that enables internet access
- Launch an instance
- Connect to the instance
- Add and attach a block volume

Migrating DB to cloud

https://docs.us-phoenix-1.oraclecloud.com/Content/Database/Tasks/mig-11g-12c.htm

Different methods are available to migrate

Launching instances

Instances leverage SSH key pair instead of a password for purpose of to authenticating a remote users, first task is to create key pair, prepare instances by launching cloud network with subnets, launch instances in any of the subnets which has been created, connect to it, if storage needs to be provisioned, follow the same step san image, a cloud network, a subnet, etc,and such resources can co-exist in the same compartment with the instance or in other compartments, prerequisite being, should have requisite levels of access to individual compartments, so as to launch instances, same steps needs to be performed in case of attaching a volume to an instance, besides,

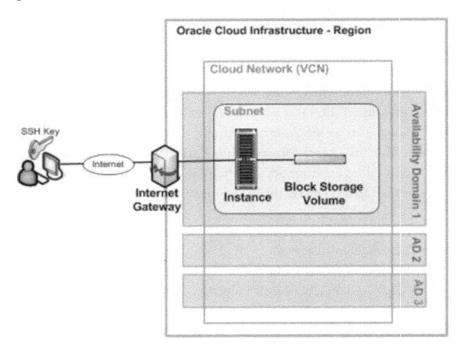

Launching instances 1

It isn't necessary instances must to reside within same compartment, supposing if they don't, administrators need to grant on necessary permissions on to individual compartments, and steps are:

Prepare:

1. Create a key pair.
2. Choose a compartment for your resources.
3. Create a cloud network.

Launch and connect:

4. Launch an instance.

5. Connect to your instance.

Add storage and clean up:

6. Add a block volume (optional).
7. Clean up your resources.

Database services

https://docs.us-phoenix-1.oraclecloud.com/Content/Database/Concepts/databaseoverview.htm

DB service, permits users to quick-launching of Oracle DBMS,create single or multiple databases on it, on which users are granted complete control over resources, operations, but Oracle exercises control of it, both hosting, management. DB service supports multiple types of systems which range in size, price, and performance.

Exadata DB Systems

Bare Metal and Virtual Machine DB Systems

License types

Oracle cloud offer support for licensing model with two license types. With License included, the cost of the cloud service includes a license for the Database service. With Bring Your Own License (BYOL), Oracle Database customers with an Unlimited License Agreement or Non-Unlimited License Agreement can use their license with Oracle Cloud Infrastructure, it is not mandatory to possess exclusive supports a licensing model with two license types. With License included, the cost of the cloud service includes a license for the Database service. With Bring Your Own License (BYOL), Oracle Database customers with an Unlimited License Agreement or Non-Unlimited License Agreement can use their license with

Oracle Cloud Infrastructure, besides not having hard need to have separate on-premises licenses and cloud licenses, besides neglecting the need for a exclusive on-premises licenses and cloud licenses, BYOL DB instances integrate well with all prominent DB service management capability functionalities, that which include backup, restore of DB system, patching, and Oracle Data Guard, supposed BYOL editions are

- Bare Metal Shapes: BM.DenseIO1.36 and BM.DenseIO2.52
- Virtual Machine Shapes:
  o VM.Standard1 (X5 with remote storage): 1, 2, 4, 8, and 16 core
  o VM.Standard2 (X7 with remote storage): 1, 2, 4, 8, 16, and 24 core
- Exadata X6: Quarter, Half, and Full racks

Few restrictions are in place

If BYOL is activated users are deprived of freedom of switching BYOL and license-included licensing model on the same instance but, instances need to be terminated and then create instances anew, Database service supports BYOL only for, clients who have contracted for Universal Credit Plan, Non-metered customers are barred from using instances, however Oracle offers such customers option to from a non-metered model to a Universal Credit Plan Existing customers can migrate from a non-metered model to a Universal Credit Plan, which freely allows use of options which has been purchased as a part of ULA. if organization has purchased Standard or Enterprise Licenses with additional options, it is compulsory that, only Standard Edition or Enterprise Edition license be deployed, in case of any additional DB option which is not RAC, Active Data Guard, Database In-Memory, or Multitenant, it is mandated to use Enterprise Edition - High Performance. instead in case of presence of Active Data Guard, Database In-Memory, or Multitenant, it is compulsory to use Edition - Extreme Performance other hand, if exists Active Data Guard, Database In-Memory / multitenant, it is best to use Enterprise Edition - Extreme Performance, and in such case, especially for a 2-node RAC on virtual machine configuration, then the additional OCPUs will be charged at the RAC OCPU pricing.

Authentication, authorization

Every service within Oracle cloud integrates with IAM for authentication, authorization for all interfaces - Console, SDK or CLI, and REST API. It is job of administrators, to establish groups, compartments, policies, which control which users can access which services, what resources, type of access, for instance, policies control, who are authorized to create policies, control who should create new users, manage, monitor resources, create buckets, etc

Steps

https://docs.us-phoenix-1.oraclecloud.com/Content/Database/Tasks/migrating.htm

User can migrate on-premise DB instances into cloud, by adopting multiple methods combined with utilities, decision on which method to be used is based on factors which include version, character set, and platform Endian format of the source and target databases, listed below are some steps

- On-premises database version
- Database service database version
- On-premises host operating system and version
- On-premises database character set
- Quantity of data, including indexes
- Data types used in the on-premises database
- Storage for data staging
- Acceptable length of system outage

- Network bandwidth

For sake of deciding suitability of methods it is necessary to collect following information

1. Database version of your on-premises database:

    o Oracle Database 12c Release 2 version 12.2.0.1
    o Oracle Database 12c Release 1 version 12.1.0.2 or higher
    o Oracle Database 12c Release 1 version lower than 12.1.0.2
    o Oracle Database 11g Release 2 version 11.2.0.3 or higher
    o Oracle Database 11g Release 2 version lower than 11.2.0.3

2. For on-premises Oracle Database 12c Release 2 and Oracle Database 12c Release 1 databases, the architecture of the database:

    o Multitenant container database (CDB)
    o Non–CDB

3. Endian format (byte ordering) of your on-premises database's host platform. Some platforms are little Endian and others are big Endian. Query V$TRANSPORTABLE_PLATFORM to identify the Endian format, and to determine whether cross-platform tablespace transport is supported.
   The Oracle Cloud Infrastructure Database uses the Linux platform, which is little endian.

4. Database character set of your on-premises database and the Oracle Cloud Infrastructure Database.
   Some migration methods require that the source and target databases use compatible database character sets.

5. Database version of the Oracle Cloud Infrastructure Database you are migrating to:

    o Oracle Database 12c Release 2
    o Oracle Database 12c Release 1

o   Oracle Database 11g Release 2

Oracle Database 12c Release 2 and Oracle Database 12c Release 1 databases created on the Database service use CDB architecture. Databases created using the Enterprise Edition software edition are single-tenant, and databases created using the High Performance or Extreme Performance software editions are multitenant, listed below are migration methods

- Data Pump Conventional Export/Import
- Data Pump Full Transportable
- Data Pump Transportable Tablespace
- Remote Cloning a PDB
- Remote Cloning Non-CDB
- RMAN Cross-Platform Transportable PDB
- RMAN Cross-Platform Transportable Tablespace Backup Sets
- RMAN Transportable Tablespace with Data Pump
- RMAN DUPLICATE from an Active Database
- RMAN CONVERT Transportable Tablespace with Data Pump
- SQL Developer and INSERT Statements to Migrate Selected Objects
- SQL Developer and SQL*Loader to Migrate Selected Objects
- Unplugging/Plugging a PDB
- Unplugging/Plugging Non-CDB

Domain Naming Service DNS

https://docs.us-phoenix-1.oraclecloud.com/Content/DNS/Concepts/dnszonemanagement.htm

Oracle Cloud Domain Name System (DNS) service permits creation, management of with varying degrees of granularity., can create and manage your DNS zones, can also create zones, add records to zones, and allow Ole Cloud Infrastructure's edge network to manage domain's DNS queries, users see the query reports for each zones, from a common console.

DNS Service Components

The following list describes the components used to build a DNS zone and make it accessible from the internet.

Domain

Domain names identify a specific location or group of locations on the Internet as a whole. A common definition of "domain" is the complete portion of the DNS tree that has been delegated to a user's control, examples are, *example.com* or *oracle.com*.

Zone

A zone is a portion of the DNS namespace. A Start of Authority record (SOA) defines a zone. A zone contains all labels underneath itself in the tree, unless otherwise specified.

Label

Labels are pretended to the zone name, separated by a period, to form the name of a sub-domain. For example, the "www" section of www.example.com or the "docs" and "us-ashburn-1" sections of docs.us-ashburn-1.oraclecloud.com are labels. Records are associated with these domains.

Child zone

Child zones are independent sub-domains with their own Start of Authority and Name Server (NS) records. The parent zone of a child zone must contain NS records that refer DNS queries to the name servers responsible for the child zone. Each subsequent child zone creates another link in the delegation chain.

Resource records

A record contains specific domain information for a zone. Each record type contains information called record data (RDATA). For example, the RDATA of an A or AAAA record contains an IP address for a domain name, while MX records contain information about the mail server for a domain.

Delegation

Name servers where your DNS is hosted and managed.

Methods to access DNS servers

Users can gain control to the resources, by connecting to console, or REST API, for which standard desktop, internet connection, is needed, along with supported browser, subscription to required platform provider. Console, APIS, customized scripts are few methods to accessing servers. Administrators' must establish groups, compartments, and policies which can control user's privileges, access, ex. which users can access which services?, Which resources, the type of access. In case of regular users, there are certain limitations too, which is NS service is limited to 1000 zones per account and 25,000 records per zone. No SDK or CLI is available for the Oracle Cloud Infrastructure DNS service currently. The Console or the REST API with an SDK, CLI, or other tool

Service policy

For purpose of connecting to cloud, it is mandatory to get assigned the right set of access privileges, in a policy scripted d by administrators, irrespective of using console, REST API, with SDK, CLI, or other tool. if an user attempts to execute an action, gets message that not authorized, consult the administrator, regarding the access controls that has been assigned.

DNS

https://docs.us-phoenix-1.oraclecloud.com/Content/DNS/Concepts/dnszonemanagement.htm

The Oracle Cloud Infrastructure Domain Name System (DNSOracle DNS, allows creation, management of DNS zones, add record service allows for creation of DNS zones, which can be self-managed, and permit Oracle Cloud Infrastructure's edge network to manage domains, DNS queries, can also view query report for the zones, which exhibit different levels of granularity.

DNS Service Components

The following list describes the components used to build a DNS zone and make it accessible from the internet.

Domain

Domain names identify a specific location or group of locations on the Internet as a whole. A common definition of "domain" is the complete portion of the DNS tree that has been delegated to a user's control. For example, *example.com* or *oracle.com*.

Zone

A zone is a portion of the DNS namespace. A Start of Authority record (SOA) defines a zone. A zone contains all labels underneath itself in the tree, unless otherwise specified.

Label

Labels are pretended to the zone name, separated by a period, to form the name of a sub domain. For example, the "www" section of www.example.com or the "docs" and "us-ashburn-1" sections of docs.us-ashburn-1.oraclecloud.com are labels. Records are associated with these domains.

Child zone

Child zones are independent subdomains with their own Start of Authority and Name Server (NS) records. The parent zone of a child zone must contain NS records that refer DNS queries to the name servers responsible for the child zone. Each subsequent child zone creates another link in the delegation chain.

Resource records are record contains specific domain information for a zone. Each record type contains information called record data (RDATA). For example, the RDATA of an A or AAAA record contains an IP address for a domain name, while MX records contain information about the mail server for a domain.

Delegation

The name servers from where, where DNS is hosted and managed.

Methods of access DNS

SSH, console, REST APIs, scripts are few means to access oracle instances, with supported browser,

Authentication, authorization

IAM is deployed for authorization, authentication for for all interfaces (the Console, SDK or CLI, and REST API).IT department has to establish, compartments, and policies which is deployed to control user access viz which user gets access to which service, which can create new users, create and manage the cloud network, launch instances, create buckets, download objects, resources, and the type of access. For instance policies regarding who get to control who can create new users, create and manage the cloud network, launch instances, create buckets, download objects, etc. besides, if you are regular an user is supposed to utilize cloud, has to contact systems administrator for creating, establishing, user credentials, on behalf of users' admistrator's then shall identify which compartment or compartment to be allocated.

Database service

https://docs.us-phoenix-1.oraclecloud.com/Content/Database/Concepts/databaseoverview.htm

DB system, allows users to swiftly launch, a Oracle Database System (DB System), create one or more databases on it, over which users will have full access, to features, operations which comes with DB. DB service offers support to multitude of DB Systems, of varied type, size, and performance. Users are bestowed complete access to features, operations, however, Oracle owns, manages, infrastructure.

You have full access to the features and operations available with Oracle Database, but Oracle owns and manages the infrastructure, major types are

Exadata DB Systems

Bare Metal and Virtual Machine DB Systems

License types

Oracle supports a licensing model with two license types. With License included, the cost of the cloud service includes a license for the Database service. With Bring Your Own License (BYOL), Oracle Database customers with an Unlimited License Agreement or Non-Unlimited License Agreement can use their license with Oracle Cloud Infrastructure, which implies, that there is no necessity of procuring separate on-premises licenses and cloud licenses. Furthermore, BYOL DB instances support all advanced Database service manageability functionality that includes backup/restore, systems patching. Oracle

Guard users, themselves can activate BYOL during launching of DB instances, enabling of which affects methods as how utilization data for instances is metered, billed, listed below are versions of supported DB versions

Bare Metal Shapes: BM.DenseIO1.36 and BM.DenseIO2.52

- Virtual Machine Shapes:
    - VM.Standard1 (X5 with remote storage): 1, 2, 4, 8, and 16 core
    - VM.Standard2 (X7 with remote storage): 1, 2, 4, 8, 16, and 24 core

Exadata X6: Quarter, Half, and Full racks

Restrictions

Restrictions that apply are

- In event of enabling BYOL, users can't make a switch between BYOL and license-included licensing model on the same instance, and don't have other option than terminating
- DB service that supports BYOL exclusive for users who have subscribed to Universal Credit Plan,
- The Database service supports BYOL only for customers who use the Universal Credit Plan. Non-metered customers are barred from using
- BYOL, however permitting residing tenants to migrate from a non-metered model to a Universal Credit Plan.
- users are provided access to that has been purchased, which is listed in the ULA

In case of holding Standard or Enterprise Licenses which includes extra options, it is mandatory to use a Standard Edition or Enterprise Edition license.

- And in case of requirements of extra any database option except RAC, Active Data Guard, Database In-Memory, or Multitenant; it is must to deploy you Enterprise Edition - High Performance. If the environment is installed with Active Data Guard, Database In-Memory, or Multitenant, it is compulsory to adopt Enterprise Edition - Extreme Performance., besides if the choice is made for Extreme Performance edition for a 2-node RAC on virtual machine configuration, extra CPUs will be billed according to RAC OCPU pricing. Access can be gained through Console (a browser-based interface) or the REST API. Instructions for the Console and API

Exadata DB systems

https://docs.us-phoenix-1.oraclecloud.com/Content/Database/Concepts/exaoverview.htm

Single Exadata DB System consists of a quarter rack, half rack, or full rack of compute nodes and storage servers, tied together by a high-speed, low-latency InfiniBand network and intelligent Exadata software. Users can conveniently configure auto backups, optimize them for various workloads, scale systems up to address increasing demands, listed below are supported software releases

- Oracle Database 12c Release 2 (12.2)
- Oracle Database 12c Release 1 (12.1)
- Oracle Database 11g Release 2 (11.2)

System configurations

Exadata DB Systems are offered in quarter rack, half rack or full rack configurations, and each configuration consists of compute nodes and storage servers. Compute nodes are each configured with a Virtual Machine (VM), for which users are provided root access for compute node empowering VMs to load, execute additional software on them, by default, users are not granted admin privileges to access to the Exadata infrastructure components that includes switches, power distribution units (PDUs), integrated lights-out management (ILOM) interfaces, or the Exadata Storage Servers, which are all administered by Oracle. Users are provided with complete rights to databases, and users can make connections to databases by installing Oracle Net Services from outside the Oracle Cloud, Users need to take responsibility for administrative actions viz creating tablespace, managing database plus taking ownership of database administration tasks such as users. In built utilities are provide using which customization of default automated maintenance set up task can be achieved, and establish recovery process in the event of a database failure

Storage configuration

In an event of a user, launching a system, storage space within, configured for use by Oracle Automatic Storage Management (ASM).As default, below mentioned disk groups are created

- The DATA disk group is intended for the storage of Oracle Database data files.
- The RECO disk group is primarily used for storing the Fast Recovery Area (FRA), which is an area of storage where Oracle Database can create and manage various files related to backup and recovery, such as RMAN backups and archived redo log files.
- The DBFS and ACFS disk groups are system disk groups that support various operational purposes. The DBFS disk group is primarily used to store the shared cluster-aware files (Oracle Cluster Registry and voting disks), while the ACFS disk groups are primarily used to store Oracle Database binaries. Compared to the DATA and RECO disk groups, the system disk groups are so small that they are typically ignored when discussing the overall storage capacity. You

should not store Oracle Database data files or backups inside the system disk groups.

The disk group names contain a short identifier string that is associated with your Exadata Database Machine environment. For example, the identifier could be C2, in which case the DATA disk group would be named DATAC2, and the RECO disk group would be named RECOC2, and so on

Launching

https://docs.us-phoenix-1.oraclecloud.com/Content/Database/Tasks/exalaunchingDB.htm

Whenever an instance is launched, by default system is provisioned to support oracle DB, prerequisites are listed

- The public key, in OpenSSH format, from the key pair that you plan to use for connecting to the DB System via SSH. A sample public key, abbreviated for readability, is shown below.
  ssh-rsa AAAAB3NzaC1yc2EAAAABJQAA....lo/gKMLVM2 xzc1xJr/Hc26biw3TXWGEakrK1OQ== rsa-key-20160304
- The name of a virtual cloud network (VCN) to launch the DB System in.
- Exadata DB systems require two separate VCN subnets: a client subnet for user data and a backup subnet for backup traffic.
- Never chose subnet which overlaps with 192.168.128.0/20., configuration holds good for both the client subnet and backup subnet.
- Users can define the client subnet as either a private subnet or a public subnet, but it is essential to define backup subnet as a public subnet to back up the database to Object Storage.

- Exadata warrants the use use a VCN Resolver for DNS name resolution for the client subnet, can automatically resolves the Swift endpoints required for backing up databases, patching, and updating the cloud tooling on an Exadata DB system.

Default Options for the Initial Database

Certain default options, for launching system in the Console are listed

- Console Enabled: False
- Create Container Database: False for version 11.2.0.4 databases. Otherwise, true.
- Create Instance Only (for standby and migration): False
- Database Home ID: Creates a database home
- Database Language: AMERICAN
- Database Sizing Template: odb2
- Database Storage: ACFS for version 11.2.0.4 databases. Otherwise, ASM.
- Database Territory: AMERICA
- Database Unique Name: The user-specified database name and a system-generated suffix, for example, dbtst_phx1cs.
- PDB Admin Name: pdbuser (Not applicable for version 11.2.0.4 databases.)

Configuring static routes

Entire traffic in an Exadata DB system by default, routed through the data network., and order to create round-trip to bring route backup traffic to the backup interface (BONDETH1), it is essential static route on *each* of the compute nodes in the cluster is designed,

Pre-requisites

- The Exadata DB system's cloud network (VCN) must be configured with an internet gateway. Add a route table rule to open the access to the Object Storage Service Swift endpoint on CIDR 0.0.0.0/0.

- Oracle recommends that you update the backup subnet's security list to disallow any access from outside the subnet and allow egress traffic for TCP port 443 (https) on CIDR Ranges 129.146.0.0/16 (Phoenix region), 129.213.0.0/16 (Ashburn region), 130.61.0.0/16 (Frankfurt region), and 132.145.0.0/16 (London region).
- The network traffic between the system and Object Storage does not leave the cloud and never reaches the public internet.

Access

DNS facilitates use host names instead of IP, for communicating with DB system, *Internet and VCN Resolver* (the DNS capability built into the VCN) as described in DNS in Your Virtual Cloud Network. Oracle recommends using a VCN Resolver for DNS name resolution for the client subnet. It automatically resolves the Swift endpoints *to talk to DB systems,* user can the *Internet and VCN Resolver* (the DNS capability built into the VCN), Oracle recommends deploying Resolver for DNS name resolution for the client subnet, which automatically resolves the Swift endpoints, which is a pre-requisite for backing up databases, patching, and updating the cloud tooling on an Exadata DB system, technical details are listed

https://docs.us-phoenix-1.oraclecloud.com/Content/Database/Tasks/examonitoringDB.htm

Accessing Enterprise Manager Database Express 12c

Enterprise Manager Database Express 12c (EM Express) is available on Exadata DB system database deployments created using Oracle Database 12c Release 1 (12.1) or later. Means of access

- To manage the CDB. When a database deployment is created, Database automatically sets port 5500 on the deployment's compute nodes for EM Express access to the CDB.
- To manage a PDB. For an Oracle Database 12.2 or later deployment, a single port (known as the global port) is automatically set on the deployment's compute nodes. The global port lets you use EM Express to connect to all of the PDBs in the CDB using the HTTPS port for the CDB.
- For an Oracle Database 12.1 deployment, you must manually set a port on the deployment's compute nodes for each PDB you want to manage using EM Express.

Accessing Enterprise Manager 11g Database Control

Enterprise Manager 11g Database Control (Database Control) comes with on Exadata DB system database deployments which has been created using Oracle Database 11g Release 2. Database Control is allocated a unique port number for each database deployment. Standard policy, access to Database Control is routed through 1158 for the first deployment, next set of deployments Subsequent deployments are allocated ports in a range starting with 5500, 5501, 5502, for which users directly needs to confirm Users need to confirm DB control port for DB by creating a search for REPOSITORY_URL in the $ORACLE_HOME/host_sid/sysman/config/emd.properties file. Prior to accessing DB controls, add suitable network ports for database to list associated with the Exadata DB system's client subnet. After configuring, and is important to update security list, which is the correct process to update security list using which user access can be granted in such a manner, users can directly access database control by directing browser to https://<node-ip-address>:<port>/em wherein node-ip-address is the public IP address of the compute node hosting Database Control, and port is the Database Control port used by the database

Updating security list

Even before, users can gain access to EM express or database control, it is essential to assign port for database to security list linked with Exadata DB system's client subnet, below steps lead needs to be followed

1. In the Console, click Database and locate the DB system in the list.
2. Note the DB system's Client Subnet name and click its Virtual Cloud Network.
3. Locate the subnet in the list, and then click its security list under Security Lists.
4. Click Edit All Rules and add an ingress rule with source CIDR=*<source CIDR>*, protocol=TCP, and port=*<port number or port range>*.

The source CIDR should be the CIDR block that includes the ports you open for the client connection.

Managing DB on Exadata system

https://docs.us-phoenix-1.oraclecloud.com/Content/Database/Tasks/examanagingdatabases.htm

Administrators can apply dbaasapi command line utility to create and delete databases on an Exadata DB System. The utility operates like a REST API, which t reads a JSON request body and produces a JSON response body in an output file. The utility is located in the /var/opt/oracle/dbaasapi/ directory on the compute nodes and must be run as the root user, some of prerequisites are Exadata DB System needs access the object store. It is essential that, DB System's cloud network (VCN) is being configured with internal gateway, to compete configuration, add routing table rule provide access to the Object Storage Service Swift endpoint on CIDR 0.0.0.0/0DB System's cloud network (VCN) must be configured with an internet gateway. Add a route table rule to open the access to the Object Storage Service Swift endpoint on CIDR 0.0.0.0/0. It is recommendation from Oracle, regular update scripts be developed for updating backup subnet's security list to prohibit any access from any external subnet, permit egress traffic for TCP port 443 (https) on CIDR 129.146.0.0/16. One has to take a note; network traffic between the DB System and Object Storage does not leave the cloud and never reaches the public internet.

An existing Object Storage bucket to use as the backup destination, methods viz console, API console, to create bucket, for accessing instances, users can create or oracle can generate Swift password, AM, APIs are other ways to generate password, user credentials mentioned in backup configuration file necessarily should have tenancy-level access to Object Storage, simplest method to accomplish this is to user name to the Administrators group, which grants permission to necessary services, besides, administrator has the rights to create policies which grants tenancy-level access to just Object Storage, however it permits access to all cloud services, but administrators has privilege to create policies that permit allows tenancy-level access to just Object Storage. T

https://docs.us-phoenix-1.oraclecloud.com/Content/Database/Tasks/exabackingup.htm

Users have permissions to create backups of Exadata DB System to an existing bucket in the Oracle Cloud's object storage service, and to local disk Fast Recovery Area, steps needed to be followed:

- Create a backup configuration file that indicates the backup destination, when the backup should run, and how long backups are retained. If the backup destination is Object Storage, the file also contains the credentials to access the service.
- Associate the backup configuration file with a database. The database will be backed up as scheduled, or you can create an on-demand backup.

Pre-requisites

It is necessary that Exadata DB System needs to access the Oracle Cloud Infrastructure Object Storage service. Exadata DB System's cloud network (VCN) should be configured with an internet gateway. Configure routing table rule to open the access to the Object Storage Service Swift endpoint on CIDR 0.0.0.0/0. It is always necessary for system administrators to update the backup subnet's security list to disallow any access from outside the subnet, allowing egress traffic for TCP port 443. on the IP ranges listed under Object Storage IP Allocations, should remember that, network traffic between the system and Object Storage doesn't cross subnets, never leave the cloud and never reaches public internet An existing Object Storage bucket to use as the backup destination Swift password, administrators can login into Console or the IAM API to generate the password. It is necessary that user name specified in the backup configuration file necessarily configured to have tenancy-level access to Object Storage, simple method to accomplish is to add the user name to the Administrators group, which provides open permission to all cloud services, to regulate, administrators needs to create targeted policies, add specific user name to admin groups, which facilitates complete access to all services, but for restricting, one of the strategy is include the user name to the Administrators group, but one drawback, it opens access to all cloud services, in this circumstance one of the best ways deploy policies which is capable of allowing tenancy-level access to just Object Storage Listed below examples of such a policy.

Allow group DBAdmins to manage buckets in tenancy
Allow group DBAdmins to manage objects in tenancy

Default options

- Full (level 0) backup of the database followed by rolling incremental (level 1) backups on a seven-day cycle (a 30-day cycle for the Object Storage destination).

- Full backup of selected system files.
- Automatic backups daily at a specific time set during the database deployment creation process.

Retention period:

- Both Object Storage and local storage: 30 days, with the 7 most recent days' backups available on local storage.
- Object Storage only: 30 days.
- Local storage only: Seven days.

Encryption:

- Both Object Storage and local storage: All backups to cloud storage are encrypted.
- Object Storage only: All backups to cloud storage are encrypted.

Block Volume

https://docs.us-phoenix-1.oraclecloud.com/Content/Block/Concepts/overview.htm

Oracle Cloud Infrastructure Block Volume service facilitates, dynamic provisioning, management of block storage volumes, with help of GUI, scripts, users can create, attach, connect, move volumes as required to suit individual storage, application needs, once attached, connected to an instance, users have complete control, can utilize as regular HDD, utilize for all compatible purposes, attach/detach is simpler at any point of time, with guarantee of data safety, components needed to attach/ detach are-

- Instance: A bare metal or virtual machine (VM) host running in the cloud.
- Volume attachment: There are two types of volume attachments:

- o ISCSI: A TCP/IP-based standard used for communication between a volume and attached instance.
- o Para-virtualized: A virtualized attachment available for VMs.

<u>Two type of volumes are</u>:

Block volume: A detachable block storage device that allows you to dynamically expand the storage capacity of an instance.

Boot volume: A detachable boot volume device that contains the image used to boot a Compute instances, described are few block volume scenarios

Common use case of block volume is extending storage capacity to oracle cloud, instance, upon launching instances, establishing cloud networks, users can create block storage volumes using any standard methods, attach/detach instances can be performed by volume attachments, after doing so, users can connect to volumes from user instance's instance's guest OS using iscsi, after which volumes can be mounted, used by instances

Scenario -Persistent and Durable Storage

Block Volumes volume can be detached from running instance, moved to a different instance without any data loss, because of the inherent property of data persistence, which allows simple migration of data between instances, ensuring safety of data even if disconnected from the cloud network, in case of moving volumes to another instance, first un-mount drive from current running instance, terminate connection, attach it to the second instance, from where, users can just migrate instance, un-mount the drive from the initial instance, terminate the iscsi connection, and attach it to the second instance, then on, users can make simple connections, mount the drive from that instance's guest OS to instantly have access to all of users data, block volumes, provide high levels of durability, as against traditional drives, besides every volume is replicated, which aids in safeguarding users data

Instance Scaling

In event of terminating instances, it is technically possible to retain associated boot volumes, apply for launching new instances, using varied instance type or shape, this strategy lets easy switch from a bare metal instance to a VM instance and vice versa, or scale up or down the number of cores for an instance.

Capabilities, limits

- Block Volume volumes can be created in sizes starting from 50 GB to 16 TB in 1 GB increments. By default, Block Volume volumes are 1 TB and performances with block size. Volumes per instance: 32
- Number of backups
  - Monthly universal credits: 1000
  - Pay-as-you-go: 500

Regions, availability domains

https://docs.us-phoenix-1.oraclecloud.com/Content/General/Concepts/regions.htm

It is established in hosted, regional availability domains, Oracle Cloud is hosted in regions and availability domains. A region is a localized geographic area, and an availability domain is one or more data centers located within a region. A region is composed of several availability domains. Most Oracle Cloud Infrastructure resources are either region-specific, such as a virtual cloud network, or availability domain-specific, such as a compute instance. Availability domains in a region are connected to each other by a low latency, high bandwidth network, which makes it possible for IT department to offer high-availability connectivity to the Internet and customer premises, and to build replicated systems in multiple availability domains for both high-availability and disaster recovery. Regions are completely independent of other regions and can be separated by vast distances—across countries or even continents. Generally, you would deploy an application in the region where it is most heavily used, since using nearby resources is faster than using distant resources. However, you can also deploy applications in different regions to:

- mitigate the risk of region-wide events, such as large weather systems or earthquakes
- meet varying requirements for legal jurisdictions, tax domains, and other business or social criteria

Local Resources

- API signing keys
- compartments
- dynamic groups
- federation resources
- groups
- policies
- tag namespaces
- tag keys
- users

Regional Resources

- Buckets: Although buckets are regional resources, they can be accessed from any location if you use the correct region-specific Object Storage URL for the API calls.
- customer-premises equipment (CPE)
- DHCP options sets
- dynamic routing gateways (DRGs)
- images

- internet gateways
- load balancers
- local peering gateways (LPGs)
- reserved public IPs
- route tables
- security lists
- virtual cloud networks (VCNs)
- Volume backups: They can be restored as new volumes to any availability domain within the same region in which they are stored.

Availability Domain-Specific Resources

- DB Systems
- ephemeral public IPs
- Instances: They can be attached only to volumes in the same availability domain.
- subnets
- Volumes: They can be attached only to an instance in the same availability domain.

https://access.redhat.com/documentation/en-US/Red Hat Enterprise Virtualization/3.0/html/Technical Reference Guide/ chap-Technical Reference Guide-Introducing Red Hat Enterprise Virtualization.html

1. <u>Redhat basics</u>

<u>Red hat Virtualization</u>

RHEL Virtualization presents full-feature virtualization platform utilities that are essential for effective and efficient management and listed below are the RHEL cloud components. The Red Hat Enterprise Virtualization Hypervisor is a concise, feature rich Virtualization platform that can be considered for quick and easy method of deploying and managing virtualized guests. Hypervisor is a minimal installation of Red Hat Enterprise Linux designed especially to support virtualization workloads. Users will have to manage hypervisors with the Red Hat Enterprise Virtualization Manager. Full virtualization achieved by using a loadable Linux kernel module called Kernel-based Virtual Machine (KVM). KVM can concurrently host multiple virtualized guests running either Windows or Linux operating systems. Virtualized guests run as individual Linux processes on the host machine and are managed remotely using the Red Hat

Enterprise Virtualization Manage. RHEL enterprise manager is a centralized management system which, Which permits, administrators to view and manage virtual machines and images, This platform offers exhaustive range of properties, which includes search capabilities, resource management, live migrations, and provisioning and the Manager component runs on RHEL. The manager offers users with GUI, through which administrative and administrative tasks such as managing physical and logical resources of the virtual environment, it can also be trusted to manage provisioning, connection protocols, user sessions, virtual machine pools, images, and virtual machine high availability. Users and administrators can interact with RHEL enterprise manager by using Administration Portal, a User Portal, and an Application Programming Interface (API). With help of administration portal, administrators can create user accounts, perform configuration and maintenance tasks, and for users to Create, configure and maintain Red Hat Enterprise Virtualization environment. User Portal can also be used for start, stop, reboot, and make connections to the virtual machines, and through this portal user privileges delegation can be performed. Users can be granted "power user" access by the administrators, for specific reasons such as delegating rights to another user, if needed, and are permitted to create virtual machine templates and virtual machines from this interface, REST API offer an interface for automation of tasks, that normally carried out manually by users. Scripts that make use of the REST API can be written in any language which supports accessing HTTP and HTTPS resources.

Architecture

https://access.redhat.com/documentation/en-US/Red_Hat_Enterprise_Virtualization/3.0/html/Technical_Reference_Guide/chap-Technical_Reference_Guide-Architecture.html

Red Hat Enterprise Virtualization environment comprises s of:

- The Red Hat Enterprise Virtualization Manager,

- One or more Red Hat Enterprise Virtualization Hypervisor hosts, or Red Hat Enterprise Linux virtualization hosts,
- associated backing storage,
- the networking which t facilitates communication between all elements of the Red Hat Enterprise Virtualization environment.

And all the above mentioned entities, consists of a number of components which are transparent to users and administrators. These components interact to enable the efficient virtualization of workloads using Red Hat Enterprise

Virtualization manager

The manager, Enables s centralized management for a virtualized environment. And this platform supports user of multiple interfaces to access the Red Hat Enterprise Virtualization Manager and each interface, supports access to the virtualized environment in a different manner. Virtualization Manager generates graphical interfaces and an Application Programming Interface (API). With individual interface connects to the manager, an application delivered by an embedded instance of the JBoss Enterprise Application Platform, besides multiple such components, that offer support to Red Hat Enterprise Virtualization Manager in addition to JBoss Enterprise Application Platform.

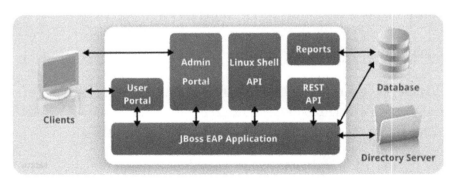

RHEL enterprise virtualization manager 1

Manager presents graphical interfaces and an Application Programming Interface (API). Individual interfaces, each interface connects to the Manager, an application delivered by an embedded instance of the JBoss Enterprise Application Platform, besides the Jboss platform, there are numerous component that offer support enterprise virtualization manager, along with JBoss Enterprise Application Platform.

Interfaces for accessing the manager

User portal

Generally administrators, use the user portal as the primary means for delivering Virtual Desktop Infrastructure to end users. and this technology gives end users, with a complete desktop environment, which is a look alike of PC''s desktop environment. Web browser can be used to access the portal, which, will provide privileges to display and access a user's assigned virtual desktops and administrator has the privileges to define the actions and the rights for the users. Standard users by default are privileged to start, stop, and use desktops that are assigned to them by the system administrator, and power users can perform administrative and configuration management tasks and the two sets of users can use the same URL, but are redirected to the respective functions, based on the assigned privileges.

Standard user access

Standard users are assigned with privileges to power their virtual desktops on and off and connect to them through the user portal. Simple Protocol for Independent Computing Environments (SPICE) or Virtual Network Computing (VNC) clients. Both protocols can be used for Direct connection to virtual machines is facilitated through h Simple Protocol for Independent Computing Environments (SPICE) or Virtual Network Computing (VNC) clients, and these two helps user with an environment similar to a locally installed desktop environment. The administrator identifies the protocol that should be configuring to connect to a virtual machine at the time of the virtual machine's creation,

Redhat Virtualization hypervisor

https://access.redhat.com/documentation/en-US/Red_Hat_ Enterprise_Virtualization/3.0/html/Technical_Reference_Guide/sect-Technical_Reference_Guide-Architecture-Red_Hat_Virtualization_ Hypervisor.html

Enterprise Virtualization environment has single or multiple hosts attached to it. A host is a server which presents the physical hardware that virtual machines can utilize. the hosts run an optimized operating system installed using a special, customized installation media customized y for creating virtualization hosts and host configuration reads like "servers running a standard Red Hat Enterprise Linux operating system that has been customized after installation to permit use as a host" and both methods leads to in a situation, where "hosts that interact with the rest of the virtualized environment in the same way, and so, will both referred to as hosts."

Kernel–based Virtual Machine (KVM)

The Kernel-based Virtual Machine (KVM) is a loadable kernel module that provides full virtualization through the use of the Intel VT or AMD-V hardware extensions. Though KVM itself runs in kernel space, the guests running upon it run as individual QEMU processes in user space. KVM allows a host to make its physical hardware available to virtual machines. Besides The Kernel-based Virtual Machine (KVM) is a loadable kernel module that offers full virtualization through the use of the Intel VT or AMD-V hardware extensions. Despite,KVM operates in kernel space, the guest instances which runs as individual QEMU processes in user space. KVM allows a host to make its physical hardware available to virtual machines

QEMU

QEMU is a multi-platform emulator, deployed for the purpose of offerring full system emulation for example,

QEMU emulates a full system, for example a PC, including one or more processors and peripherals. QEMU can be used to launch different operating systems or to debug system code. QEMU, working in conjunction with KVM and a processor with appropriate virtualization extensions, provides full hardware assisted virtualization. VDSM performs actions on virtual machines, storage, besides assisting in inter-host communication. VDSM monitors virtualized hosts' resources such as memory, storage, and networking. VDSM performs actions on virtual machines, storage, besides helping in inter-host communication, besides, the health, status of virtualized hosts' resources such as memory, storage, and networking.

Guest OS

Guest operating systems can be deployed in an Virtualization environment without modification. The guest operating system, and any applications on the guest, is isolated and run normally. However, device drivers that allow faster and more efficient access to virtualized devices are available and can be installed inside the guest, besides installation of enterprise Virtualization Agent on guests, which provides more detailed information on guests to management console Storage Pool Manager (SPM) is a role assigned to a single host in which empowers the SPM host sole authority to make all storage domain structure metadata changes for the data center which includes creation, deletion, manipulation of virtual disk images, snapshots, and templates. Besides allocation of space for seldom used block devices on SAN devices. Migrating role of SPM to other host within the datacenter, which will lead to an environment that all hosts in a data center must have access to the storage domains defined in the data center is possible

Rehat storage

https://access.redhat.com/documentation/en-US/Red Hat Enterprise Virtualization/3.0/html/Technical Reference Guide/ sect-Technical Reference Guide-Architecture-Storage.html

RHEL virtualization adopts centralized storage strategy, for virtual machine disk images, templates, snapshots, and ISO files. Further, it is also logically segregated, into storage pools, which is constituted of, storage domains and such domain aggregates storage capacity which contains images with metadata that defines the internal structure of the storage. There are three types of storage domain; data, export, and ISO. Data storage domain is the critical it is sufficient, that a single such domain is created, in each center, Data storage domain is exclusive to a particular e data center. Storage domains are shared resources and hence the design should be created such that, it is accessible to all hosts in a data center. Storage networking is recommended to be implemented that can be implemented with the help of installing Network File System (NFS), Internet Small Computer System Interface (iSCSI), or Fiber Channel Protocol (FCP). A storage domain shall consist of block devices (SAN - iSCSI or FCP) or files (NAS - NFS. Export and ISO domains are optional. NFS is used as an aggregation point, all virtual disks, templates, and snapshots are simple files. On SAN (iSCSI/FCP), block devices are aggregated into a logical entity called a Volume Group (VG) and it is performed by deploying the Logical Volume Manager (LVM) and depicted is the storage architecture. On NFS, all items that are stored viz, virtual disks, templates, and snapshots are considered simple files, but On SAN (iSCSI/FCP), block devices are aggregated into a logical entity which is termed a

Volume Group (VG).This is accomplished by configuring using the Logical Volume Manager (LVM).

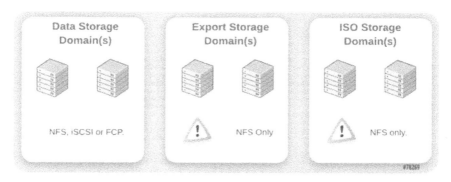

Storage architecture 1

Data storage domain

Data domains serves as the repository or storage space, holding disk images of all the virtual machines running in the environment, which includes installed operating system images, and data disks. Snapshots of the virtual machines can also stored in the data domain. However, it can't be shared between multiple datacenters, besides, the data domain in question, compulsorily of the same type as the data center. For example, a data center of a iSCSI type, must have an iSCSI data domain

Export storage domain

An export domain is a temporary storage repository that is used to copy and move images between data centers and Red Hat Enterprise Virtualization environments. The export domain can be used to back up virtual machines and templates. An Export domain can be moved between data centers, but can only be active in one data center at a time. ISO domains store ISO files, which are logical CD-ROMs that are utilized to to install operating systems and applications for the virtual machines. And as they are are logical volumes, As a logical entity that replaces a library of physical CD-ROMs or DVDs, an ISO domain removes the data center's need for physical media. An ISO domain can be shared across different data centers

Storage attributes

https://access.redhat.com/documentation/en-US/Red Hat Enterprise Virtualization/3.0/html/Technical Reference Guide/ sect-Technical Reference Guide-Storage Architecture-Storage Attributes.html

RH Enterprise Virtualization environment supports two storage formats: RAW, QCOW2.

3.3.1.1. QCOW2.QCOW represents QEMU copy on write. QCOW2 format decouples physical storage layer from virtual layer by inserting mapping between logical and physical blocks, with individual logical block mapped to its physical offset, which enables snapshots. Creating fresh snapshot, leads to creation of new copy on write layer, either, as a new file or logical volume, with an initial mapping that points all logical blocks to the offsets in backing file or volume. During writing into a QCOW2 volume, relevant block is read from backing volume, updated with new details, writing into new snapshot QCOW2 volume .Subsequently maps are updated to point to new location. Advantage that one derives when QCOW2 used over RAW,

Copy-on-write support, where "volume-only" represents changes, effected to an underlying disk image. Snapshots are supported when a volume is capable of representing multiple snapshots of images history.RAW storage format comes with performance advantage compared when compared with QCOW2,where no formatting gets applied to images stored, which has been stored in RAW. Reading, writing an image stored in RAW format doesn't necessitate any additional operations needs to be performed as part of host manager. In an event of guest file system writes to a pre-defined offset in within its virtual disk, I/O will be written into the same offset on backing file or into logical volume. Raw format demands, whole of space allocated image, should be pre-allocated, unless, externally managed thin provisioned LUNs from a storage array are installed.

Storage pool manager

https://access.redhat.com/documentation/en-US/Red Hat Enterprise Virtualization/3.0/html/Technical Reference Guide/ sect-Technical Reference Guide-Storage Architecture-Role The Storage Pool Manager.html

RH Enterprise Virtualization hosts deal with storage domain structure related metadata (image/snapshot creation, image/snapshot deletion, and volume/domain extension) based on a single writer and multiple readers configuration. RH enterprise Virtualization host, which is capable of altering structure of data domain is termed as Storage Pool Manager, with every hosts capable of reading structural metadata, however, only storage pool manager has privileges to write domain structure metadata for datacenter. It is the manager, which coordinates all metadata changes happening within datacenter viz. Creation or deletion of disk images, creation, merging snapshots, copying images between storage domains, creating templates and storage allocation for block devices. or purpose of assigning storage pool manager role manager, causes a potential SPM host to try's assuming a storage-centric lease. Manager issues spmStart command to a host, causing VDSM on that host to attempt assuming storage-centric lease. If host is successful, it retains storage-centric lease, till such time, manager makes a requisition to new host to assume role of SPM.

This can happen when, SPM host is un-able to access s all storage domains, but can access the master storage domain. Host fails to renew lease because, which could be due to connectivity issue to storage, lease volumes are full, where no write operations shall be performed.

If, Host itself crashes.FVDSM on a host uses distributed algorithms' to take a mutex (storage-centric lease) on the storage pool, for ensuring it is only host, anywhere which is SPM. Underlying algorithm is storage baseline, never communicates with neighboring hosts. Mutex communications are written into a special logical volume within data storage domain called leases logical volume.

Storage Pool Manager Selection Process

Is initiated, managed by the Virtualization Manager. First, the Red Hat Enterprise Virtualization Manager requests that VDSM confirm which host has the storage-centric lease. Manager tracks history of SPM assignment from original creation of storage domain onward. availability of SPM role is confirmed in three ways:

- "getSPMstatus": the Manager uses VDSM to check with the host that had SPM status last and receives one of "SPM", "Contending", or "Free".
- The metadata volume for a storage domain contains the last host with SPM status.
- The metadata volume for a storage domain contains the version of the last host with SPM status.
- When storage pool manager role, storage-centric lease gets frees, manager assigns them to operational hosts in an ad-hoc manner.
- In an event of role assignment failing on a new host, manager adds host to list, which contains, details of failed operations, however during
- Subsequent iterations of manager, attempts to assign role a host, which is not part of the list.
- However, manager continues request, that manager role, storage centri-lease be taken over by a randomly selected host, which is not from list of failed hosts, till such time, SPM selection is successful.
- Every instance, where running SPM, is unreachable or unable to fulfill responsibilities, virtualization manager activates
- storage pool manager selection process.

Networking

https://access.redhat.com/documentation/en-US/Red Hat Enterprise_Virtualization/3.0/html/Technical_Reference_Guide/sect-Technical_Reference_Guide-Architecture-Network.html

RHEL network architecture assists s connectivity between the different elements of the Red Hat Enterprise Virtualization environment. Which includes communication between the Red Hat Enterprise Virtualization Manager and hosts, communication between individual hosts, and storage communication between hosts and network attached storage. The architecture enables connectivity between virtual machines, communication between virtual machines and network attached storage, besides enabling and communication between virtual machine users or clients and their virtual machines and the architecture facilitates The Red Hat Enterprise Virtualization network architecture also allows optional connectivity to destinations and objects which is considered as are external to the Red Hat Enterprise Virtualization environment. Besides supporting network architecture, it also facilitates Red Hat Enterprise Virtualization network architecture not only supports network connectivity, it assists in segregation of networks. Isolation is the mainstay, where host in different clusters, can be isolated from each other, in the same manner, in which hosts in different clusters can be isolated for each other, as can be performed for virtual machines hosted in separate cluster's.VMs which can be deployed for specific reasons, can also made to connect to which can be isolated special purpose networks, which can also be isolated from general purpose virtual machines. Configurations can be created to segregate by traffic type. Storage traffic and display traffic can be carried on separate networks, In order to support all these networking possibilities, networking is defined in Red Hat Enterprise Virtualization in several layers. The underlying physical networking infrastructure should defined and configured this, enabling connectivity between the hardware and the logical components of the Red Hat Enterprise Virtualization environments

Network setup

The network architecture depends on few common hardware and software devices:

- Network Interface Controllers (NICs) are physical network interface devices which connects a host to the network.
- Virtual NICs (VNICs) are logical NICs that can be operated using the host's physical NICs and offer They networking infrastructure y to virtual machines.
- Bonds bind multiple NICs into a single interface or bridge.
- Bridges are a packet-forwarding technique for packet-switching networks. They form the basis of logical

Logical networks can be created for the purpose of segregating network traffic, depending on environment needs, also logical network can only be implemented at the host level as a software bridge device. During standard installation one logical network can be defined, during the installation of the Red Hat Enterprise Virtualization Manager, additional logical networks if required can be added when needed, as dedicated storage logical network, and a dedicated display logical network. Network Interface Controllers are physical network interface devices which creates network routes between the host and the network devices, .Virtual NICs (VNICs) are logical NICs which needs to be configured which provides network connection to between two virtual machines. Bonds are created in order to bind NICs in different machines, into a single interface or bridge. Bridges are packet-forwarding devices for packet-switching networks and this forms the fundamental for logical networks, they form the basis of logical networks.

Storage architecture

https://access.redhat.com/documentation/en-US/Red Hat Enterprise Virtualization/3.0/html/Technical Reference Guide/ chap-Technical Reference Guide-Storage Architecture.html

Described are the storage components, such as storage domains, datacenter forming the basis of storage virtualization, and sheer interaction between the components, that offers users with dynamic and flexible virtualization infrastructure.

    a. Datacenters
    b. Data center is what that offers highest levels of abstraction in RHEL virtualization and DC can be described as a huge g container which encapsulates three types of sub containers,

Storage container contains data about storage types and storage domains, which include connectivity information for storage domains. Storage is defined for a data center, and is made available to all clusters in the data center. All host clusters within a data center are configured to access to the same storage domains. Network container contains data about the data center's supported logical networks, which includes details like network addresses, VLAN tags and STP support. Logical networks that are required for are defined for a data center, and which is optionally implemented at the cluster level. Cluster container retain clusters and Clusters are groups of hosts with compatible processor cores, either AMD or Intel processors. Cluster container holds clusters. Clusters are groups of hosts with compatible processor cores, either AMD or Intel processors. Clusters are migration domains; Virtual machines are capable of migrated between and to any hosts with the same cluster, but not outside. Single data center architecture can hold multiple clusters, and each cluster can contain multiple hosts. can be migrated to any host within a cluster, and not to other clusters. One data center can hold multiple clusters, and each cluster can contain multiple hosts. File based storage types which are supported by RHEL Virtualization are NFS and file systems, that is installed on the local storage of a Red Hat Enterprise Virtualization host And this type of storage permits an entity which could also be external to Red Hat Enterprise Virtualization environment, and if NFS is in question, the storage could be NFS storage, this could be a Red Hat Enterprise Linux NFS server, or other third party network attached storage server and hosts have self managing capabilities, besides self management of local storage and file systems, host interact with files as if they were present in local storage location

Block storage utilize un-formatted block devices, and devices are aggregated to volume groups by the Logical Volume Manager (LVM) A instance of LVM that runs on all hosts and each LVM instance is does not recognize instances running on other hosts VDSM adds clustering logic on top of LVM by scanning volume groups for changes, and updating individual hosts by refreshing volume group information. For use with virtual machines, the volume groups is presented to hosts as logical volumes for using with the virtual machines In the case of additional capacity is added to the existing domain, virtualization manager triggers a refresh signal, to these volumes, and upon receiving signal the manager triggers VDSM on each host to refresh volume group information.

Storage attributes

https://access.redhat.com/documentation/en-US/Red_Hat_Enterprise_Virtualization/3.0/html/Technical_Reference_Guide/sect-Technical_Reference_Guide-Storage_Architecture-Storage_Attributes.html

COW represents for QEMU copy on write. The QCOW2 format decouples the physical storage layer from the virtual layer by adding a mapping between logical and physical block, apart from individual logical blocks its mapping to its physical offset. Such a mapping facilitates advanced features like snapshots. Creating a new snapshot creates a new copy on write layer, either a new file or logical volume, with an initial mapping that points all logical blocks to the offsets in the backing file or volume. When writing to a QCOW2 volume, the relevant block is read from the backing volume, modified with the new information and written into the new snapshot QCOW2 volume. Then the map is updated to point to the new place. Benefits QCOW2 offers over using RAW representation include: Copy-on-write support, where a volume only represents changes made to an underlying disk image. Snapshot support, where a volume can represent multiple snapshots of the image

RAW

RAW scores better than QCOW2; no formatting is applied to images stored in the RAW format. No extra setting or configuraratioins is needed for Reading and writing images stored in RAW format. In an event of guest file system writes to a given offset in its virtual disk, the I/O will be written to the same offset on the backing file or logical volume. Raw format requires that the entire space of the defined image allocated in advance, except a situation where externally managed thin provisioned LUNs from a storage array.

Pre-allocated storage

https://access.redhat.com/documentation/en-US/Red_Hat_Enterprise_Virtualization/3.0/html/Technical_Reference_Guide/sect-Technical_Reference_Guide-Storage_Attributes-Storage_Allocation_Policies.html

All of the storage needed for a virtual machine is allocated in advance. For instance, if a 20 GB logical volume is created for the data partition of a virtual machine, 20 GB is allocated on disk. Sufficient storage needs to allocated in prior to configuration, of e to each virtual machine by an administrator to manage the forecasted requirements of the virtual machine, plus sufficient buffer, which will enhance the write times, since no storage allocation takes place during runtime, which would not probably not undertaken which might impact flexibility. Doing allocation in this manner minimizes the capacity of the Red Hat Enterprise Virtualization Manager to over-commit storage. And pre-allocation, is most probably recommended

Reallocated storage is recommended for virtual machines used for high intensity I/O tasks with less tolerance for latency in storage; generally, server virtual machines fit this description.

In the case of if thin provisioning functionality offered by the storage back end is being used, preallocated storage cannot be still be selected from the administration portal when provisioning storage for virtual machines.

<u>Storage functions</u>

<u>https://access.redhat.com/documentation/en-US/Red Hat Enterprise Virtualization/3.0/html/Technical Reference Guide/sect-Technical Reference Guide-Storage Architecture-Storage Functions.html</u>

RHEL cloud storage is sturdy, durable and highly available and durable, that can be considered for any type of storage requirements. It exhibits the properties of any completive, storage technologies; Multipathing allows paths between all LUNs in the Red Hat Enterprise Virtualization environment to be mapped and alternate paths to be determined. This applies to block devices, although the equivalent functionality can be achieved with a sufficiently robust network setup for network attached storage. Provisioning storage allows the logical over-commitment of resources to a virtual machine and the physical assignment of the resource to the virtual machine on-demand.

Red Hat Enterprise Virtualization storage components interact with each Storage functions such as:

Multipathing as paths between all LUNs in the RHE Virtualization environment to be mapped and alternate paths to be determined.

- and this sort of mapping may apply to block devices, even though similar functionality can be accomplished by deploying a robust network setup for network attached storage.

Provisioning storage

Permits logical over commitment of resources to VMs and physical assignment of the resource to the virtual machine on-demand. Logical volume extension facilitates images to be provided with additional storage resources as and when are necessary. Snapshots offers backups of a virtual machine's system state at a certain point in time.

Multipathing

In the event of the RHE Virtualization Manager discovers all of the connected LUNs, multipathing is defined over the storage network.

All valid paths between the LUNs in the network are mapped and the result,

Alternate paths are defined, in order to maintain the availability, should there be an outage in the primary path Multipathing is highly recommended to be configured to take guard against any a single point of failure and simultaneously enhance the bandwidth and improving security within the network. All volume groups are created on top of multipath devices, so that, in case of any system failure or network disruptions occurs leading o an outages

Redundancy

Multipathing is self activated, which offers fail-over protection, in the circumstance of If any element of an I/O path (the cable, switch, or controller) fails, an alternate path is found. provides failover protection. Improved Performance, besides distributes I/0 operations between different network links, and by default is is configured to do a round –robin, alternative techniques like Asynchronous Logical Unit Access (ALUA) can also help.

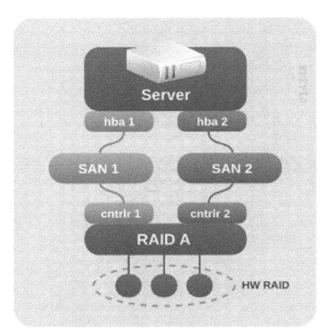

Figure 3.4. Active/Passive Multipath
Configuration with One RAID Device

In this configuration, there is one I/O path that goes through hba1, SAN1, and controller 1 and a second I/O path that goes through hba2, SAN2, and controller2. There are many points of possible failure in this configuration:

- HBA failure

- FC cable failure
- SAN switch failure
- Array controller port failure

A failure at any of these points will cause a switch to an alternate I/O

Load balancing and migration

https://access.redhat.com/documentation/en-US/Red Hat Enterprise Virtualization/3.0/html/Technical Reference Guide/ chap-Technical Reference Guide-Load Balancing Scheduling and Migration.html

Independent hosts can only be configured with limited hardware, though it can scale, but there is a threshold, as they still are prone to downtimes. And standalone hardware have limitations on the size and expansion, and also prone to failures. In order to overcome such situations, and to create safeguards, and also resource exhaustion, Hosts are grouped into clusters, that is basically is a grouping of shared resources. A RHEL, enterprise virtualization environments responds to changes in demand for host resources, by deploying load balancing policy, scheduling and migration. The Manager is in complete control and in a position to enforce, that failure of a single host in a cluster, does not bring down the virtual machines in that cluster, in other words, the manager will be able to recognize, identify, a, a faulty cluster, b,under-utilized host and migrate all such VMs off the faulty host, and at times shutting down the host itself, in order to shut down the host, for power saving, and once the necessary repair works are carried out, hosts an be activated, and if needed, instances can also be migrated, Virtual machine migration – Resources are checked in order to determine an appropriate target hosts,

Independent hosts can only be configured with limited hardware, though it can scale, but there is a threshold, as they still are prone to downtimes. And standalone hardware have limitations on the size and expansion, and also prone to failures. In order to overcome such situations, and to create safeguards, and also resource exhaustion, Hosts are grouped into clusters, that is basically is a grouping of shared resources. A RHEL, enterprise virtualization environments responds to changes in demand for host resources, by deploying load balancing policy, scheduling and migration.The Manager is in complete control and in a position to enforce, that failure of a single host in a cluster, does not bring down the virtual machines in that cluster, in other words, the manager will be able to recognize, identify, a, a faulty cluster, b,under-utilized host and migrate all such VMs off the faulty host, and at times shutting down the host itself, in order to shut down the host, for power saving, and once the necessary repair works are carried out, hosts an be activated, and if needed, instances can also be migrated, Cluster manger, responds to changes in the current resource pool,by adopting load balancing policy for a cluster to schedule the migration of virtual machines from one host in a cluster to another. The relationship between load balancing policy, scheduling, and virtual machine migration are discussed in the following sections.

Storage functions

https://access.redhat.com/documentation/en-US/Red_Hat_Enterprise_Virtualization/3.0/html/Technical_Reference_Guide/sect-Technical_Reference_Guide-Storage_Architecture-Storage_Functions.html

RHE Virtualization storage components interact, amongst themselves, delivering listed functions:

Multi-pathing opens network route between all active LUN's within virtualization environment, for purpose of mapping, for determining alternate routes to be determined Multipating applies to block devices, in-spite of an alternate, equivalent functionality can be realized by configuring sturdy network which is attached to storage.

- Using provisioning storage, (a) permits logical over-commitment of resources, to a VM,(b) physical assignment of the resource to the virtual machine on-demand.
- Logical volume extension permits images to be allocated with extra storage resources, as and when needed.
- Snapshots' must be used to create backup of a VM's state during certain point in time.

Storage domain

https://access.redhat.com/documentation/en-US/Red_Hat_Enterprise_Virtualization/3.0/html/Technical_Reference_Guide/sect-Technical_Reference_Guide-Minimum_requirements_and_supported_limits-Storage_Domain.html

Storage domain offers space for purpose of storing VM disk-images, SO images, import, export VM's. While RH permits creation of multiple storage domains inside datacenter, few restrictions apply for individual domain. Supported storage types:

- Fiber- Channel Protocol (FCP)
- Internet Small Computer System Interface (iscsi)
- Network File System (NFS)

Deployment of data storage-domain should be of same type. Type must be specified as a step within creation o domain, can be of following types:

- FCP,
- iscsi,
- NFS.

Legacy FCP or iscsi export storage domains RHEL virtualization environment 2.2,which can be attached to datacetenters' that runs RHEL virtualization 2.2,that can be attached to an environment which is running Virtualization 3.0.New ISO, export storage domains should be offered by NFS. Every data-storage domains, which reside within datacenter, must of same type. Type must be specified as a step during the process of creation of a storage domain. Data-storage domain must be either FCP, iscsi, or NFS .Legacy FCP or iscsi exports storage domains from RHEL virtualization environment 2.2,is capable of getting attached to datacenters within RHEL virtualization 3.0.New ISO, export storage domains should mandatorily should be provided by NFS. LUN's 300 LUNs are permitted for individual storage domain that is provided by iscsi or FCP.

https://access.redhat.com/documentation/en-US/Red_Hat_Enterprise_Virtualization/3.0/html/Technical_Reference_Guide/sect-Technical_Reference_Guide-Minimum_requirements_and_supported_limits-Red_Hat_Enterprise_Virtualization_Manager.html

It is compulsory that, RHEL virtualization manager servers', should run Windows Server 2008 (R2).It is essential, that, additional hardware needs to be complied with. Limitations of Enterprise Virtualization Manager are:

- RAM :Atleast, 3GB RAM must be installed
- PCI Devices: A minimum of one network controller which has a minimum bandwidth of 1 Gbps is recommended Storage
- Storage : Atleast, 3 GB of available local disk capacity is ideal

https://access.redhat.com/documentation/en-US/Red_Hat_Enterprise_Virtualization/3.0/html/Technical_Reference_Guide/References_RHEL_6_RHEVH_Support_Limits.html

Hyper-visor requirements

CPU – Supported limits

- At least 1 physical CPU is required, with all of them supporting

- Intel® 64 or AMD64 CPU extensions, AMD-V™ or Intel VT® hardware virtualization extensions.
- RH supports maximum of 128 physical CPUs

RAM : A minimum of, additional 512 MB of RAM is needed and it is recommended for individual VM. Quantity of RAM neede for individual guests varies depending on:

- guest operating system's requirements,
- guests' application requirements,
- Memory activity utilization of guests.
- KVM's possess capability for over-committing physical RAM for virtualized guests, which is accomplished by only allocating RAM for guests,only when needed, moving
- It does this by only allocating RAM for guests as required and shifting underutilized guests into swap up, to 1 TB of RAM is supported.

The minimum supported internal storage for a Hypervisor is the total of the following list:

Storage

- The root partitions require at least 512 MB of storage.
- The configuration partition requires at least 8 MB of storage.
- The recommended minimum size of the logging partition is 2048 MB.
- The data partition requires at least 256 MB of storage. Use of a smaller data partition may prevent future upgrades of the Hypervisor from the Red Hat Enterprise Virtualization Manager. By default all disk space remaining after allocation of swap space will be allocated to the data partition.

- The swap partition requires at least 8 MB of storage. The recommended size of the swap partition varies depending on both the system the Hypervisor is being installed upon and the anticipated level of overcommitted for the environment. Overcommitted allows the Red Hat Enterprise Virtualization environment to present more RAM to guests than is actually physically present. The default overcommitted ratio is 0.5.

The recommended size of the swap partition can be determined by:

- o Multiplying the amount of system RAM by the expected overcommitted ratio, and adding
- o 2 GB of swap space for systems with 4 GB of RAM or less, or
- o 4 GB of swap space for systems with between 4 GB and 16 GB of RAM, or
- o 8 GB of swap space for systems with between 16 GB and 64 GB of RAM, or
- o 16 GB of swap space for systems with between 64 GB and 256 GB of RAM.

Example B.1. Calculating Swap Partition Size

For a system with 8 GB of RAM this means the formula for determining the amount of swap space to allocate is:

https://access.redhat.com/documentation/en-US/Red_Hat_Enterprise_Virtualization/3.0/html/Technical_Reference_Guide/sect-Technical_Reference_Guide-Minimum_requirements_and_supported_limits-Red_Hat_Enterprise_Virtualization_Manager.html

Red Hat Enterprise Virtualization Manager

It is mandatory, that RHE Enterprise virtualization manager servers must execute Widows server 2008 R2.Besides, additional requirements must also be met.

RAM: Atleast 3 GB of RAM is necessary

PCI devices: Atleast a single network controller, with bandwidth of 1 Gbps is recommended.

Storage: User's must ensure availability 3 GB of free local disk space

Directory services

https://access.redhat.com/documentation/en-US/Red_Hat_Enterprise_Virtualization/3.0/html/Technical_Reference_Guide/chap-Technical_Reference_Guide-Directory_Services.html

RHEL Virtualization platform utilizes directory services for user authorization, authentication. Interaction between manager interfaces, which includes User Portal, Power User Portal, Administration Portal, REST API are limited to authenticated, authorized users. VM's, housed within virtualization environment is granted option for utilizing existing AD, for authentication, authorization, but suitable configurations has to be applied. Supported AD Service providers are Identity, Policy, Audit (IPA), Microsoft Active directory service for

- Portal logins (User, Power User, Administrator, REST API).
- Queries to display user information.
- Adding the Manager to a domain.

Authentication is process of verification, identification of an entity which generates some data, integrity of the generated data. A principal is an entity, whose identity should be verified. Verifier is same entity which demands offering assurance of the principal's identity. For RHE virtualization, Manager functions as verifier, user turns principal .Data integrity is a guarantee, which ensures data received is same as data generate by principal. Confidentiality, authorizations are closely associated with authentication.

Confidentiality is safeguard's data from not being shared with un-intended recipients. Strong authentication methods are capable of offering confidentiality. Authorization methods are implemented for determining whether a principal can or cannot be allow performing operations. RHEL Virtualiatization utilizes AD, for associating users with corresponding roles, authorize accordingly. It is recommended, that authorization, be performed once principal has been authenticated, which occurs based on information contained in local or remote to the verifier. Is best practice, for authorization is performed, after principal has been authenticated and based on whether information local or remote to the verifier. While installation process is on, automatically, an internal domain gets automatically configured for management or administration of virtualization environment..Once installation is over, additional domains can be added.

Local Authentication: Internal Domain

RHEL virtualization manger creates a limited, internal administration domain during installation, which should be confused with AD domain, because, directory exisistance depends on a key in RHE virtualization, postgres database as against a directory service user on a directory server. Internal, external domain differs, with internal domain contains a single user, the admin@internal user. extending this approach to initial authentication permits virtualization to be examined without need for fully functional directory server, which guarantees that administrative accounts are available for troubleshooting any problems with external directory services.admin@internal user must be created for performing initial configuration of environments, which includes installing, accepting hosts, addition of external AD,IPA authentication domains, delegation of privileges for users from external domains.

https://access.redhat.com/documentation/en-US/Red Hat Enterprise Virtualization/3.0/html/Technical Reference Guide/ sect-Technical Reference Guide-Directory Services-Remote Authentication Using GSSAPI.html

Remote Authentication Using GSSAP

In context of RHEL virtualization, remote authentication refers to authentication refers to a specific type which is managed from remotely from virtualization manger. Term Remote authentication is used in context of connections are used for user or API connections entering to Manager from within an AD,IPA domain, coming into the Manager from within an AD or IPA domain. It is necessary that manager should be configured by administrator's or using rhevm-manage-domains tool, which is a part of AD or IPA domain, which requires that, Managers be granted appropriate credentials for an account for AD or IPA directory server for a suitable domain, with sufficient privileges for adding systems to domain. Once domain is added, domain users can be authenticated by the manager, against the directory server using a password.SASL,Simple Authentication and Security Layer must be used,which subsequently uses Generic Security Services Application Program Interface (GSSAPI)for performing secure verification of users, also determine authorization level, granted to user.

https://access.redhat.com/documentation/en-US/Red Hat Enterprise Virtualization/3.0/html/Technical Reference Guide/ chap-Technical Reference Guide-Advanced Tasks and Options. html

Templates

RH virtualization environment by design has tools for simplifying process of simplifying provisioning process for users. Templates, tools are short-cuts, which allow administrators configure, deploy fresh VM's based on an existing, pre-configured virtual machine, sidelining OS installation, configurations. These configurations will be useful for VM's, that will be utilized as appliances, ex. web server VM's. If the environment demands deployment,administrator's must create VM's, that can be utilized as templates, performing an OS installation, necessary web-server, supporting packages, then apply unique configuration changes. Now, administrators' should create necessary templates, depending on operational VM, which will then to use for creation of fresh, identical as required. VM pools are groups of VM's, designed for working with specific templates, which can be provisioned in short span of time. Requisite permissions for accessing, using VM's within a pool must be granted at pool level, users, who have been granted permissions to utilize poll, are assigned virtual machines randomly from pool. Within pool, VM's exhibit transitory nature.

Since, user's are assigned VM's, without caring for allocation of such VM's within pool which has already been used earlier, pools aren't recommended for use, which requires data persistance.VM pools are best fit for scenarios' (a) user data is stored in a central location, where VM's are used as methods for accessing, using data, (b) where data-persistence doesn't take precedence. Creating pools leads to creation of appropriate VM's, which populate pool in stopped state, which are re-started on user's request. For purpose of creation of template, administrator must create, customize a single VM. Install desired packages, customized configurations needs to be applied,once this is done, VM is ready for indented use, and for minimizing number of changes that needs be performed on VM's after deployment. It is recommended, but optional step ahead of creation of template from a VM is creating generalization, purpose being, removal of details viz. System user names, passwords, time-zones information, which is bound to change post deployment, and which doesn't impact customized configurations. When a VM, which offers basis for templates, created VM is configured successfully configured, generalized, paused. Administrators are empowered for creating a template from a VM. Creation of template from VM's causes read–only copy of specifically configured VM disk–image to be created.

Read–only image will form backing image for any VM which will be created in future, based on template first created. Template is customized read only disk image, comes with associated virtual hardware configuration. Hardware, if necessary, can be changed within VM's, which are created from templates. Examples are for instance provisioning two gigabytes of RAM for an virtual machine created from a template which has one gigabyte of RAM. Template disk image, shouldn't be altered, if done, changes will be propagated to every machine, which is running based in new templates.

Pools

https://access.redhat.com/documentation/en–US/Red_Hat_Enterprise_Virtualization/3.0/html/Technical_Reference_Guide/sect-Technical_Reference_Guide-Advanced_Tasks_and_Options-Pools.html

VM pools facilitate raid provisioning of vast numbers of identical VM's to users as desktops. Such user's, for whom permissions are granted for accessing, utilizing VM's from a pool, receive an active VM depending on respective position within the queue of requests, those users', for whom permissions granted for access, use VM's from any pool receives an available VM, depending on position within the queue of requests. Intrinsically, VM's inside pools prohibit data-persistence,during every instance a VM gets assigned from pool and gets allocated to base state, suited for environments of user's data storage is centralized. A technical support company employs certain number help desk staff, but only few of them are operating at given point of time, instead of creating VM's for individual employee, a pool of requisite VM's can be created, with support staff allocating themselves to each VM, when work starts, return VM to the pool when finished work. VM Pools are created from a template. VM's within a pool, utilize existing backing read–only image only, use's temporary copy on write image for retaining changes, besides serving as destination for newly created data. VM's within a pool are totally different with actual VM's, where a copy on write layer which holds user generated, altered data is lost during shutdown. In order to avoid this situation, VM pools doesn't ask for higher storage capacity than templates, which backs it, besides provisioning extra space for date which is generated or even altered, during use. universally acknowledge as proven method for supplying compute power to end-users', especially for specific tasks, without incurring extra spending on provisioning of exclusive compute power, for specific actions to be performed, without having to assign desktop for users'. Example Pool Usage - a company employs certain number of staff, however only few are active at any point of time, in this circumstance, instead of creating same number of VM's as matching number of staff, pool of corresponding number of VM's equal to user's can be created, with support-staff, allocating themselves as VM's, at start of respective work timing, return it to pools when signing-off. Minimum requirements, supported limit. There exists, sizable count of physical, logical limitations which applies to RHEL virtualization environments with configurations outside of such e limitations are currently not supported.

Data center

https://access.redhat.com/documentation/en-US/Red_Hat_Enterprise_Virtualization/3.0/html/Technical_Reference_Guide/appe-Technical_Reference_Guide-Minimum_requirements_and_supported_limits.html

For managed virtual environments, highest level container for all resources is the data center, with substantial restrictions, which gets applied to such resources, which is being capable of contained within respective datacenter.

Storage domains

Atleast, minimum of 2 storage domains per data center is recommended. Minimum of one data-storage domain is mandatory, single ISO storage domain for each data center is recommended.

Hosts

Maximum of 200 hosts per data center is supported.

Cluster

https://access.redhat.com/documentation/en-US/Red Hat Enterprise Virtualization/3.0/html/Technical Reference Guide/ sect-Technical Reference Guide-Minimum requirements and supported limits-cluster.html

Clusters' are described as group of physical hosts which t are treated as a resource pool for a set of VM's. A Host within a cluster must share common infrastructure, storage. Typically clusters must be treated as migration domain, inside which VM's can be moved from one host to another. For ensuring stability, Mentioned limitations apply for individual cluster. Which are, every managed hypervisor must compulsorily reside within a cluster, with all of them powered by same CPU type and isn't possible for Intel, AMD CPU's o-exist within same cluster.

https://access.redhat.com/documentation/en-US/Red Hat Enterprise Virtualization/3.0/html/Technical Reference Guide/ appe-Technical Reference Guide-Virtualized Hardware.html

Virtualized hardware

Enterprise Virtualization presents three unique types of system devices for purpose of virtualzing guests. These are all hardware devices, made to appear as physically attached hardware devices to virtualized guests, however device drivers, function in different method.

Emulated devices

In certain contexts, are also termed as virtual a device, which exists completely within software. Emulated device drivers act as translation layer between OS, which runs on host, which manages source devices and OS running on guests. Device level instructions directed to and forth between emulated devices are intercepted, translated by the hypervisor. Any device of e same type as one's which is being emulated, recognized Linux kernel, can be used as backing source device for emulated drivers'.

Para–virtualized Devices

Are those ones which necessitatates' installation of device drivers on guest OS, thereby providing an interface for communicating with hyper-visor, is housed within host machine. A generic use of this interface is, permitting traditionally intensive tasks like I/O operations, to be performed outside virtualized environment.

Physically shared devices

A select hardware platform permits virtualized guests to gain direct access to different hardware resources, components. This process in virtualization is known as pass-through or device assignment. Pass-through allows devices to appear and behave as if they were physically attached to the guest operating system. Central Processing Unit (CPU)

Individual Hyper-visor, which is inside a cluster, holds a certain virtual CPUs (vCPUS), which gets exposed to guests, which runs on hypervisors. Individual CPU's that are exposed by Hypervisors inside a cluster must be of same type, as one selected when Cluster was initially created using RH virtualization. Users, administrators must avoid mixing of virtual CPU types within a Cluster, as it is not possible technically. Active virtual CPU types, displays properties based on physical CPUs, having same name. Virtual CPU's are indistinguishable from physical CPU to the guest operating system. Supported processor's are:

AMD Opteron G2
AMD Opteron G3
Intel Xeon Core 2
Intel Xeon 45nm Core2
Intel Xeon Core i7
System devices

https://access.redhat.com/documentation/en-US/Red Hat Enterprise Virtualization/3.0/html/Technical Reference Guide/ sect-Technical Reference Guide-Virtualized Hardware-System devices.html

System devices are an integral part of system, critical for guest's to be executed, which can't be re-located individual system device, which is attached to a guest, equally occupies a free PCI slot, default system devices are:

- host bridge,
- ISA bridge, USB bridge, with USB, ISA bridges being same device,
- Graphics card, using either the Cirrus or qxl driver, memory balloon device.
- ISA bridge, USB bridge, with USB, ISA bridges being same device,
- Graphics card, using either the Cirrus or qxl driver, memory balloon device.

Network devices

https://access.redhat.com/documentation/en-US/Red Hat Enterprise Virtualization/3.0/html/Technical Reference Guide/sect-Technical Reference Guide-Virtualized Hardware-Network devices.html

Type of network interface controller that must be configured for exposing to a guest is decided during creation of guest; however it can be altered, through virtualization manager.

- 1000 network interface controller exposes a virtualized Intel PRO/1000 (e1000) to guests
- virtio network interface controller exposes a paravirtualized network device to guests
- rtl8139 network interface controller exposes a virtualized Realtek Semiconductor Corp RTL8139 to guests.

Several interface controllers', can be configure per guest. One controller added, occupies one available PCI slots on guest. Refer to network devices documentation, for knowing about number of PCI devices, which can be exposed to individual guest.

https://access.redhat.com/documentation/en-US/Red Hat Enterprise Virtualization/3.0/html/Technical Reference Guide/sect-Technical Reference Guide-Virtualized Hardware-Graphics devices.html

Graphics devices

- Two emulated graphics devices are provided shall be connected to SPICE protocol or with VNC.
- ac97 emulates a Cirrus CLGD 5446 PCI VGA card.
- vga emulates dummy VGA card with Bochs VESA extensions (hardware level, comprising all non-standard modes

https://access.redhat.com/documentation/en-US/Red_Hat_Enterprise_Virtualization/3.0/html/Technical_Reference_Guide/sect-Technical_Reference_Guide-Virtualized_Hardware-Storage_devices.html

Both, Storage devices,storage pools are permitted to use block device drivers for purpose of attaching storage devices to virtualized guests. There is a clear distinction between storage servers, storage devices Primarily drivers' should be used for attaching a backing storage device, file or storage pool volume to a virtualized guest. Backing storage device shall be any supported type of storage device, file, or storage pool volume. It is task of drivers to expose an emulated block device to guests. An emulated IDE driver is capable of attaching any combination of up to four virtualized IDE hard disks or virtualized IDE CD-ROM drives to individual virtualized guest. An emulated IDE driver is also capable of offering virtualized DVD-ROM drives. VirtIO driver's, exposes a para-virtualized block device to guests, which functions for all storage devices supported by hypervisor, which is attached to virtualized guest, with exception of floppy-drive, which should be emulated. Primary functionality of a balloon-driver is to permit guests to communicate to hypervisor, details about memory requirements. Balloon driver, help the host to perform efficient allocation of memory to guests, besides permitting read-only memory to be allocated for neighboring guest, processes .Such guests using balloon driver's, are permitted to identity portion's of guest's RAM to be designated as not in use. Hypervisors' then can release excess memory capacity, utilize memory of host processes or other guest on other guests on that specific host. In an event of guest's needing a portion of free memory again, hypervisor shall reallocate RAM to guest (balloon deflation).

Balloon driver

https://access.redhat.com/documentation/en-US/Red_Hat_Enterprise_Virtualization/3.0/html/Technical_Reference_Guide/

sect-Technical Reference Guide-Virtualized Hardware-Balloon driver.html

Primary functionality is to permit guests to express to hypervisor's, quantity of memory which is required. It allows hosts to perform efficient allocation of allocated memory to guests, permit free memory to be distributed to other guests, processes. Guests', using balloon drivers, can identify portion of guest's RAM as unavailable, which is

Balloon inflation

Hypervisor shall release memory, which can be utilized for performing other host process or any other guests within same host and in an event of guest wanting to access that free memory again, hypervisor will reallocate RAM to that particular guest, which is (balloon deflation).

2. Cloud platform

https://www.redhat.com/en/technologies/cloud-computing/cloud-infrastructure

Redhat Cloud Infrastructure

Is a combination of tightly integrated Red Hat technologies, that can be utilized to design, create, manage a open, private Infrastructure-as-a-Service (IaaS),cloud environment, which cheaper solution,compared to any alternate solutions. Components can be installed, configured at any time, from anywhere. Listed below are features:

Open platform

All products are designed based on open a standard, which liberates your dependency on a single-service provider.

- Flexibility: Is provided by management components which spawns multiple platforms viz. Redhat OpenStack, besides public cloud providers viz. AWS, Azure.
- Economy of scale: It is now simple for designing a traditional private cloud using datacenter virtualization traditional workloads, using RHEL virtualization.
- Integrated management: Cloud Forms presents a open hybrid cloud management platform, using which an must be able to deploy, monitor, manage cloud services across multiple virtualization platforms.
- Cost-effective, secure virtualization
- RHE cloud accelerates deployment of traditional private cloud, with assistance of datacenter virtualization traditional workloads, assisted by RHE virtualization.
- Automated provisioning: RHE offers automated provisioning capabilities—as besides, configuration, software management—of Red Hat Enterprise Linux, and those applications, based on Red Hat package manager.
- Deploy those entire environment's that are required: RH cloud infrastructure is architected for managing, simultaneously, different virtualization technologies viz. RH, OpenStack, besides pubic clouds like AWS, Azure.
- Ability to manage multiple environments: Cloud Forms, is an open hybrid cloud management platform that offers visibility, control over existing independent virtual infrastructures. Cloud forms can be used for deploying, monitoring, managing cloud services, across different virtualization platforms viz. AWS, RHE Virtualization, VMware vSphere, Google Cloud.

https://www.redhat.com/en/resources/cloud-suite-datasheet

Red Hat Cloud Suite

Key product advantages include:

- Offer's comphrennsive application development, containers via Red Hat OpenShift Container Platform.
- Offers full integration with all supported components, which together, presents a hybrid cloud.
- Delivered with one, single unified management framework across infrastructure, application development layers, complete operation, life-cycle management along with proactive risk mitigation.
- Exposure to Open API's, provides customers choice for upgrade, replace current running components with own choice of technology, platform, vendors, with no vendor lock-in or with any platform technology, or any Red Hat and third-party products
- RH cloud suite is suited to operate with wide range of commodity hardware, public cloud options.

Technical requirements

- RHEV Manager: Recommended. 1-2 quad core Intel 64 processors, 16GB random access memory (RAM), 50GB disk, 1Gbps Ethernet network interface controller (NIC).
- RH Virtualization Hypervisor: 1 central processing unit (CPU) with Intel 64 or AMD64 CPU extensions, and AMD-VTM or Intel VT hardware virtualization extensions, 2GB RAM, 10GB local disk storage, 1GB Ethernet NIC. OpenStack Platform compute nodes: 64-bit x86 processor supporting
- Intel 64 or AMD64 CPU extensions, AMD-V or Intel VT hardware virtualization extensions are enabled. 2GB RAM, 50GB is available disk space, 2 x 1Gbps network interface cards are installed

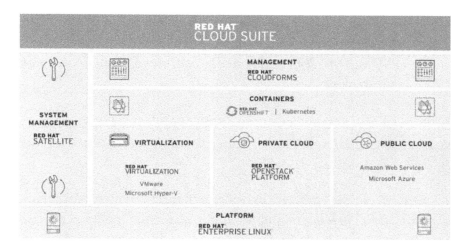

- OpenStack Platform controller nodes: Are 64-bit x86 processor, that support Intel 64 or AMD64 CPU extensions, AMD-V or Intel VT hardware virtualization extensions enabled. RHE Linux® 6.5 or later, 2GB RAM, 50GB available disk space, 1Gbps network interface cards.
- CloudForms: Delivered as virtual appliance in Open Virtualization Format (OVF) for operating with majority of virtual infrastructures.
- RH Satellite:

64-bit architecture, RH Enterprise Linux 6.5 or later, with atleast 2 CPU cores, minimum of 8GB memory is basic requirement, but ideal is 12GB.

During installation, any additional YUM repositories other than those specified in RedHat Satellite installation documentation should be disabled.

Red Hat Insights:

Minimum: 64-bit architecture, RH Linux 6 or later.

RH OpenShift Container Platform: Minimum hardware is 2 Intel x64 servers, each powered by 2 cores, 4GB RAM, with actual sizing performed based on capacity requirements

- Red Hat OpenShift Container Platform:
- Minimum hardware is 2 Intel x64 servers each with 2 cores, 4GB RAM. With actual sizing performed based on capacity requirements.

https://www.redhat.com/cms/managed-files/cl-red-hat-cloudforms-unified-management-for-hybrid-environments-inc0451306lw-201611-en.pdf

Order of the day is hybrid structures, which comprises virtualization, private or public cloud platforms, container-based infrastructures. As platform changes, so does requirements for IT operations. Management of IT operations implies process of prioritizing services, rather than managing those, establishing trusted processes for compliance rather than try to control everything, automating infrastructure for delivering higher responsiveness'. Cloud Forms, is one amongst best-in-class, unified management, designed for hybrid environments, delivering consistent processes functionality across multiple layers of infrastrucucture which is Self-service ordering combined automated provisioning, policy enforcement strategy that guides in designing strategies for accelerating service delivery. IT managers are bestowed with comprehensive operational, life-cycle control over services that has been deployed this enables customers to enhances, and simultaneously withholding operation control. Listed are features.

- Complete lifecycle management
  - o Administrators' can explore beyond self-service's, thus gaining on provisioning, integration, resource management, operational management, retirement, and financial reporting.
- Operational visibility
  - o Cloud Forms provides necessary utilities for discovering, mapping resources, and corresponding relationships.
- Compliance, governance

- Oversees, default enforcement of policies across all environments, ably supported by comprehensive insights and detailed logging.

Cloud Forms are recommended for enhancing operations with higher-levels of visibility, by performing constantly discovering, monitoring, performing deep-inspection of resources. This service must be utilized for provisioning new resources, perform discovery of existing ones, enabling IT staff to visualize,understand relationships between them, analyze root-causes, plans for subsequent scenarios', by collecting data. By doing so, Cloud Forms ensures compliance, governance, aided by automated policy enforcement, remediation.

Listed are features

- Policies' must be framed to ensure, resources stay compliant with corporate regulatory requirements. In case of Cloud Forms detecting, out-of-compliance state, Cloud Forms either raise an alert or automatically remediates issues. During the entire cycle, CloudForm constantly tracks actions, maintains audit logs for generating clear actionable time-frame of events to occur.
- Virtual appliance format, agent-less design permits it to perform continuous or timed scan on existing infrastructure, within short span of time.
- Robust integration features, permits to be get connected to an existing IT operations environments enabling completely automated IT process to be executed.

Deliver's a unified, consistent set of management features across Virtualization platforms viz.

- Red Hat Virtualization, VMware VRealize, Microsoft Hyper-V
- Private cloud platforms based on Red Hat OpenStack® Platform-V)

- Private cloud's based on Red Hat OpenStack® Platform
- Public cloud platforms (e.g. Amazon Web Services, Microsoft Azure, Google Cloud Platform
- Container-based environments like OpenShift
- Software-defined networking environments, viz. Native networking capabilities for OpenStack Neutron, AWS, Azure, Google Cloud
- Comprehensive life-cycle management, which includes, provisioning, reconfiguration, de-provisioning, retirement
- Operational management features, which are mandatory for starting, stop, flex, scale, deploy services
- Performs, Forensic analysis using SmartState on VM instances and timeline, event-tracking which communicates root cause analysis.
- Performs Relationship-mapping, for all infrastructure levels which includes's application containers, physical systems, networks.
- Users, administrators are recommended to use Resource trend tracking for informing capacity, what-if scenario planning

https://www.redhat.com/en/technologies/jboss-middleware/3scale

API management

Simple, flexible Cloud-native development

APIs's play key roles' in integrating, delivering business values for cloud operations, agile integration thereby delivering business value in digital worlds, supports innovation, enables cross-enterprise agility, assists in creation of new innovative product, revenue streams. Red Hat 3scale API Management simplifies, management of API's .Facilitates sharing, securing, distributing, control, monetizes APIs in infrastructure platform, which is designed for delivering high-performance, simplistic customer control, future growth.

Recommend is 3scale components on-premise, in the cloud, or on any combination of the two.

Features

- API traffic control Utilizes, self-controlled or cloud components, which are capable of offering an efficient traffic management, security, access policy enforcement.
- API program management
  - Utmost efficiency can be achieved by centralizing control of API program—including analytics, access control, monetization, developer workflows.
- OpenShift integration
- Designed to build, execute high-performance applications in a contained, in an automated fashion.
- Hybrid cloud support across for individual components
- RH allows API managemement to be customized, to suit operations of components, be it in cloud, or in on-premised, or for any combination of these two.
- Comprehensive security
- A large set of encryption, authentication, authorization protocols are supported.
- High-availability, performance
- Web-scalable architecture delivers, high availability with an assured uptime guarantees of 99.99%, carrying millions of API calls per day. Application, services don't experience any latency, no round trips between datacenter, RH 3scale API Management.
- Red Hat Fuse integration
  It is recommended to integrate with Fuse for creating API's, configuring of API gateway on OpenShift, for controlling, distributing gateways within local, cloud, on-cloud, on-premise deployments using utilizing the existing stack.
  - OpenShift integration

Architects must capitalize on power of Linux® containers—delivered at scale for APIs for delivering container's availability, efficiency. Gain the power of Linux® containers—delivered at scale for APIs. User's should utilize 3scale API gateway, for developing, executing high-performance applications in contained, automated methods.

https://www.redhat.com/en/technologies/storage/hyperconverged-infrastructure

Hyper-Converged infrastructure

RHEL Hyper converged Infrastructure, is designed using OpenStack, virtualization platforms, those architected for providing co-located, scalable, software-defined compute storage, which is powered by Red Hat Ansible®Automation on economical, industry-standard hardware. Eventually, organizations get an integrated software-defined compute, storage in a compact footprint.

Features

- Maximum resources
  Reduces, deployment time and operating costs, streamlines roll-out process in an compact footprint.
- Centralized administration
  Single-interface, multi-featured front-end, which offers centralized control, administration
- Flexible infrastructure
  Hyper-convergence is designed to support complex workloads with scalable architectures on industry-standard hardware.
- Single-support software stack
  Using a single RHE subscription, consolidate planning, design, procurement, training, management, upgrades, support using single RH subscription.

Opensource

It is necessary to capitalize on innovation of upstream communities with a guarantee of delivering enterprise-ready capabilities, without being locked-in with proprietary components, solutions.

Infrastructure consolidation for cloud & virtualization

Industry verticals viz.energy,retail,banking, telecom depend on critical applications, that should be deployment of which comes with restrictions viz. space, financial constraints, paucity of skilled IT staff, infra-consolidation warrants, that application spread should be from data center core to edge of the network. RH Hyper-converged Infrastructure features' is outcome of years of customer deployment, conducting exhaustive QE testing of components. Current versions of converged infrastructure are containerized with RH Storage, streamlined by RH Ansible® Automation, which is customized for deployment of targeted use-cases, which is completely opensource.

https://www.redhat.com/cms/managed-files/st-red-hat-hyperconverged-infrastructure-virtualization-overview-f15168-201811-en.pdf

Hyper-converged infrastructure for virtualization

Hyper converged infrastructure (HCI), displays ability for consolidating, simplifying compute, storage, network infrastructure for providing an efficient platform which will enhance efficiency. Hyper converged Infrastructure for Virtualization is most ideal solution for hosting business-critical applications within a virtualized environment, besides compatible for multiple edge deployment scenarios. With strong foundation provided by enterprise virtualization, Gluster Storage, Redhat AnsibleAutomation, Hyper-converged Infrastructure for Virtualization simplifies planning and procurement, streamlines deployments, management. Users can experience single life-cycle experience for virtual compute, virtual storage resources. Compute, storage, management components are all open source. Architects are free to select any industry-standard hardware or implement validated configurations, which best qualifies workload requirements.

Powered with advanced data reduction capabilities, virtual graphics processing unit (vGPU) support, software-defined networking functionality, Hyper-converged Infrastructure for Virtualization empowers architects, deploy an open, rugged software-defined infrastructure with minimal footprint.HCI is primarily configured for virtualzing business applications, maximize resource utilization by performing infrastructure consolidation, which leads results in realization of increase in operational efficiencies. It is recommended IT managers' manage integrated compute-plus-storage resources with a single management interface, which leads to increased operational efficiency. RH hyper-converted infrastructure for virtualized compute, storage are always in demand, with different stakeholder, user-groups, departmental, lines of business teams, DevTest operators, teams' those are executing remote facilities in industry verticals viz. Retail, manufacturing. Remote

Operations include untrained IT professionals or individuals 'whose isn't associated with cloud. Such industries are constantly in search of appropriate solutions, which deliverers reduced physical footprints. It is essential to develop simplified procurement, deployment, manageability, backup. HCI is comprised of Redhat stack. compute components are configured to be deployed on same servers, thus reducing physical footprint, reducing time consumed for deployments, streamlining overall operational proceseess.HCI, is recognized for delivering higher levels of flexibility, that falls within range of deployable configurations, which is achieved by utilizing foundation provided by:

- Redhat virtualization
- Gluster storage,

HCI for virtualization significantly simplifies traditional network, compute, storage infrastructure, yielding substantial benefits which includes:

- Cost-savings, accrued from consolidating infrastructure, standardization
- Small initial investments for creating proof-of-concepts.
- Simplified procurement using a prepackaged product.
- Simplified deployment, management, upgrades
- Offers cohesive purchasing, support using single vendor relationship
- Deliver's Built-in predictability from use case-specific performance, testing

Data reduction capabilities

Data reduction

Integrates Virtual Data Optimization (VDO) module for Linux device mapped as delivered along-with RHEL.VOD, delivers in-line, real-time, block-level de-duplication, compression at 4KB level, along-with management of VDO data reduction.

vGPU support

Oil, gas companies, have to develop methods for delivering complex graphics with highest possible levels of performance within virtualized environments. GPU's assist in enhancing increase visual clarity, enhanced performance, and substantially reduced lag time during the process of delivering virtualized graphics to users at remote sites.

Open Network Virtualization (OVN).

Software-defined networking is one of the critical component of hyper converged infrastructure.OVN is a open source virtual switching project, which separates physical network topology from logical networks. Configuring OVN greatly enhances scacalability facilitating live migration of virtual networking components, without intervention of a hypervisor.

https://www.redhat.com/en/technologies/management/insights

Redhat Insights

Facilitates admistrators' users', to proactively identify, remediate threats to security, performance, availability, scalability, which can be achieved by configuring Redhat insights, which offers advanced predictive analytics. Mitigate issues and un-planned downtimes within RHEL environment.

Features

Predictive analytics

With exhaustive assessment, by performing intelligent prediction across physical, virtual, container, private, public cloud environments, it is highly feasible for reducing costs, time, proactively addressing issues.

Heightened visibility for environment

RH Insights, is packaged along with Enterprise Linux subscription, which gives option for begin proactive identification, remediation of risks across entire RH infrastructure, which starts from time OS gets deployed.

• Minimal human touch

It is prudent for capitalizing on advantages of SaaS deployments and scale swiftly, without having to requisition additional infrastructure, enabling teams to instantaneously start reducing security vulnerabilities for avoiding unplanned downtimes

- Automated, real time remediation

By utilizing, real-time views into hybrid environments, operational teams, doesn't require error reports, as administrator's in periodic basis, communicated about potential problems that might arises and provides suitable remediation steps for fixing them, even before problems turn critical. Insights are capable of automating remediation of problems which arises through Ansible Playbooks.

- Performs live analysis of deployments

RH insights, permit users' perform review's on systems located in on-premise, public clouds, with inclusion of targeted rules for AWS, Azure. More can also be included.

https://www.redhat.com/cms/managed-files/rh-insights-optimize-infrastructure-datasheet-f18088cs-201907-en.pdf

Product overview

In current circumstance, where current workloads evolve, number of deployments, complexity increase, managing risks has become a key focus area for architects. To ensure continuity of operational efficiency, it is necessary for deploying fresh environments, which guarantees' swift scalability, reliability .RH insights, assists clients derive benefits from past learning, technical knowledge of Red Hat Certified Engineers (RHCEs®), which simplifies users' tasks in indentifying, prioritizing, resoling any problems, before t impacts business operations. Insights offer highly scalable, prescriptive analytics across entire hybrid environment. Insights is bundled with all supported versions of RHEL, which enables users' proactively detect issues, provides enhanced visibility into deployments, enhances security, recommends remediation using Redhat satellite.

Is, delivered as SaaS offering. Insights, makes use of expertise of open source software for generating customized remediation in real time. Utilizes, intelligent data for purpose of pinpointing technical risks, besides assisting administrator's, in resolving issues, before problem impacts business. This is sophisticated, integrated platform, which supports operational, analytics, automated resolution across physical, virtual, containers, private, public cloud environments.

Advantages

Capabilities of RH Insights include offering continuous, exhaustive analysis of Redhat infrastructure, enabling system administrators, in advance, identity major threats, security incidents, of company's RH cloud's performance, stability for purpose of ensuring performance, stability. By way of combining granular risk assessment, customized remediation steps, together with automated resolution, RHinsights, transform IT reacting in proactive manner, than reactivate towards all issues, transforming them to offer proactive, intelligent infrastructure management.

Features

- Perform continuous in-depth analysis
- In-sights, facilitates, obtaining comphrensive analysis of entire RH environment, with predictive analytics, for resolving issues, well ahead of issues impacting environment, business. Insights are programmed to identify any security lapses, mitigate them, on bare metal, virtual, container, or private or public clouds. Streamlines, performance of applications, with aim of minimizing system uptime.
- Offers, heightened visibility into RHEL environments
- RHinsights, in individual RHEL subscription, delivers Linux's latest version.

- Power of predictive analytics, embedded within RHEL, guides user's in proactive identification, remediation of threats, resulting in minimizing outages, un-expected downtimes.
- Redhat teams' can access RH exhaustive knowledge base. It is beneficial for resolving any issues, using more than 100,000 verified solutions designed for threats, configuration problems. Prioritize issues, on the basis of a comphrensive risk assessment, resulting risk score, which includes probability, potential impact Utilize, time diligently by prioritizing issues based on an overall risk score that includes probability and potential impact.

A clean, customized, step-by-step remediation

It is recommended avoid complexities, by replacing them with simple to execute issue resolution. It is necessary for identification, prioritization, and assignment of re-meditation task to individual systems or groups to for enhancing response. It is suggested, to minimize risks for under or over-staffed operation teams, with customized, verified solutions.

Comprehensive risk assessment

Prioritize time, resources on to be spent on solving issues, which maximum impact risk reduction, by performing a comprehensive risk assessment, which combines probability risk with potential impact per issues

Supported platforms

RHinstights, offers, predictive analytics, remediation procedures for RHEL6.10, subsequent versions, latest being 8, introdcuced in May 2019, with Insights packed.

https://www.redhat.com/en/technologies/storage/hyperconverged-infrastructure

RH HCI- Hyper-converged infrastructure

HCI, is designed based on OpenStack, virtualization platforms, which delivers co-located, scalable, software-defined compute, storage, which is powered by RH AnsibleAutomation,delivered on cost-conservative, industry standard hardware,along with Integrated software-defined compute and storage in an compact footprint.

Features

Maximize resources

HCI minimizes deployment times, minimize OPEX, streamline roll-out, with a compact footprint.

- Single-support software stack
- It is mandatory for consolidating planning, procurement, training, management, upgrades, with support of single RH subscription.
- Delivers enhanced performance at edge
- It is necessary to install more power on network edge, where human resources, space are constrained.
- Open source
- It is a best practice to utilize innovation of upstream communities, which guarantee enterprise-ready capabilities, without getting locked with proprietary offerings.

Industry verticals viz,retail, banking, telecommunications, public sector's, depend on critical applications, which needs to be deployed with constraints viz. space limitations, budgets, scarcity of skilled personnel. And business necessitates extending of such applications from datacenter core to edge of networks. Hyper-converged infrastructure, benefit from vast experience of customer deployments, QE testing of components. Such components, are containerized with RH storage, streamlined using, RH Ansible Automation, with suitable customizations, being applied for specific use cases, which is completely open source.

- RH Hyper-converged Infrastructure for Cloud, Virtualization
- Built on Red Hat Virtualization and Red Hat Gluster® Storage, Red Hat Hyper-converged Infrastructure for Virtualization provides a single support stack for virtual compute and virtual storage resources for departmental and lines-of-business teams, remote sites, DevTest, and other resources.
- Is entirely open source.

Redhat satellite

https://access.redhat.com/documentation/en-us/red_hat_satellite/6.4/html/release_notes/pref-red_hat_satellite-release_notes-introduction

Redhat Satellite was designed to offer system management features, which enables users' to deploy, configure, manage systems across physical, virtual, cloud environments. Also offers features viz. provisioning, remote management, monitoring of multiple RHEL Linux deployments from a centralized location, using a single console, tool. Satellite, server performs synchronization of contents from Redhat Customer Portal, besides different sources, offering functionalities viz. Fine-grained life cycle management, user and group role-based access control, integrated subscription management, advanced GUI, CLI, or API access. RH Satellite Capsule Server mirrors contents from RHEL satellite server, to enable occurrence of content federation across multiple geographical locations. Host systems, if need arises, are capable of pulling content, configuration from Capsule server installed in respective locations, but not from central Satellite Server. Another functionality offered is, providing localized services viz, Puppet Master, DHCP, DNS, or TFTP .Capsule server, facilitates scaling of RH satellite, when quantity of managed systems, Capsule Servers assist in scaling of RH Satellite, in concurrence with number of managed systems being increased within environment.

Satellite6 Component Versions

RH Satellite, is architected as collection of sizable upstream projects, complete details are published in appropriate URL. For getting to know about details of number of projects that has been identified to be a part of major projects included, RH Satellite, Proxy Server Life Cycle. To gain an overview of different lifecycle phase pertaining to RH Network satellite, RH satellite, status of support for supported products, refer to RH Satellite,

https://access.redhat.com/support/policy/updates/satellite

Ansible enhancements

https://access.redhat.com/documentation/en-us/red_hat_satellite/6.4/html/release_notes/chap-red_hat_satellite-release_notes-new_features_and_enhancements.

Latest version of Satellite installer is capable of installing Ansible Core, requisite Foreman modules. Remote execution of Ansible jobs are managed by Capsule Server. Several enhancements have been implemented for Ansible integration in Satellite for performance enhancement. Insights, is capable of being deployed in targeted host(s), using Ansible, during process of provisioning of hosts, or can also be provisioned later, as and when needed. Support for Ansible in Satellite. Latest version of Satellite, is archichted for supporting imports import of RHEL system roles, which are part of latest RHEL version 7.4, which supports Linux system role for adding Ansible roles for simplifying configuration procedures, and also simpler. Version 6.4 doesn't support different roles or playbooks, until enterprise purchases a valid Ansible Engine subscription. However, it is possible for importing, custom Ansible roles from external locations like Ansible Galaxy. However, such extra roles, playbooks are outside purview of Satellite support or Smart Management subscription. Playbooks thus created from support perspective are deemed to be part of a scripting framework .RH support team, can provide assistance in usage, syntax of commands. When an enterprise seeks assistance in debugging or authoring of a playbook on company's behalf, RH consulting service partner, will engage with Cloud team to design appropriate methods, in listed areas.

- Auditing Enhancements. Audits' are performed to identify, perform any remediation if needed to following:
- Changes that has been done, to role-based access control configuration
- Changes that has been effected to content management life cycle
- Any change to Satellite's taxonomy
- User interactions

Discovery plug-in

For enhancing discovery, administrators' can consider enabling a Capsule Server, to assume role of Template Capsule purposefully created for a discovery subnet. Template Capsule can also be configured to perform role of proxy service that can provision templates' for specific discovery subnet.

- Composite Content View Republishing
- A Composite Content View gets republished, when an component Content View also gets republished.
- Custom Configuration Enhancements

- In latest version of Satellite, a Custom configuration value, which has been recommended by RH, doesn't gets overwritten by satellite installer.
- Load–Balancing Capsule pool
- It is recommended to create a load–balanced Capsule pool, for providing adequate resiliency against planned, unplanned shutdowns.
- Manifest, Subscription Management Enhancements
- With built–in tools, users are provided choice of editing the imported manifest, simultaneously managing subscription allocations directly in the Satellite web UI.
- Provisioning on AWS GovCloud
- AWS GovCloud regions can be considered for purpose of hosting, provisioning.
- RHV 4 API Support
- For purpose of evaluating new engine API, user's can use RHV 4 API's, which is presented as a technology preview feature. RSS Feed Support
- Using latest versions of RSS feed, it is now possible for accessing RH satellite blog, by connecting to RH satellite blog for Satellite web UI. If required, administrators' shall activate or deactivate update notifications for specific RSS feeds.
- Supports external Databases

https://www.redhat.com/en/technologies/jboss-middleware/3scale

Middleware

RH 3scale API Management

API's form bedrock of agile integration, delivery of business values in a digital world. API's play significant role in innovation, simplifying cross-enterprise agility, while encouraging creation of new products, revenue streams. RH 3scale API Management simplifies task of managing API's User's can share, protects, distributes, manages, monetize API's, in a infrastructure platform built, which is designed for delivering higher levels of performance, offering customized controls, supports future growth. Deploy 3scale components can be provisioned in on-premise, cloud, or any combination of two.

Benefits

- API traffic control

3scale utilizes self-managed or cloud components which offer for providing traffic control, security, access policy enforcement.

API program management

Users' are a permitted to own centralize control of API program—including analytics, access control, monetization, developer workflows.

OpenShift integration

Is, Architected, for executing high-performance applications in a controlled and in an automated manner.

RH Fuse integration

RH fuse, which integrates with all components, must be used for creating API', effortlessly, swiftly .Offers, Comprehensive security.
Large number of encryption, authentication, authorization protocols is supported.

Hybrid cloud's supported across all components

3scale extensively supports each and every component, which resides any cloud model viz. on-premise, in cloud, or on any combination of the two. This environment lets users to design customized API management.

https://www.redhat.com/en/technologies/jboss-middleware/amq

Middleware - AMQ

Extends integration to outer edges of business operations

In order to offer swift response for increasing business demands, in a swift, efficient methods, it is necessary for inventing newer methods to integrate large number of applications, vast quantity of applications, which are distributed across environment.AMQ is designed on lines of open-source communities viz. Apache Active, Apache Kafka, a flexible messaging platform which delivers information in reliable, secure manner, which leads to real-time integration, connecting Internet of Things (IoT),becoming a reality.

Features

Stringent Data propagation in a micro serviced environment

Users can freely share data between micro-services, applications, simultaneously delivering high levels of throughputs, lower latencies. AMQ streams component makes Apache Kafka "OpenShift native", with assistance of powerful operators' that simplifies deployments, configuration, management, use of Apache Kafka on OpenShift.

Self-service messaging, on-demand

With AMQ online, enabled, it is necessary for developers to provision messaging, whenever it is necessary, which can be done using browser console.AMQ online component is developed on top of foundation of OpenShift, which itself is a container platform, designed for delivering HA, enhanced scalability,besides guaranteeing availability of cloud-native applications.

Real-time integration

Aided by different messaging patterns for supporting real-time messaging, AMQ integrates, AMQ performs integration of applications, endpoints, devices, efficiently, resulting in environment turning more responsive, agile.

Multilingual client support

RH AMQ support connectivity from client programs, scripted in multiple languages. Also, supports Java clients' native connectivity from C, C++, Python, .Net and more. Streaming Text Oriented Messaging Protocol (STOMP) support, results in establishing message connections from scripting languages viz. JavaScript and Ajax.

Multiprotocol, language-based support

AMQP defines a open-wire protocol, to support messaging interoperability.MQ is a result of collaboration between prominent messaging vendors, end-user organization. With AMQP, developers can deploy multiple, different messaging solutions, and receive appropriate responses to growing business needs.

High performance, security, reliability

Architected for delivering High-performance, reliability, security and delivered, aided by professional support services. Many mission critical applications have been supported by AMQ.AMQ design is based on open source projects from Apache Software Foundation.

Middleware

https://www.redhat.com/en/technologies/jboss-middleware/fuse

Fuse constitutes a part of agile integration solution. Distributed approach, guides teams to deploy integrated services, where it is most needed. Fuse comes with API-centric, container-based architecture, which decouples services, allowing them to be created, extended, deployed independently.

Features

Hybrid deployment

It is a best practice for utilizing on-premise, in public/private clouds, or as a hosted service for supporting diverse set of users', using single integration platform.

Built-in iPaaS with low-code UI/UX

Application developers, business users are recommended to make use of drag-and-drop interface, as portion of a comprehensive Integration Platform-as-a-Service (iPaaS) solution.

Container-based integration

To achieve better performance, throughputs, it is recommended that, Application developers create, extend, deploy, scale micro services independently.

Complete integration

Starting from legacy systems to IoT devices, everything can be integrated with large set of connectors

UBUNTU

https://www.ubuntu.com/

U buntu is the platform of choice for most production Open Stack clouds, with Canonical providing consulting, training, support and fully managed cloud services for many of the world's leading companies. And a open cloud platform from Canonical, which has been deployed for both prod and non-prod environments, comes with Canonical offering comprehensive including training many environments have adopted this. Make user of fully managed cloud service and get complete operational control remotely for the cloud services, even without the need for bootstrapping. The swiftest route to get connected to production environment And with Foundation cloud built, one can be sure of building on –premise cloud within 3 weeks,

Automate physical service

Turn your data center into a physical cloud with MAAS bare-metal provisioning. On premises, open source and supported.

Consulting packages

With Foundation Cloud Build, we will build you a fixed-price cloud on your premises, with a proven reference architecture in 3 weeks

Automate physical servers

Turn the data center into a physical cloud with MAAS bare-metal provisioning. On premises, open source and supported.

Modeling

Hundreds of services and pre-configured applications are available for single-command deployment to any cloud.

Fully manage clouds

Canonical operates large number of private Open Stack clouds on behalf of customers, facilitates, getting advantages of OpenStack on premise while concentrating on business workloads, performance. Boot Stack is a "build, operate and transfer" service which lets users to take control of the private environment any time. The fastest path to production OpenStack, with the most widely used OS for cloud computing. Canonical operates large number of private OpenStack clouds on behalf of customers, facilitates, getting advantages of OpenStack on premise while concentrating on business workloads, performance. Boots tack is a "build, operate and transfer" service which lets users to take control of the private environment any time. The fastest path to production OpenStack, with the most widely used OS for cloud computing. Services also include, co-creation of the architecture, design and construct OpenStack setup DC of customers choice, operate according to SLAs https://www.ubuntu.com/cloud/foundation-cloud

Canonical operates large number of private OpenStack clouds on behalf of customers, facilitates, getting advantages of OpenStack on premise while concentrating on business workloads, performance. BootStack is a "build, operate and transfer" service which lets users to take control of the private environment any time. The fastest path to production OpenStack, with the most widely used OS for cloud computing. Services also include, co-creation of the architecture, design and construct OpenStack setup DC of customers choice, operate according to SLAs and the properties are

Designed to deliver

Canonical adopts user's requirements to design unique cloud architecture that turns concentrate on developing business applications, delivered with all it is needed to maintain the efficiency of systems.24/7 support assures of high availability, Canonical provides phone, mail and web based support, the deployments. Listed below are the features:

- Two-day onsite requirements gathering workshop
- Includes tools for ongoing operations management
- KVM and LXD hypervisors
- Ceph-based storage
- Full HA implementation of all control services in converged or discrete architecture
- Automation and monitoring packages such as Juju, Prometheus, Nagios and more are included as standard
- Integrated log management with Elastic, Logstash, and Kibana
- Complete handover with tenant on boarding, documentation, and details of ongoing support

https://www.ubuntu.com/openstack

Characteristics

- Ubuntu is the most adopted Linux distribution for OpenStack
- Big business entities like AT&T, Bloomberg, PayPal, eBay, Sky and Wal-Mart design OpenStack with Canonical on Ubuntu
  - Ongoing operations like upgrading OpenStack are simplified with Canonicals' reference architecture
- Boot-Stack is a fully managed OpenStack cloud, on IT infrastructure hardware, inside the datacenter, that managed by, by Canonical
- Foundation Cloud consists of s set-up, design, architecture and training in one package by Canonical

Methods to obtain

CTO can rely on Canonical to design, build and operate a production OpenStack cloud in your premise, starting as low as $15 per server per day. Also offers training and support packages, which is also the recommended strategy way to get to production fast, enabling, IT team ramp workloads, and efficiency, let mangers focus on performance and not on the logistics. Completely managed by Canonical,

Delivered in weeks

Canonical guarantees to, build and operate a production OpenStack cloud on users premises, starting at low @15 per server per day. This is the recommended way to get to production fast, enabling you to ramp your workloads efficiently and focus on cloud consumption not infrastructure.

Installation

Deploy Use Canonicals' conjure-up to deploy a multi-node OpenStack. With LXD containers, it can fit into laptop, in VMware or public cloud.Compatile for developers attempting cloud, who wishes to learn how each components work, and is suggested to be deployed with MAAS ('Metal as a Service') to deploy across many servers and scale it to many racks.

Characteristics

Boot-Stack a private OpenStack cloud managed remotely by Canonical, which Is the best method to run production environment. Has the flexibility of being loaded into any compatible hardware of choice, with 24/7 support.

- Highly customizable
- Organization has individual choice of Ubuntu- certified server and network hardware
- Monitoring can be setup using existing machine using the existing facilities
- Committed availability, supported by defined SLA
- Guaranteed availability backed by a clear SLA
- Transfer operations at will

Production environment in 3 weeks

Deploying Foundation Cloud Build service has the potential of getting a full production OpenStack cloud up and running in 3 weeks using the reference architecture and by offering model driven operations and upgrades to future OpenStack releases guaranteed, this platform has proven to deliver higher efficiencies that can be customized. Adopt Canonicals' conjure-up to deploy a multi-node OpenStack. With, LXD containers, as it can suit the needs. That fits into your laptop and it ideally suits the requirement of first time users/ developers who would want to experiment the components, In action. It is suggested to be deployed with MAAS ('Metal as a Service') to deploy across many servers and scale it to many racks. Services offered are

- SLAs and support services
- On-site engineering and support
- Access to Reference architectures
- OpenStack feature development at the time of actual need
- Customized architecture service placement
- Repeatable automated deployment
- Hardware assistance

Ubuntu core

https://www.ubuntu.com/core

Ubuntu Core is a miniature transactional version of Ubuntu designed for host of IoT devices and large container deployments, besides running new breed of super-secure, remotely upgradeable Linux app packages known as snaps – and it's trusted by leading IoT players, from chipset vendors to device makers and system integrators.

Why to use?

Ubuntu Core shares the same kernel, libraries and system software as classic Ubuntu, one can develop snapshots on Ubuntu PC as is done for any other application, however there difference is that it's been built for the Internet of Things.

Smallest

Ubuntu Core is smaller than competing "micro" container OS offered by other platforms and it is tiny since it just a base file system. Applications s are delivered as snaps, alongside a free choice of container runtimes and coordination systems which is reality because it's got a smaller attack surface, it's much more secure

Tamper proof

Snaps on the file system are immutable and next to impossible to hack since they are read-only and digitally signed, besides Their integrity can be verified any point of time, and the system is bound to be secure from start to shut

Freedom of choice

Snaps are optional extensions to the base Ubuntu Core system which can be offered by vendors besides being integrated with other snaps through secure, well-defined interfaces, which ensures no-locking

A range of target platforms

Ubuntu Core supports an unrivalled range of SoCs and single-board computers, from the 32-bit ARM Raspberry Pi (2 and 3) and the 64-bit ARM Qualcomm Dragon board to Intel's full range of IoT SoCs.

Which can be executed on prominent the leading clouds — Amazon, Microsoft and Google include Ubuntu Core images for production container deployments and minimal OS operations.

Internet of things

https://www.ubuntu.com/internet-of-things

Beginning from home control to industrial controls including robotics, core offers highly tight security application stores and reliable updates, development effort are made simpler, snap packages make Ubuntu core, secure and trustworthy for distributed services, few application areas are:

- Digital Signage -Miniature footprint and full OpenGL. Combined with reliable updates across wide array of hardware make Ubuntu Core a perfect platform for millions of digital signs
- Robotics: With ROS and snapcraft, it becomes simpler for enabling applications for robots and drones, creating new ecosystems and business models. Configuring / deploying Gateways – Feature rich network and support protocols makes Ubuntu core industrial scale gateways one can create future next wave of industrial control and intelligence with Ubuntu Core

Regular updates for the OS, and applications protects devices from ongoing attacks, remedies security threats automatically .and The role of the update controller is to ensure that changes are certified by manufacturers or ISV's and updates needs to be monitored periodically as even, since single lapse has the potential to place device in the frontend attack line, and put to risk millions of devices and bad update has the potential of product recall, thus it is must to create fool-proof

Snaps for security

Ubuntu Core is an all-snap version of Ubuntu. A snap is a secure, easily upgraded, universal Linux package for an app and all its dependencies. Snaps are:

- Confined for strict security
- Transactional for reliable updates
- Compressed to save disk space
- Easy to create and distribute
- Widely adopted by industry leaders

https://www.ubuntu.com/internet-of-things/digital-signage

Digital signatures

Secure, reliable besides having the choice of upgraded remotely, Feature Rich ecosystem of hardware, software solutions. Multitude of devices are currently is currently deployed

Digital signage players need the power of Ubuntu

Even With a small footprint and serious power, Ubuntu Core cut costs of hardware cost even running high definition videos, offers economic solution while still running 4K video. Designed to provide cheaper options, this technology builds from its heritage on servers to bring a secure and stable platform, designed for 24/7 availability and resistant to screen takeovers and other attacks. Users can configure auto upgrade automatically and promises timely delivery of new features. For purpose of software development one can utilize : existing libraries and codebase, flexibility in development, all the way down to the device drive Faster innovation: wide peripheral support, Wi-Fi, 3G/4G, NFC, Bluetooth, software-defined radio, deep learning, audio and camera support (including RealSense Application isolation, enabling security, robustness and simpler maintenance Remote maintenance: No physical presence required, remotely managed from datacenter.

Managed cloud

https://www.ubuntu.com/cloud/managed-cloud

Boot-Stack creates swiftest is the fastest path to a production private OpenStack cloud.

- Can be deployed on servers at individual locations, managed by Canonical, 24/7

- Design is based on proven architectures that will facilitate the setup running in 3 weeks
- Supports high levels of customization of architecture, in a series of iterations, based on workloads
- Demand SLA for the cloud
- focus on your business applications first
- Ensure that team has been provided with complete access to all machines at all times
- Ensure tight integration with monitoring systems

Factors' that needs consideration:

Economics

CapEx optimization essentially begins from automation, with efficient operations offering the advantages of complete ownership, over rentals.

Scale

Ubuntu is considered as the platform for large number of business especially with requirement to deliver on high levels of complexity at scale and at speed.

Efficient

This stack offers ready to use, fully converged designs, that leads to space optimization, easing out of the server numbers, offering completely containerized OpenStack.

Highly resilient

High availability and resilience in storage and networking across environments, lays guarantee our Boots tack SLA
And this platform fits into the business strategy

Managed Open Stack

Provides Controlled density and performance so that, performance can be monitored Containers are designed to offer bare metal performance and speed, offers Capex, optimization, over long term for workloads, meets all regulatory compliance, ensures high levels of data sovereignty, and the existing hardware and network can be used to host services Provides Controlled density and performance so that, performance can be monitored Containers are designed to offer bare metal performance and speed, offers Capex, optimization, over long term for workloads, meets all regulatory compliance, ensures high levels of data sovereignty, and the existing hardware and network can be used to host services, it meets the needs of host of regulatory compliances, and standards, ensures data sovereignty and can operate over the existing links and other characteristics are

- Designed to manage Elasticity for highly variable load
- Commissioned multiple regions for low latency
- Users can opt for the providers of their choice
- OPEX as needed
- Privacy of data and applications are ensured by configuring Network isolation
- Guaranteed SLAs

BootStack-ing is the efficient route to modern VIM. As a VNF vendor; Boots tack enables users to test individual VNF on widely adopted Telco production OpenStack. Boot Stack team actively monitors Opens tack 24/7, offering monitoring, alerting, capacity planning and continuous service checks to guarantee healthy environment, Operated for achieving high standard of Canonicals home grown production OpenStack, supporting critical public services for 60m users and device to thus guaranteeing higher uptimes. Boots tack team actively monitors customers OpenStack 24/7; monitoring, alerting offering views on performance, health status, and reports back to administrators for collective action. And canonical offers BOT – build, operate, transfer model Ubuntu owns responsibility for remote management and 24/7 availability customers platform, offering multiple support options

Managed Cloud

https://www.ubuntu.com/cloud/managed-cloud

Securely managed it offers easier route to production on private Open cloud, mangers can focus on business, while canonical mange business operations. Runs s organizations r servers, in your premise, but managed by Canonical, 24/7 Designed adopting Canonical authorized reference, the environment can be made go-live within 3 weeks, utilities are offered free of cost, customize architecture, run as many iterations based, and then finalize the design. Sign comprehensive SLA for the cloud infrastructure, while designers focus on developers focus business application, It offers compressive 24/7 access and support. Can easily adopt with the existing management systems, where only minimal efforts and changes are required.

Features

Budget

CAPEX economics calls for complete automation. Operating efficiently has potential to benefits of ownership, over public cloud rentals,

Scale

Ubuntu has been one of choice of mainly internet operators and cloud service providers, web operators who select this platform to fit the requirements of complexity and speed, scale

Efficiency

Squeeze majority of servers and other cloud components, with proven Canonical reference architecture who leads market in containerized OpenStack.

Resilient

The manner in which Ubuntu offers highly-availabilible, resilience in storage and networking across the board underpins our Boots tack SLA,re-affirms, that this platform can deliver for any sort of requirements,

https://www.ubuntu.com/cloud/public-cloud

Public loud

Ubuntu Servers are regarded most prominent Cloud OS which is made possible of futures like security, versatility and policy of regular updates, this platform leads the chart for running most workloads in public clouds today. With certified images available on clouds from partners like AWS, Microsoft Azure, Google Cloud Platform, Rackspace, Oracle and IBM Softlayer, besides of having distinction one being only free cloud operating system with the option of enterprise-grade commercial support.

Reasons for use

Established as a reliable technology for enterprise-scale workloads on all leading public clouds

Not necessary to pay for licenses, irrespective of number of images that runs

Users receive Enterprise-grade support, besides management tools that can be directly accessed from Canonical, Ubuntu LTS Guarantees support for five years, complete Maintenance and security updates. Recognized as one of the fastest method for scaling up workloads on public cloud, with Juju users can launch entire cloud environment in single click, or using a single command line, deploy Juju for all deployment purposes. Juju allows launching an entire cloud environment with one click, or just one command using the CLI, besides Juju can be deployed for umbrella deployment.

Storage

https://www.ubuntu.com/cloud/storage

Ubuntu Advantage Storage from Canonical is delivers software-defined storage (SDS) technology - Ceph, NexentaEdge, Swift and Swift Stack, which adopts basic concepts any cloud storage. It embeds proven software-defined storage (SDS) technology - Ceph, NexentaEdge, Swift and Swift Stack, into a round the clock -supported software solution with a unique metered pricing model. Current cloud environment, stairs at increasing pace of data creation, as structured and unstructured data occupies disks and data retention policies lengthen, IT management, has to invent effective and cost effective methods to encounter the growing storage needs. Even though cost effective, traditional storage strategies, which included SAN and NAS has to an, extend outdated the utility as a concept even though small and medium business are counting with it, the current device needs to meet such needs. Ubuntu storage offers one such choice. Ubuntu offers below choices.

Swift: High performance S3-compatible object store developed and shipped with OpenStack, meets the requirements of storing unstructured data

Ceph: converged storage framework which especially designed to present object, block, and file storage from a single distributed computer cluster.

Swift stack

Designed for object storage, built on OpenStack Swift, built on OpenStack Swift, innovative storage controller for global management and NFS and SMB/CIFS file gateways

Metered pricing

Traditional storage types are either charged on per-node or as per the total disk capacity, which has possibility of penalizing for techniques such as high durable applications here is where Ubuntu offers differential on pricing, and it based on the quantity of data that has been recorded in storage pool irrespective of how was it recorded or how much consumed and users don't get bill for unused space.

Why is this an advantage?

https://www.ubuntu.com/cloud/storage

Ubuntu storage choices follow standard properties of cloud grade storage, but obviously differ from other storage, and to understand the benefits, the same has been enlisted

Swift-With high performance coupled high performance S3-compatible object store developed and shipped with Open Stack, is a perfect option for storing unstructured data. Different variants are listed

Block and object_storage - presents developers with feature of offering inline de-duplication & compression, low latency block services, instant snapshots, and enterprise grade, end-to-end data integrity.

Ceph_– Is a converged storage framework which has specifically architected to present object, block, and file storage from a single distributed computer cluster.

NexentaEdge_- Block and object storage offering inline de-duplication & compression, low latency block services, instant snapshots, and enterprise grade, end-to-end data integrity.

Swift Stack_-_An object storage system which has built on OpenStack Swift, powered an innovative storage controller for global management and NFS and SMB/CIFS file gateway

Metered pricing

Commonly, usage of legacy storage solutions are charged on per-node or according to total disk capacity, which at times result in penalizing good practices viz as high durability replication Ubuntu Advantage Storage is different, users are charged on the basis of quantity of data that has been recorded in individual storage pool, irrespective of how data is written or even how much space is utilized, which also means, users aren't charged empty spaces,

Characteristics

Pre- Plan, build and expand production-grade SDS infrastructure on commodity hardware using proven open source solutions. Deploy and scale Ubuntu Advantage Storage cluster within hours, using Juju and MAAS. Billed for actual data storage, besides Ubuntu doesn't impose penalty in case of increased replication or high-durability erasure coding or early build out of capacity Premium (landscape) customers can activate Autopilot to design, deploy and manage t storage clusters in a completely automated manner. World-class support is offered from Canonical, experts in large-scale, multi-site-replicated deployments, Canonical offers with Ubuntu 16.04 LTS with five years of support for every component in the stack

Containers

https://www.ubuntu.com/containers

To provide services – From LXD to Kubernetes to Docker canonical has created extensive partner chain, which is in a position to provide compressive full range of technologies and services to run containers at scale on public, private and hybrid or bare metal clouds. From LXD to Kubernetes to Docker, Canonical has established tie-ups with leading technology and platform providers, who enables to full range of technologies and services to run containers at scale on public, private, and hybrid or bare metal clouds and LDX offers pure hypervisor. Migrate existing Linux VMs directly to containers, even without modifying the applications or operations. . LXD's machine containers operate just like virtual machines..Users will be able to execute Run an unmodified Linux operating system and applications with VM-style operations at incredible speed with zero latency. Users with ease can run an unmodified Linux operating system and applications with VM-style operations with zero latency, high speed. LXD's pure-container architecture designed for Linux virtualization offers high levels of density advantages over VMware ESX and Linux KVM for private and public cloud infrastructure. If one is considering container orchestration system to assist to construct micro service-based app canonical can be considered or usage, as it offers simple steps and high elasticity. And it is cheaper, Modeled by adopting Juju, Canonicals' Kubernetes combines multiple operational scripting and tooling that are required to manage a long-lived cluster, including upgrades and elastic scaling. Offers simple integration,(including scripts, codes), with Prometheus for purpose of monitoring, Ceph for storage and Elastic Stack including Kibana for analysis and visualizations.

Docker engine on Ubuntu

https://www.ubuntu.com/containers/lxd

10x the density of ESX, 25% faster, zero latency

Migrate effortlessly Linux VMs straight to containers, without having to modify any applications, amending administrative process; LXD is a pure-container hypervisor which runs unmodified Linux guest operating systems with VM-style operations at un-parallel speed and density. Offers dependable are-metal performance for guests, facilitates, sharing of hardware resources in minimal steps, provides simple monitoring of guest processes Delivers precise quality-of-service and quotas Utilities are provided for snap-shot creation, evn during live migration is in progress, besides supporting ARM, POWER, X86 and Z. Restful API and simple CLI, assist developers to create utilities to assist in enhancing deployment process. Supports Rapid provisioning, instant guest boot remote image services, help developers to launch images, sitting from a different location, and administrators to configure monitoring rules, to mange images, default protected with AppArmor, user namespaces, SECCOMP, offers elastic storage and networking feature, that ensures, continuous service availability XD containers are considered similar to any other physical VM. Users privileges allow for remote login monitor guest OS to control guest OS in standard procedure viz, install applications, secure them, and operate them with the same tools while gaining raw performance and density of containers. LDX is capable of launching instances in seconds, thus facilitating of initiating hundreds on a single server. Connect them separately and securely to networks, live-migrate between hosts and drive all of this through a clean REST API. LXD is designed to operate as the next-generation hypervisor for Linux at scale By design XD can perform to "lift and shift" Linux VMs to containers without modifying the application or operations.

https://www.ubuntu.com/containers

Lifts and- shifts the existing VM workloads, it gives option to users to migrate existing Linux VMs straight to containers, easily, without modifying the apps or your operations. LXD's machine containers operate just like virtual machines, besides offering performance of

25% faster than legacy VM, by executing an unmodified Linux operating system and applications with VM-style operations at incredible speed with zero latency By permitting, this task, users get 10x the density of ESX And having the freedom to execute Run an unmodified Linux operating system and applications with VM-style operations at incredible LXD's pure-container strategy to Linux virtualization offers benefits of dramatic density advantages over VMware ESX and Linux KVM for private and public cloud infrastructure. And Canonical distribution of Kubernetes comes with following characteristics:

Universal: Delivers consistenent, compatibilble throughputs across public clouds and your private data centers, besides offering VE updates and TLS encryption across all components, besides being fault-tolerant guaranteed. Google and Canonical in collaboration, aims to create seamless operations between Google's Container Engine (GKE) service with Ubuntu worker nodes, and Canonicals' Distribution of Kubernetes. Deploy Kubernetes to ensure smooth migration, of the container workloads be able to container workloads can migrate to owing to kernel-to-k8s alignment. Few reasons for selecting Kubernetes:

Cloud Neutral

AWS, Azure, Google, Oracle, Racks pace, SoftLayer, or private VMware, OpenStack or bare metal are platforms where Kubernetes can be deployed, besides deploying and operating consistently on, Azure, Google, Oracle, Rackspace, SoftLayer, or private VMware, OpenStack or bare metal.

Current

With canonical, users can plan migration to latest version, whenever wanted and will lesser complexity, while upgrades to each new stable release as well as edge build

Support

Enterprise support which is given, cover a range of SLA's and choice of physical / virtual / cloud, and also support the full stack from kernel to k8s.

GPU and CUDA ready

By default it is delivered with the automatically detect and configure GPGPU resources for accelerated machine learning, AI, transcoding HPC workloads on K8s.

Extensible

Kubernetes facilitates simple integration of custom monitoring, storage, networking, and container runtimes. We offer consulting for deeper customization

Completely managed

Canonical also offers to manage your setup, operations, remotely, besides build and operate Kubernetes, with option of transferring control of cluster operations to in-house team

Converged storage

Components viz storage, networking and computers is overlaid by hyper-converged reference architecture, which can ensure efficient use of resources, besides high availability failover

Compliant

Kubernetes has been rated top performer leader in K8s test suite performance and API standards compliance

Besides, canonical offers consulting packages - : Kubernetes Explorer and Kubernetes Discover however individual Kubernetes that has being built is designed with future expansions, future-proof with automated upgrades to newer versions on demand.

Cloud Neutral

AWS, Azure, Google, Oracle, Rackspace, SoftLayer, or private VMware, OpenStack or bare metal are platforms where Kubernetes can be deployed, besides deploying and operating consistently on, Azure, Google, Oracle, Rackspace, SoftLayer, or private VMware, OpenStack or bare metal.

With canonical, users can plan migration to latest version, whenever wanted and will lesser complexity, while upgrades to each new stable release as well as edge build

Support

Enterprise support which is given, cover a range of SLA's and choice of physical / virtual / cloud, and also support the full stack from kernel to k8s.

GPU and CUDA ready

By default it is delivered with the automatically detect and configure GPGPU resources for accelerated machine learning, AI, transcoding and HPC workloads on K8s.

Extensible

Kubernetes facilitates simple integration of custom monitoring, storage, networking, and container runtimes. We offer consulting for deeper customization

Completely managed

Canonical also offers to manage your setup, operations, remotely, besides build and operate Kubernetes, with option of transferring control of cluster operations to in-house team

Converged storage

Components viz storage, networking and computers is overlaid by hyper-converged reference architecture, which can ensure efficient use of resources, besides high availability failover

Compliant

Kubernetes has been rated top performer leader in K8s test suite performance and API standards compliance

https://www.ubuntu.com/containers/docker-ubuntu

Docker engine on Ubuntu

Integrated support service with enterprise SLAs

Docker Engine is a lightweight container runtime with robust tooling which builds and runs the container. Vast majority of all Docker-based scale out operations runs on Ubuntu. Docker and canonical in joint development, in order to deliver an integrated Docker Enterprise Edition offering on Ubuntu Which presents customers with fastest and simplest path for the task of supporting of Ubuntu and Docker Engine in enterprise Docker operations.

Why run Docker Engine on Ubuntu?

Single partner:

Eases many tasks viz managing multiple agencies and contacts, minimize, relationship complexity and the potential for friction, will just have single point of contact rather than multiple.

High levels of security

The manner Ubuntu packages Docker engine as a single snapshot results in extra additional isolation and confinement benefits which significantly improve the security of your Docker app.

Faster, more reliable

Docker Engine image snaps are more agile to installation besides, automatically updates transactions, ensuring continuity in transactions and below is described how Docker support offering works

Agile

Docker Engine image snaps are more agile to installation besides, automatically updates transactions', ensuring continuity in transactions, besides being fast of install update automatically in order to maintain the Docker upto date, never broken. And this is how Docker support work

Docker and Canonicals' integrated support offering for Docker Engine running on Ubuntu thereby streamlining operations and support experience:

Stable, maintained releases of Docker are published and updated by Docker as snap packages on Ubuntu, which facilitates direct access to the official Docker Engine for all Ubuntu users

Offers Level 1 and Level 2 technical support for Docker Enterprise Edition and are backed by Docker Inc. for Level 3 support, besides guaranteeing universal availability of secure Ubuntu images on Docker Hub

Ubuntu for desktops

https://www.ubuntu.com/desktop

Ubuntu desktop is packed with a bunch of features, that will help to run an organization, school, home, Most of the essential applications such as an office suite, browsers, email and media applications are pre-installed besides plethora of games are delivered through Ubuntu software center, Always free for downloads, primarily to use and share, and Ubuntu thrives on contribution of millions of voluntary developers

Listed below are features

Secure

With a built-in firewall and virus protection software, Ubuntu is one of the most secure operating systems around. And the long-term support releases give you five years of security patches and updates

Accessible

This is one of the platforms which address linguistic, disabilities, irrespective of nationality, gender or disability. Ubuntu is fully translated into over 50 languages and includes essential assistive technologies.

Available on range of hardware

Canonical works with the world's leading computer manufacturers to certify that Ubuntu works on a huge range of devices. It means that Ubuntu is now available at thousands of retailers across China, India, South East Asia and Latin America. And Ubuntu isn't just for the desktop; it is used in data centers around the world powering every kind of server imaginable and is by far, the most popular operating system in the cloud.

Support and management

Ubuntu Advantage is the professional support package from the experts at Canonical. Get 24x7 support with access to engineers with first-hand experience of your issues. It includes Landscape, the Ubuntu systems management tool, for monitoring, managing, patching, and compliance reporting on all your Ubuntu desktop

https://www.ubuntu.com/download/ubuntu-flavours

Canonical is associated s with leading computer manufacturers who certify that it can operate over a wide range of devices which concludes, that it been deployed across continents, besides offering services to desktop deployed in datacenters, and has ability to power any kind of server imaginable and is by far, the most popular operating system in the cloud

Ubuntu flavors

https://www.ubuntu.com/download/ubuntu-flavours

Kubuntu flavors offer distinct means to experience and, each with its r own preference of default applications and settings. Ubuntu flavors are supported d by an exhaustive Ubuntu archive for packages and updates listed below are the choices

Kubuntu

Kubuntu presents the KDE Plasma Workspace experience, a user friendly technology which offers good-looking system for home and office use.

Lubuntu

Is a prudent, swift, energy saving and lightweight variant of Ubuntu using LXDE and it proven OS on PC and laptop users running on low-spec hardware.

Mythbuntu

Is a standalone MythTV based PVR system, which can be standalone or can be integrated with an existing MythTV network

Ubuntu budgie

Ubuntu Budgie provides the Budgie desktop environment that just focuses on offering simplicity besides elegance, simultaneously offering traditional desktop metaphor based interface utilizing a customizable panel based menu driven system

Ubuntu Gnome

Ubuntu GNOME adopts GNOME Shell along with a exhaustive of applications from the GNOME Desktop Environment

Ubuntu Kylin

The Ubuntu Kylin project is tuned to meet the requirements of Chinese users offering a visonfull and elegant Chinese experience out-of-the-box.

Ubuntu mate

Ubuntu MATE showcases the simplicity of a classic desktop environment. Ubuntu MATE is the extension of the GNOME 2 desktop which was Ubuntu's default desktop until October 2010.

Ubuntu Studio

Ubuntu Studio is a multimedia content creation flavor of Ubuntu that has been written for meeting the requirements of audio, video and graphic enthusiast or professional

Xubuntu

Xubuntu presents an elegant and simple to adopt use operating system. Xubuntu comes is delivered with Office that is a stable, light and configurable desktop environment.

Installation

Deploy Use Canonicals' conjure-up to deploy a multi-node OpenStack. With LXD containers, it can fit into laptop, in VMware or public cloud.Compatile for developers attempting cloud, who wishes to learn how each components work, and is suggested to be deployed with MAAS ('Metal as a Service') to deploy across many servers and scale it to many racks.

Characteristics

BootStack a private OpenStack cloud managed remotely by Canonical, which Is the best method to run production environment. Has the flexibility of being loaded into any compatible hardware of choice, with 24/7 support

- Highly customizable
- Organization has individual choice of Ubuntu- certified server and network hardware
- Monitoring can be setup using existing machine using the existing facilities
- Committed availability, supported by defined SLA
- Guaranteed availability backed by a clear SLA
- Transfer operations at will

Production environment in 3 weeks

Deploying Foundation Cloud Build service has the potential of getting a full production OpenStack cloud up and running in 3 weeks using the reference architecture and by offering model driven operations and upgrades to future Opens tack releases guaranteed, this platform has proven to deliver higher efficiencies that can be customized. Adopt Canonicals conjure-up to deploy a multi-node OpenStack. With LXD containers, as it can suit the needs. That fits into your laptop and it ideally suits the requirement of first time users/ developers who would want to experiment the components, In action. It is suggested to be deployed with MAAS ('Metal as a Service') to deploy across many servers and scale it to many racks. Services offered are

- SLAs and support services
- On-site engineering and support
- Access to Reference architectures
- OpenStack feature development at the time of actual need
- Customized architecture service placement
- Repeatable automated deployment
- Hardware assistance

Ubuntu core

https://www.ubuntu.com/core

Ubuntu Core is a miniature transactional version of Ubuntu designed for host of IoT devices and large container deployments, besides running new breed of super-secure, remotely upgradeable Linux app packages known as snaps – and it's trusted by leading IoT players, from chipset vendors to device makers and system integrators.

Why to use?

Ubuntu Core shares the same kernel, libraries and system software as classic Ubuntu, one can develop snapshots on Ubuntu PC as is done for any other application, however there difference is that it's been built for the Internet of Things.

Smallest

Ubuntu Core is smaller than competing "micro" container OS offered by other platforms and it is tiny since it just a base file system. Applications s are delivered as snaps, alongside a free choice of container runtimes and coordination systems which is reality because it's got a smaller attack surface, it's much more secure

Tamper proof

Snaps on the file system are immutable and next to impossible to hack since they are read-only and digitally signed, besides Their integrity can be verified any point of time, and the system is bound to be secure from start to shut

Freedom of choice

Snaps are optional extensions to the base Ubuntu Core system which can be offered by vendors besides being integrated with other snaps through secure, well-defined interfaces, which ensures no-locking

A range of target platforms

Ubuntu Core supports an unrivalled range of SoCs and single-board computers, from the 32-bit ARM Raspberry Pi (2 and 3) and the 64-bit ARM Qualcomm Dragonboard to Intel's full range of IoT SoCs.

CLOUD FOUNDRY

https://docs.cloudfoundry.org/concepts/overview.html

Industry standard cloud platform

The basic tenet of cloud is to permit users deploy network applications, services and expose the same to the users within a short span of time. And when the same application gains prominence, Cloud algorithm automatically scales consummates to stage, the same is quickly, swiftly scales to handle additional traffic, replacing with a few keystrokes which builds-out and migration efforts, which in traditional environment consumed months.

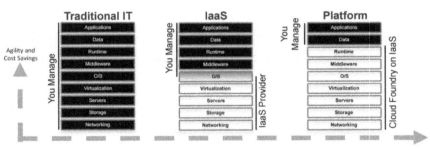

IaaS=Infrastructure as a Service (AWS, vSphere, OpenStack, etc.)

It is absolutely impossible to design a-one-size-fit all architecture, and loaded with umpteen restrictions, few have limited language, framework support; some may have deficits in application services, or even restrict deployment to a single cloud. CF is one of the prominent open source platforms, that can be trusted to execute applications, within the company's existing datacenter or deploy on any IaaS services. Alternatively PaaS can also be adopted by commercial providers viz. AWS, VSphere, OpenStack .Alternatively one can also chose PaaS services, that has been hosted by commercial providers. CF is supported globally, receiving huge support for by vast designer, developer community. Platform exhibits extensitibiliy, openness, elasticity, that forbids users from being locked-in, within solitary framework, standard set of services, applications or even different platforms. CF can be one of the best choices for any IT manager whose target is to eliminate, cost complexities of configuring infrastructure for those applicatations hosted within the environment. CF offers light-weight scripts, rich UI, that developers can make use of design, deploy their applications, on to the Cloud foundry, which can also be utilized for running utilities, and with zero modifications, being effected to the codes.

How does it work?

One of the functionality is to balance processing loads over multiple machines, thereby optimizing for efficiency, resilience against any sort of single or multi-point failures, and this is made possible by executing the following steps:

- BOSH creates and deploys virtual machines (VMs) on top of a physical computing infrastructure, and deploys and runs Cloud Foundry on top of this cloud. To configure the deployment, BOSH follows a manifest document.
- The CF Cloud Controller runs the apps and other processes on the cloud's VMs, balancing demand and managing app lifecycles.
- The router routes incoming traffic from the world to the VMs that are running the apps that the traffic demands, usually working with a customer-provided load balancer.

Applications can run freely

By architectural principle Cloud Foundry designates two types of VMs: the component VMs which constitutes the platform's infrastructure, besides the host VMs which are designated for purpose of hosting applications, which are designed to be deployed in public cloud. Within CF, the Diego system spreads the hosted application loads across the entire host VMs landscape, and ensures continuous operations, balancing unexpected traffic surges, outages or any other pertinent changes, and complete process is managed through configuring an auction algorithm. CF utilizes git system on GitHub to version-control source code; build packs, documentation, and other resources.

Cloud foundry components

https://docs.cloudfoundry.org/concepts/architecture/

The constitution of Cloud Foundry comprises of self-service application execution engine, an automation engine for application deployment and lifecycle management, and a scriptable command line interface (CLI), besides providing services for integration with development tools, in order to simplify deployment steps. CF is architected as Open Architecture, which is delivered with buildpac mechanism, which is instrumental in adding frameworks, an application services interface, and a cloud provider interface.

Description

Router

Functionality of the router is to direct all incoming traffic towards designated target components, be it potent or a hosted application running on a Diego Cell. The router is programmed in such a manner, that it sends regular queries to Diego Bulletin Board System

(BBS), to ascertain which cell, containers, individual application is currently being executed. Based on the information generated, router, if necessary re-computes new routing tables based on the IP addresses of each cell virtual machine (VM), host-side port numbers for cell containers.

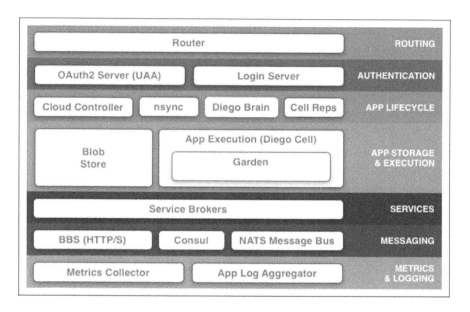

Cloud foundry fundamental components 1d

Authentication

Is provides by OAuth2 Server (UAA) and Login Server, both of them operate in unison to provide identity management.

Cloud Controller CC and Diego Brain

Functionality of CC, is to perform redirection of applications, based on the defined rules and for the purpose of pushing an application to CF, it is necessary to target the CC, after which CC sends instructions to Diego Brain through the CC-Bridge components, directing them to coordinate between individual Diego cells to stage and run applications.CC is also used as a storage location for storing, managing records of orgs, spaces, user roles, services.

nsync, BBS, Cell Reps

In order to maintain service availability, it is essential that applications don't experience outages, and hence it is a must that, deployments must be under continuous watch of the status, and if necessary reconcile with expected state, by terminating, re-starting process, as appropriate. Both, nsync, BBS, Cell Rep components are designed in such a manner, that they operate alongside a chain, in order to maintain the availability of applications. One end of the chain is end-users, other end being instances of applications, that is executed on largely-distributed VMs, which has a probability of crashing or turning redundant. And described are actual operations. a nsync receives a message from the Cloud Controller when the user scales an app. It writes the number of instances into a DesiredLRP structure in the Diego BBS database. BBS uses its convergence process to monitor the DesiredLRP and ActualLRP values. It launches or kills application instances as appropriate to ensure the ActualLRP count matches the DesiredLRP count. Cell Rep monitors the containers and provides the ActualLRP value.

Blobstore

The blobstore is a repository for large binary files, which Github cannot easily manage because Github is designed for code. The blobstore contains the following:

- Application code packages
- Buildpacks
- Droplets

And is necessary, users configure the blobstore as either an internal server or an external S3 or S3-compatible endpoint.

Build & Application staging

https://docs.cloudfoundry.org/concepts/how-applications-are-staged.html

1. At the command line, the developer enters the directory containing her application source code and uses the Cloud Foundry Command Line Interface (cf CLI) to issue a push command.
2. The cf CLI tells the Cloud Controller to create a record for the application.
3. The Cloud Controller stores the application metadata. Application metadata can include the app name, number of instances the user specified, and the buildpac, and other information about the application.
4. Before uploading all the application source files, the cf CLI issues a resource match request to the Cloud Controller to determine if any of the application files already exist in the resource cache. When the application files are uploaded, the cf CLI omits files that exist in the resource cache by supplying the result of the resource match request. The uploaded application files are combined with the files from the resource cache to create the application package.
5. The Cloud Controller stores the application package in the blobstore.
6. The cf CLI issues an app start command.
7. The Cloud Controller issues a staging request to Diego, which then schedules a Diego cell ("Cell") to run the staging task ("Task"). The Task downloads buildpacks and the app's buildpac cache, if present. It then uses the buildpac that is detected automatically or specified with the –b flag to compile and stage the application.
8. The Cell streams the output of the staging process so the developer can troubleshoot application staging problems.

9. The Task packages the resulting compiled and staged application into a tarball called a "droplet" and the Cell stores the droplet in the blobstore. The Task also uploads the buildpack cache to the blobstore for use the next time the application is staged.

10. The Diego Bulletin Board System reports to the Cloud Controller that staging is complete. Staging must complete within 15 minutes or the staging is considered failed. Apps are given a minimum of 1GB memory to stage, even if the requested running memory is smaller.

11. Diego schedules the application as a Long Running Process on one or more Diego cells.

12. The Diego cells report the status of the application to the Cloud Controller.

Application stacks

https://docs.cloudfoundry.org/devguide/deploy-apps/stacks. html#cli-commands

A can stack be termed as a pre-built, pre-configured root file system (rootfs), which supports a a specific operating system, that is capable of hosting, configuring, an Linux-based systems, which is mandatory for configuring,creating Linux-based systems need /usr and /bin directories at their root and these stacks operate in unison with a buildpacks for the purpose of supporting applications, that are being executed in specific compartmetns.Diego architecture is designed in such a manner, that cell VMs, are capable of supporting multiple stacks. The stacks which are being supported are:

- cflinuxfs3: The Linux cflinuxfs3 stack is derived from Ubuntu Bionic 18.04. cflinuxfs2: The Linux cflinuxfs2 stack is derived from Ubuntu Trusty 14.04.
- flinuxfs3: The Linux cflinuxfs3 stack is derived from Ubuntu Bionic 18.04

- flinuxfs2: The Linux cflinuxfs2 stack is derived from Ubuntu Trusty 14.04.

CF provides utilities for creating, customizing indivual stacks

Restaging Applications on a New Stack

For purpose of securing applications, CF core, sends out periodic updates, to resolve any issues that might arise for any sort of vulnerabilities, from any sources. To enhance the protection, CF core, sends out periodic updates which are designed to to prevent, resolve common Vulnerabilities, Exposures (CVEs). With Frequent updates and release, applications pick up on such stack changes through new releases of Cloud Foundry, but on contrary, if users applications are designed to links statically to a library which is already present in rootfs,it is necessary to manually restage, in order to synchronize with the changes. In some situations, it could out to be difficult proposition, to be aware of which library(s), an application is statistically linked to. And many a times, it depends on the languages that is being used and case could be, an application which uses a Ruby or Python binary, and links out to part of the C standard library, and when a situation arises where, updates have to be installed, there are fair chances, than one need to recompile the application, and restage.

2 common steps are needs to be followed

- Utilize the cf stacks command to list the stacks available in a deployment.
- And in an event of alrering stack, re-staging the applications, make use of cf push command. Sample of that could be, restaging user applications n the default stack cflinuxfs2 and execute cf push MY-APP:

Deployment

https://docs.cloudfoundry.org/deploying/index.html

Following steps needs to be completed for preparing domain for cloud foundry

- Choose a DNS domain name for Cloud Foundry instance, which will be used in the process of deploying applications. To cite a use case, if an user names the domain, ABC.com, CF specifically deploys each of such applications as "APP-NAME.cloud.example.com.
- From the AWS Route 53 dashboard, click Hosted zones.
- Click Create Hosted Zone.
- Under Domain Name, enter the domain name, that was chosen earlier, or AWS to host. Under Type, select Public Hosted Zone, which in-turn creates four name server (NS) records for your hosted zone.
- From the company's
- Domain registrar, delegate DNS authority for company' hosted zone into internet four Amazon Route 53 name servers.
- And in order to achieve this, replace company's Domain registrar's NS records for the domain with the NS record values which has been created in the previous step.

Deployment

https://docs.cloudfoundry.org/deploying/common/aws.html

Prior to deploying loud Foundry with cf-deployment, Architects needs do prepare suitable environment to be laid out, with deploying a BOSH Director, steps to perform this vary, which depends on the local IaaS., following steps are mandatory:

- Decide a DNS domain name for Cloud Foundry instance, which is used as identifier in the process of application deployment. For example, IT management chooses the name cloud.example.com,then, CF deploys each of individual applications as APP-NAME.cloud.example.com.
- From the AWS Route 53 dashboard, click Hosted zones.
- Click Create Hosted Zone.
- Under Domain Name, enter the domain name you selected above, for AWS to host.
- Under Type, select Public Hosted Zone, which leads to creation of four name server (NS) records for your hosted zone.
- Accessing the company's domain registrar, delegate DNS authority for company's hosted zone to four Amazon Route 53 name servers.
- And in order to perform all of this, replace local registrar's NS records for the domain with the NS record values, which was created earlier steps. Alternatively, it is possible to locate NS record values by selecting your domain under the Hosted zones tab.

Other steps are:

Download dependencies

- Download Terraform, latest version, unzip, store in a different location, with the PAT.
- Download BOSH CLI v2+. Transform, it to t binary executable, shift to somewhere in local PATH:
- Perform either of the procedures, to download, instal bosh-bootloader:
  a. On Mac OS X, use Homebrew:
  b. $ brew install cloud foundry/tap/bbl

Create an IAM user

Following steps needs be carried out

a. Configure the AWS CLI with the information and credentials from your AWS account:
b. Create the IAM user for bosh-bootloader with the AWS CLI:
c. Create Infrastructure, Bastion, BOSH Director, and Load Balancers
d. Connect to the BOSH Director, LBs
e. Connect to BOSCH director
f. Destroy BOSCH resources

https://docs.cloudfoundry.org/deploying/common/dns_prereqs.html

Establishing an environment

It is a best practice, to create multiple wildcard DNS records to point towards the load-balances, routers.CF, assigns individual applications, its own hostname, within the application domain. By creating wildcard DNS records, individual hostnames within the domain resolves to local IP address of the router or load balancer, which frees up administrators from configuring individual IP for router or LB, besides removing the need for assigning a record for each app host-name.Ex. When a administrators creates a DNS record for system domain *.example.com, that points to the router, every application, every application deployed to the example.com domain resolves to the IP address of users router. Below listed are sample examples.

TCP: handles TCP traffic destined for the TCP Router.

HTTP: t handles HTTP traffic for system components destined for the Grouter.

Web sockets: his is an optional domain that handles WebSocket traffic destined for the Grouter.

SSH: optional domain that provides SSH access to application containers

A sample topology is shown

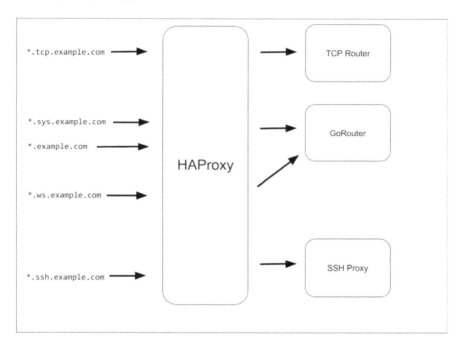

DNS configured to point five domains to 1

In reality, the actual configurations can vary depending on the local IaaS, LB configurations. Listed below are sample topologies:

- An Amazon Web Services (AWS) deployment using Elastic Load Balancer (ELBs)
- A deployment that uses HAProxy for load balancing

The above image indicates, which are the jobs that will have traffic routed towards them from LB. Architects can chose to assign different names to to these groups and in execute bosh instances command to view the instance groups. For instance, in a default cf-deployment, the ssh_proxy job is deployed to an instance group name scheduler. Your load balancers must route traffic to that VM.

Deployment of BOSCH on AWS

https://docs.cloudfoundry.org/deploying/common/aws.html#destroy-environment

Step 1: Prepare a Domain

Listed steps needs to performed

Step 1

- Select a DNS domain name specific Cloud Foundry instance, which CF utilizes as Domain name, during deployment of applications. For, instance, if name is to be test.com. CF deploys every applicication as cloud.example.com
- From the AWS Route 53 dashboard, click Hosted zones.
- Click Create Hosted Zone.
- Under Domain Name, input the domain name which has been chosen, for AWS to host.
- Under Type, select Public Hosted Zone, which creates four name server (NS) records for your hosted zone.
- From company's registered domain registrar, delegate DNS authority for all hosted zones to company four Amazon Route 53 name servers, which can be done by replacing the existing registrar's NS records for the domain with the NS record values which has been created earlier

Step 2:

1. Download Terraform v0.9.1 or later. Unzip the file and move it to somewhere in your PATH:

2. $ tar xvf ~/Downloads/terraform★
3. $ sudo mv ~/Downloads/terraform /usr/local/bin/terraform
4. Download BOSH CLI v2+. Make the binary executable and move it to somewhere in your PATH:
5. $ chmod +x ~/Downloads/bosh-cli-★
6. $ sudo mv ~/Downloads/bosh-cli-★ /usr/local/bin/bosh
7. Perform one of the following procedures to download and install bosh-bootloader:
    o   On Mac OS X, use Homebrew:
    o $ brew install cloudfoundry/tap/bbl
    o   Download the latest bosh-bootloader from GitHub. Make the binary executable and move it to somewhere in your PATH:
    o $ chmod +x ~/Downloads/bbl-★
    o $ sudo mv ~/Downloads/bbl-★ /usr/local/bin/bbl
8. Install the AWS CLI.

Steps

Create IAM user
Create Infrastructure, Bastion, BOSH Director, and Load Balancers
Connect to the BOSH Director
Destroy the BOSH Resources

Managing custom build packs

https://docs.cloudfoundry.org/adminguide/buildpacks.html

Described below are the procedures to be followed, for managing additonal build packs, using CF Command line interface tool. And in case of the applications, use language or framework which CF system doesn't support, one of the below actions can be initiated:

•   Write your own buildpack

- Customize an existing buildpack
- Use a Cloud Foundry Community Buildpack
- Use a Heroku Third-Party Buildpac
- Managing custom build-packs

Deploying Docker

https://docs.cloudfoundry.org/adminguide/docker.html#enable

By default, those applications deployed with push commands, generally are executed in standard Cloud Foundry Linux containers. And with Docker support, CF has the capabilities to deploy, execute, and manage applications that are running in Docker containers. In order to deploy, developers run cf push with the docker-image option, the location of a Docker image in order to create containers from.

Configure Docker registry access

In order to execute Docker containers, CF has to possess the necessary capabilities for accessing Docker registry with help of a Certificate Authority.

Docker image contents

A Docker image comprises of a collection of layers, and individual layers houses, one or both of the following:

- Raw bits, for the purpose of to downloading and mounting, and these bits constitute the file system.
- Metadata contains description of commands, users, environments that are stipulated for the layer. This metadata includes the ENTRYPOINT, CMD directives, which are encoded in the Dockerfile.

Steps how Garden-runC Creates Containers

How Garden-run Creates Containers

Diego utilizes Garden-run C for purpose of constructing Linux containers. Both Dockers, Garden-run C make use of libraries, supplied from the Open Container Initiative (OCI) for the purpose of creating Linux containers. Post creation, such containers use name space isolation, or namespaces, and control groups, or groups, for the task of isolating processes in containers, besides limiting resource utilization. Such resources are typically are common kernel resource isolation features, which are utilized by all Linux containers.

In the process of creation of containers, Docker, Garden-runC executes listed actions:

- Fetch and cache the individual layers associated with a Docker image
- Combine and mount the layers as the root file system which leads to creation of containers, the contents of which exactly match contents of the associated Docker image.

The monitoring process

After Garden-runC creates a container, Diego executes, manages, and monitors these processes, which are running inside of it. And purpose of deciding which process needs to be executed,

- Cloud Controller fetches, stores the metadata that associated with that particular the Docker image. Cloud Controller utilizes this metadata to execute the following actions:
- Executes, the start command as per parameters configured for individual Docker images. Also, sends out instructions to Diego, Grouter to redirect traffic to the lowest-numbered port, which is been exposed in the Docker image, or default to port 8080, in the event of Docker files are openly not

able to expose a listener port. In the process of launching applications on Diego, by cloud controller honors any user-specified overrides viz. Custom start command or custom environment variables.

For the purpose of mitigation of any perceived or actual security concerns CF recommends, that user's execute only trusted Docker containers on the platform; however Cloud Controller prohibits Docker-based applications to run on the platform.

By default, CC executes Docker containers on Diego with user namespaces enabled, and this security restriction disables few features viz. the ability to mounFuseFS devices, from working in Docker containers.

Managing custom build-packs

https://docs.cloudfoundry.org/adminguide/buildpacks.html#add

Listed below are the steps that an administrator, can use to create, manage build pack with assistance of CF CLI. n case of the users application uses a language or framework. Which CGa language or framework which CF system buildpack offer no support, one of the below actions can be initiated

- Write your own buildpack
- Customize an existing buildpack
- Use a Cloud Foundry Community Buildpack
- Use a Heroku Third-Party Buildpack

Add a buildpack

If is required to add a buildpack, execute cf create-buildpack BUILDPACK PATH POSITION [--enable|--disable] command. The arguments to cf create-buildpack specify the following:

- BUILDPACK specifies the buildpack name.

- PATH specifies the location of the buildpack. PATH can point to a zip file, the URL of a zip file, or a local directory.
- POSITION specifies where to place the buildpack in the detection priority list.
- It is must enable or disable specifies that specifies rules for allowing or blocking applications to be pushed with buildpac and is also necessary for default be enabled, only then, developers can push applications using that specified buildpac.
- And in order to ensure that a buildpack a successfully added, run CF build packs.

https://docs.cloudfoundry.org/buildpacks/custom.html

Creation of custom buildpac

CF application Runtime buildpacks, are capable are functioning with limited or even no broadband connectivity, and with buildpack-packager provides exactly same levels of the same flexibility to custom buildpacks, allowing them the freedom to operate in partially or completely disconnected environment s.Buildpacker guarantees, users are properly installing buildpack-packager. Steps are:

- Make sure, users have installed the buildpack-packager.
- Create a manifest.yml. in user's in buildpack.
- Execute, the packager in cached mode: $ buildpack-packager build -cached -any-stack. It is job of the packager to add all necessary details, in individual buildpack directory into a zip file, and exclude anything marked for exclusion in user's manifest. And in a cached mode, packager downloads, inserts dependencies as per defined in the manifest.
- Use and Share the Packaged Buildpac
- Once users have packaged build-pac, with help of −package, users shall use .zip file locally, or share it with others, by means of uploading into any network locations, which is available for access using CLI, and use resulting .zip file

locally, or share with others by the way of uploading the same, into any compatible network location, that is more accessible to CLI, after which users shall proceed to specify the build pack with the –b option, while applications are being pushed..

Core build–pac communication contract

IDX is the zero-padded index, which matches position of buildpack in the priority list. MD5 is the MD5 checksum of the buildpack's URL.

For all buildpacks, which supply dependencies via /bin/supply, It is mandatory for buldpack to create /tmp/deps/IDX/config.yml,to assign name to the subsequent buildpacks, the file can also store miscellaneous configuration for subsequent buildpacks, and is also essential to, config.yml file should be formatted as follows, which shall replace BUILDPACK with the name of the buildpack, which provides dependencies, YAML-OBJECT with the YAML object which houses buildpack-specific configuration: name: BUILDPACK config: YAML-OBJECT

Listed directories shall be created inside of /tmp/deps/ IDX/,inorder to provide, dependencies to subsequent buildpacks:

/bin: Contains binaries intended for $PATH during staging and launch

/lib: Contains libraries intended for $LD_LIBRARY_PATH during staging and launch

/include: Contains header files intended for compilation during staging

/pkgconfig: Contains pkgconfig files intended for compilation during staging

/env: Contains environment vars intended for staging, loaded as FILENAME=FILECONTENTS

/profile.d: Contains scripts intended for /app/.profile.d, sourced before launch

The buildpack may make use of previous non-final buildpacks by scanning /tmp/deps/ for index-named directories containing config.yml.

For purpose of taking advantage of dependencies, which are being offered by

The previously applied buildpacks, it has to be configured in such a manner that, last buildpac necessarily scan /tmp/deps/ for index-named directories containing config.yml.

To make use of dependencies presented by previous buildpacks, the last buildpac:

> May use /bin during staging, or make it available in $PATH during launch
>
> May use /lib during staging, or make it available in $LD_LIBRARY_PATH during launch
>
> May use /include, /pkgconfig, or /env during staging
>
> May copy files from /profile.d to /tmp/app/.profile.d during staging
>
> May use the supplied config object in config.yml during the staging process

https://github.com/cloudfoundry/cf-deployment/tree/master/iaas-support/bosh-lite

Deployment of Cloud Foundry against bosh-lite using bosh-boot loader - bbl

Prerequisites

- In case environment, where GCP or AWS - bbl only supports thesebbl is installed, it is essential to establish the requisite environment variables, suitable that suits, company's IaaS environment as recommended in bbl up --help and also the README of bosh-boot loader, and ensure, that administrators are only using

- GCP or AWS - bbl only supports these bbl is installed.
- Ensure, to configure the appropriate environment variables for the IaaS environment, precisely documented in bbl up --help and also the README of bosh-bootloader, besides having cf-deployment and bosh-deployment repos available anytime

1. Obtain the plan patch, bbl upr

bbl, permits users to alter IaaS resources, configurations, it creates and the ops files, which it utilizes by passing it a plan-patch. and for purpose of deploying BOSH lite to GCP,it is necessary to installbosh-lite-gcp plan patch. Besides, it is compulsory to execute bbl plan, ahead of enforcing any changes to plan patch. One of the first step is to point git clone bosh-bootloader repository to a local directory, subsequently execute listed commands:

- mkdir -p my-env/bbl-state && cd my-env/bbl-state
- Bbl plan --name my-env
- Cp -r /path/to/patch-dir/. .

Reference to the plan path, typically should written as ~/workspace/bosh-bootloader/plan-patches/bosh-lite-gcp/Bbl up

2. Establish DNS

For purpose of, both applications, system performing proper resolution, it is a must to establish a DNS that points to the BOSH Director, it is compulsory for administrators to discover a unique value of director__external_ip,by way of running bbl outputs. Simultaneously, Create a wildcard A record *.<SYSTEM_DOMAIN> and configure it to point towards external IP of the BOSH director, as described earlier. There a several ways to target a bosh director. This doc will use environment variables. eval "$(bbl print-env)"

3. Tagging

CF offers multiple methods to target a bosh director and by using different multiple environment variables, for ex.eval "$(bbl print-env)" Upload a runtime-config It is necessary, that cf-deployment, ensures satisfyin the pre-requisite of users having to uploaded a runtime-config for BOSH DNS. CF strongly recommends, user configure one of the DNS. that is by default offered by a. Bosh-deployment repo:, b. bosh update-runtime-config bosh-deployment/runtime-configs/dns.yml --name dns

Upload a stemcell

With the configured bosh director targeted:
STEMCELL_VERSION=$(bosh interpolate cf-deployment/cf-deployment.yml --path /stemcells/alias=default/version)
bosh \
Upload-stemcell \
https://bosh.io/d/stemcells/bosh-warden-boshlite-ubuntu-xenial-go_agent?v=${STEMCELL_VERSION}

Deploying CF

With user bosh director targeted:

bosh \
-d cf \
deploy \
Cf-deployment/cf-deployment.yml \
-o cf-deployment/operations/bosh-lite.yml \
-v system domain=<SYSTEM_DOMAIN>

Backup and restore

https://docs.cloudfoundry.org/bbr/index.html

BBR orchestrates the steps of initiating backup or restore steps on BOSH deployment or BOSH Director, subsequently transferring backup artifacts to and fro from BOSH deployment or BOSH Director. Supported components BBR is designed as a binary which is designed to perform the task of archiving, restoring BOSH deployments, BOSH Directors and it is necessary that BBR necessitates, that backup targets supply scripts which implements the backup, and restore functions. Specialty of BBR, is that, itns't depend on specific versions of BOSCH,but it is a necessity that, BOSH deployment must have a dedicated backup, restore scripts, packages in the release version, which had to archived, restored with BBR. Users are free to backup, restore listed below

- BOSH Director, including UAA and CredHub, with either Basic Auth or Client/Client-Secret UAA authentication
- Cloud Foundry with specific configuration

<u>Contract</u>

BBR signs a contract with BOSH release authors to call designated backup and restore scripts in a specific order, the method provides benefits of encapsulating the knowledge, regarding process of backup, restoration of deployments. As per design, and as the control for writing, maintaining scripts rests with release author, scripts can be changed to match deployment changes, besides ensuring that changes doesn't go out of sync.

Backup Scripts

1. Pre-backup-lock: The pre-backup lock script locks the job so backups are consistent across the cluster.
2. Backup: The backup script backs up the release.
3. Post-backup-unlock: The post-backup unlock script unlocks the job after the backup is complete.

Restore Scripts

1. Pre-restore-lock: The pre-restore-lock script locks the job so the restore is consistent across the cluster.
2. Restore: The restore script restores the release.
3. Post-restore-unlock: The post-restore-unlock script unlocks the job after the restore is complete.

In an event of BBR backup commands, executed, following action occurs

- BBR connects to instances in the deployment/director, which was listed in BBR command invocation, by utilizing these connections, BBR collects details pertaining to the scripts that needs to be executed, during eacg stage in backup.
- Subsequently, BBR executes pre-backup-lock, backup, post-backup-unlock scripts in defined intervals. It needs to be programmed in such a manner, that scripts in the same stage, are completely executed before the initiation of next stage starts. For example, BBR triggers waits for completion of all pre-backup-lock scripts before it fires any other any backup scripts. Execution of scripts doesn't follow any specific sequence. Release author have complete control over the process of configuring, ordering for scripts in the locking, unlocking stages, however any scripts which are not constrained by the ordering, shall also occur in any in any order within the respective stage.

Syntax for BBR binary is:

bbr [command] [arguments...] [subcommand]
<u>The options for [command] are:</u>
Deployment: Specifies that the target of BBR is a BOSH deployment
Director: Specifies that the target of BBR is a BOSH Director

help: Prints help text

Version: Prints the version of the bbr binary

The [arguments] are specific to the command.

Deployment

https://docs.cloudfoundry.org/deploying/cf-deployment/deploy-cf.html

Clone the cf-deployment repository:

$ git clone https://github.com/cloudfoundry/cf-deployment.git

Above mentioned repository, houses canonical manifest, which is necessary for deployment of CF, alongside with multiple ops files, which dictate, which operation needs to be performed on CF deployment manifest.

Chose suitable OpsFiles

https://docs.cloudfoundry.org/deploying/cf-deployment/deploy-cf.html#ops-files

- It is highly important to that ops files specifies,
- IaaS-specific configuration, besides for adding custom functionalities. into company's CF deployments. And as a pre-requisite, it is essential to ensure, that BOSH reads ops files from the operations folder. applies the operations to the manifest, and it is essential that all ops files are housed in operations directory of the cf-deployment repository, listed configurations requires ops files:
- Deploying Cloud Foundry to any IaaS except Google Cloud Platform (GCP Deploying Windows Diego cells to Cloud Foundry And in order to decide, that which opsfiles, IaaS needs refer to Ops-files table in the cf-deployment repository

and for purpose of deploying windows Diego cells, make use of the windows2016-cell.yml ops file.

Determine Variables

https://docs.cloudfoundry.org/deploying/cf-deployment/deploy-cf.html#determine-vars

Cf-deployment needs, extra details, in order to provide environment-specific or sensitive configuration. BOSH CLI saves these details in a variables store file, which is assigned by operator and that which contains vars-store flag, during the deployment process. This configured flag, projects name of anYAML file, which the BOSH CLI is bound to read, write into. And for some reason, if this file is missing, BOSH CLI shall create it, and even after requisite credential variable are missing, BOSH CLI will generate new values based on the type information stored in cf-deployment.yml. Even BOSCH faces hurdles in generating certain variables, but and by default, this is the sole system domain which exists, and certain situation might arise, that users need to supply variables, which is in addition to system domain.

- Perform Review of the details, available in the Step 2: Determine name, location of Ops Files,
- Create a list of variables which are needed for the ops files which has been selected. It is a must, to assign values for every t variable, For instance, aws_region variable required by the use-s3-blobstore.yml ops file has the possibility to contain the value of us-west-2.
- It is mandatory to chose, either of below mentioned methods, for purpose of assigning variables in the process of deploying Cloud Foundry, which is listed below:
- Supply variables in a YAML file specified with the --vars-file flag during deployment phase and this is method CF

recommends, for tasks of configuring external persistence services.

- Input variables by passing individual –v arguments for each variable. The syntax is –v VAR-NAME=VAR-VALUE.
- Variables passed with either –v or --vars-file shall override those already in the var store, however, it won't store there. Insert variables directly in the variables store file alongside BOSH-managed variables.

https://docs.cloudfoundry.org/deploying/cf-deployment/deploy-cf.html#upload-stemcell

Open the Cloud Foundry deployment manifest, cf-deployment. yml. In the final lines of the deployment manifest, locate the top-level property stemcells and retrieve the values for OS and version. The following example specifies an Ubuntu Trusty 3421.11 stemcell:

```
stemcells:
- alias: default
os: ubuntu-trusty
version: "3421.11"
```

Given is an example,Windows Server, version 1709 stemcell:

```
stemcells:
- alias: windows2016
os: windows2016
version: "1709.13"
Browse to URL on bosh.io.
```

identify, the stemcell which matches with users IaaS and to the version specifie, and copy the URL to the stemcell.

Upload the stemcell:

```
$ bosh upload-stemcell YOUR-STEMCELL-URL
```

Step 5: Deploy

Deploy cf-deployment:

```
$ bosh -e YOUR-ENV -d cf deploy cf-deployment/cf-
deployment.yml \
--vars-store env-repository/deployment-vars.yml \
-v system_domain=YOUR-SYSTEM-DOMAIN \
-o cf-deployment/operations/YOUR-OPS-FILE-1
-o cf-deployment/operations/YOUR-OPS-FILE-2
[...]
```

Base on earlier selection, Determine Variables section, offer extra variables with -v or --vars-fileAnd in a situation, where variable files stored are gone missing, BOSCH generates new ones, in the path which is being specified with ars-store and such a store location, should be completely secured, as is required for all subsequent deployments.

Upload Stemcell

Ensure administrator is logged into BOSH Director: $ bosh -e YOUR-ENV log-in When prompted to review the deployment manifest press enter, to continue. Deploy usually goes-on for minutes. When the command completes, execute bosh VM's. In order to make sure CF VMs are running. Usually deployment process goes on for several minutes, and when command completes, execute VMs to cross-check whether CF VMs are still alive and it is necessary to generate pull request or raise an issue on the source for this page in GitHub

https://docs.cloudfoundry.org/uaa/uaa-user-management.html

Creating and Managing Users with the UAA CLI (UAAC)

With the assistance of UAA Command Line Interface (UAAC),administrator will be able create users in the User Account and Authentication (UAA) server UAAC just helps in creation of user accounts in UAA,but doesn't possess the authority for assigning roles in cloud controller database. (CCDB).Typically, it is responsibility of administrators to user accounts with the help of CF command line interface, cFCLI .The cf CLI both creates user records in the UAA, links the two,org and space roles in the CCDB.It is necessary that an user login using Apps Manager or the cf CLI for the user record to populate the CCDB. Predominant function of UAA is to act as an OAuth2 provider, issuing tokens for client applications to be used in the event when UAA ct on behalf of Cloud Foundry users and in co-ordination with logserver, UAA functions as an authentication agent, providing authentication users with CF credentials, perform SSO service, using those, or other, credentials.UAA is designed to having end-points for purpose of managing user accounts, registering OAuth2 clients, besides authenticating different management functions.

<u>UAA projects</u>

Listed below are the projects that are made available

- Common: A module containing a JAR with all the business logic. common is used in the web apps listed below.
- Uaa: The UAA server. uaa provides an authentication service and authorized delegation for back-end services and apps by issuing OAuth2 access tokens.
- api: A sample OAuth2 resource service that returns a mock list of deployed apps. api provides resources that other apps might want to access on behalf of the resource owner.
- app: A sample user app that uses both api and uaa. app is a web app that requires single sign-on and access to the api service on behalf of users.
- scim: The SCIM user management module used by UAA.

Authentication service, uaa, is a Spring MVC web application. which is free to be deployed in Tomcat or in any compatible container of choice? Users are free to ./gradlew run to run it directly from the uaa directory in the source tree and it should be made to listen on 8080 and has URL http://localhost:8080/uaa.

UAA Server supports APIs; those are defined in the UAA-APIs document which includes the following:

- The OAuth2 /authorize and /token endpoints
- A /login info endpoint. for purpose of permitting queries to be to
- authorizing querying for required login prompts
- A /check token endpoint to, for purpose of permitting
- resource servers to gatherdata, pertaining to an access token submitted by an OAuth2 client
- SCIM users are liberty to provisioning endpoint
- Offers OpenID connect endpoints, for purpose of supporting, automating /userinfo and /check_id
- Command line clients, are authorized to perform authentication by submitting credentials directly to the / authorize endpoint.
- An ImplicitAccessTokenProvider exists in Spring Security OAuth, to utilize if your client is Java.
- By default, uaa will launch with a context root /uaa.

https://docs.cloudfoundry.org/bbr/index.html#overview

Backup, restore

Primary operation of BBR is to initates, sustain backup or restore process on the BOSH deployment or BOSH Director, besides transferring backup artifacts, from and to BOSH deployment or BOSH Directors. Supported Components.BBR is a binary, which is designed to back up, restore BOSH deployments, BOSH Directors. BBR necessitates, that backup targets, provide with scripts, which are used to implement the backup and restore functions. BBR is independent, doesn't depend on any specific BOSCH versions. But it is compulsory that a BOSH deployment should necessarily have its backup and restore scripts packaged in the releases, which are designated to be backed up and restored with BBR. By default, users shall backup, restore the mentioned deployments with BBR: BOSH Director, including UAA and CredHub, with either Basic Auth or Client/Client-Secret UAA authentication or Cloud Foundry with specific configuration

- BBR enters into a contract with BOSH release authors, for of invoking designated backup; restore scripts in a particular order, which delivers benefits:
- Even as by design, deployment encapsulates knowledge, regarding backup, restore the deployments, and since the responsibility for writing, maintaining scripts, is vested with release author, it becomes simple to for scripts to be modified, in line with the deployment changes, which ensures the system, deployment stays in sync.

Supported Components

BBR is a binary that, which is capable of performing task of backup, restore of BOSH deployments, BOSH Directors and BBR mandates, backup targets provide with scripts, which can be implement backup, restore functions. Besides, BBR doesn't depend on any specific version of BOSCH, however it is a must that, BOSCH deployments, needs to have its own backup, restore script packages embedded in the release, for purpose of performing backup and restore with BBR.BBR is not dependent on a particular version of BOSH. However, a BOSH deployment must have its backup and restore scripts packaged in the releases to be backed up and restored with BBR. Users shall back up, restore the following BOSH deployments with BBR:

- BOSH Director, including UAA and CredHub, with either Basic Auth or Client/Client-Secret UAA authentication
- Cloud Foundry with specific configuration

Contract

BBR announces a contract with BOSH release authors, to make necessary calls to marked backup, restore scrips, which is programmed to executed in a pre-determined sequence, and deployments automatically encapsulates information about backup, restore of deployments, since the onus of writing, maintaining scripts rests with release author, it becomes simpler to alter deployment sequence, thus ensuring changes doesn't go out of sync.

Backup Scripts

- Pre-backup-lock: pre-backup lock script locks jobs, ensuring consistency is maintained, during the backup processes, which are effected across, guaranteeing consistency is maintained during the process, and across clusters. backup script backs up the release.
- Post-backup-unlock, the functionality of which is to unlock script unlock the jobs, immediately once backup is completed.
- Restore Scripts :pre-restore-lock: pre-restore-lock script lock jobs, ensuring consistency of restore process across clusters, besides restoring script restores the release
- Post-restore-unlock: These scripts unlock jobs. once restore process is finished

https://docs.cloudfoundry.org/credhub/index.html

CredHub

This is a component, that has designed to deliver centralized credential management for (CF), which is capable of manage multiple scenarios within CF ecosystem. CredHub centralizes, protects credential generation, storage, lifecycle management, and access. Listed below are the functionalities, which it assists in generating, protecting credentials within any individual CF deployments

- Securing data for storage
- Authentication
- Authorization
- Access & change logging
- Data typing
- Credential generation
- Credential metadata
- Credential versioning

Deployment Architecture

Two prominent architectures are a.colocated on the BOSH Director, b .performing independent deployment, as a service. Users are free to select appropriate methods, that suits company's identified architecture. Collocated with the BOSH Director It is a best practice, for deploying CredHub on the same VM as the BOSH Director, and to meet the needs of lightweight credential storage instance, opt for collocated deployment, this configuration doesn't guarantee HA, significantly, in collocation, BOSH Director, CredHub, UAA Director database gets installed on a single VM.

Deployed as a Service

Users have the choice, to perform CredHub installations, as standalone service in single or multiple VMs'.To satisfy needs of HA credential storage instance for multiple components, it is recommended to deploy CredHub as a service. CredHub being stateless–application is easy to perform scaling instances that shares common database cluster along with an encryption provider.

CredHub Credential Types

Credentials are located in multiple locations with CF components utilizing credentials for purpose of providing authentication to connections between components. CF installations typically are packed with lots of active credentials, and with leaked credentials turing out to prominent reasons of security, data violations, so it is essential to design, implement fool-proof security strategy.

Backing, Restoring CredHub Instances

By default, CredHub applications aren't storage location for system state, but it is essential to ensure dependent components are protected, does not hold state, but you must ensure its dependent components are backed up. Redundant backups can help in pre-empting, preventing data loss, in an event of any individual component fails.

https://docs.cloudfoundry.org/credhub/backup-restore.html

CredHub isn't designed to store any stateful data, but, it heavily depends on components, which stores statefull data. First action to be taken is to; create a backup structure, which will help in quick recovery in an event of component failure, also in parallel offering the required resiliency features. Important components that necessarily need to be backed up are:

- Deployment Manifest
- Encryption Keys
- Database

Backing- up deployment manifest

It is mandatory to backup CredHub deployment manifest, every instance it undergoes a revision, it is highly recommended to bring backups under revision control, facilitating auto-management.

For downloading latest manifest, browse $ bosh manifest -d MY-DEPLOYMENT > MY-MANIFEST.yml.

Backing-up encryption keys

Procedures for backing up CredHub encryption keys differs based on the encryption provider you use. CredHub offers support to both internal, Luna HSM.

Internal

Primarily role of internal provider is to encryptions, decryptions, with help of symmetrical AES key, which in itself, encodes a hexadecimal value, which needs to be shared with application during deployment using a symmetrical AES key. This key is a hexadecimal value provided to the application during deployment, store key in a secure environment, so that the same can be accessed in future, in case administrators need to perform recovery actions, and recovery deployments. Luna Hardware Security Modules (HSMs) doesn't support traditional data export, besides it is not designed to release key material once it is placed on the device. But this doesn't imply that data lost from a Luna HSM is unrecoverable, users create deployments in order to ensure that data cease to exist in case of a failure. in case of HSM are used to store sensitive data, configure resiliency by performing the configuration:

Setting up a redundant HSM configuration, or managing a Luna Backup HSM device.

CredHub supports management, integration with a high availability (HA) Luna HSM cluster, and if this configuration is deployed, multiple HSMs use mirrored partitions for purpose of processing incoming requests. Individual HSM contains a copy of an encryption key, which offers redundancy, trying to ensure, atleast, if not all, shall fail without losing availability of key content, In case, users select Luna HSM,for storing sensitive information, resiliency can be ensured by establishing redundant HSM configuration, or Managing a Luna Backup HSM device. CredHub supports integration, managing of HA, Luna HSM cluster, if this configuration is uses, multiple HSM's also use the mirrored partitions, for processing incoming requests. Individual HSM's stores a copy of encryption key, that offers redundancy, thus guaranteeing that all but one of the HSMs could fail without the losing the availability of key material. In case of users using Luna HSM with from AWS, it is permitted to refer to their reference documentation on HA and backup, Database. CredHub stores majority of state-ful data in the configured database, that is either deployed or manageged by CredHub, resulting in backup steps differ depending on chosen database provider.

Security event logging

https://docs.cloudfoundry.org/loggregator/cc-uaa-logging.html#cc

Described is steps to enable, decode security logging for CC,user account, Authentication (UAA) server,redHub.Operators need to utilize these logs for retrieving information regarding subset of requests to the Cloud Controller, UAA server, CredHub for enforcing security compliance. Cloud Controller Logging

CF, by default, doesn't activate feature of Controller request logging, for enabling administrator needs to configure "cc.security_event_logging.enabled" setting in CF manifest to "true", then deploy. CC logs security incidents into syslog subsequently administrators need to configure syslog drain, for purpose of forwarding syslogs to management service. Format for Log Entries. Cloud Controller logs security events in the Common Event Format (CEF). CEF specifies the following format for log entries:

```
CEF:CEF_VERSION|cloud_foundry|cloud_controller_ng|CC_
API_VERSION|
SIGNATURE_ID|NAME|SEVERITY|rt=TIMESTAMP
suser=USERNAME suid=USER_GUID
```

cs1Label=userAuthenticationMechanism cs1=AUTH_MECHANISM cs2Label=vcapRequestId cs2=VCAP_REQUEST_ID request=REQUEST requestMethod=REQUEST_METHOD cs3Label=result cs3=RESULT cs4Label=httpStatusCode cs4=HTTP_STATUS_CODE src=SOURCE_ADDRESS dst=DESTINATION_ADDRESS cs5Label=xForwardedFor cs5=X_FORWARDED_FOR_HEADER

- CEF_VERSION: The version of CEF used in the logs.
- CC_API_VERSION: The current Cloud Controller API version.
- SIGNATURE_ID: The method and path of the request. For example, GET /v2/app:GUID.
- NAME: The same as SIGNATURE_ID.
- SEVERITY: An integer that reflects the importance of the event.
- TIMESTAMP: The number of milliseconds since the Unix epoch.
- USERNAME: The name of the user who originated the request.
- USER_GUID: The GUID of the user who originated the request.
- AUTH_MECHANISM: The user authentication mechanism. This can be oauth-access-token, basic-auth, or no-auth.
- VCAP_REQUEST_ID: The VCAP request ID of the request.
- REQUEST: The request path and parameters. For example, /v2/info?MY-PARAM=VALUE.
- REQUEST_METHOD. The method of the request. For example, GET.
- RESULT: The meaning of the HTTP status code of the response. For example, success.

- HTTP_STATUS_CODE. The HTTP status code of the response. For example, 200.
- SOURCE_ADDRESS: The IP address of the client who originated the request.
- DESTINATION_ADDRESS: The IP address of the Cloud Controller VM.
- X_FORWARDED_FOR_HEADER: The contents of the X-Forwarded-For header of the request. This is empty if the header is not present.

Example of log entry

An anonymous GET request:

CEF:0|cloud_foundry|cloud_controller_ng|2.54.0|GET   /v2/
info|GET
/v2/info|0|rt=1460690037402 suser= suid= request=/v2/info
requestMethod=GET src=127.0.0.1 dst=192.0.2.1
cs1Label=userAuthenticationMechanism cs1=no-auth cs2Label=vcap
RequestId
cs2=c4bac383-7cc9-4d9f-b1c0-1iq8c0baa000 cs3Label=result cs3=
success
cs4Label=httpStatusCode cs4=200 cs5Label=xForwardedFor
cs5=198.51.100.1

GET request with basic authentication:

CEF:0|cloud_foundry|cloud_controller_ng|2.54.0|GET   /v2/
syslog_drain_urls|GET
/v2/syslog_drain_urls|0|rt=1460690165743 suser=bulk_api suid=
request=/v2/syslog_drain_urls?batch_size\=1000 requestMethod=
GET
src=127.0.0.1 dst=192.0.2.1 cs1Label=userAuthenticationMechanism
cs1=basic-auth cs2Label=vcapRequestId cs2=79187189-e810-33dd
-6911-b5d015bbc999

::eat1234d-4004-4622-ad11-9iaai88e3ae9 cs3Label=result cs3=success
cs4Label=httpStatusCode cs4=200 cs5Label=xForwardedFor cs5=198

A GET request with OAuth access token authentication:

CEF:0|cloud_foundry|cloud_controller_ng|2.54.0|GET /v2/routes
|GET
/v2/routes|0|rt=1460689904925 suser=admin suid=c7ca208f-8a9e-
4aab-
92f5-28795f86d62a request=/v2/routes?inline-relations-depth\=
1&q\=
host%3Adora%3Bdomain_guid%3B777-1o9f-5f5n-i888-o2025cb
2dfc3
requestMethod=GET src=127.0.0.1 dst=192.0.2.1
cs1Label=userAuthenticationMechanism cs1=oauth-access-token
cs2Label=vcapRequestId cs2=79187189-990i-8930-52b2-9090b2c5
poz0
::5a265621-b223-4520-afae-ab7d0ee7c75b cs3Label=result cs3=success
cs4Label=httpStatusCode cs4=200 cs5Label=xForwardedFor cs5=198
.51.100.1

A GET request that results in a 404 error:

CEF:0|cloud_foundry|cloud_controller_ng|2.54.0|GET /v2/apps/7
f310103-
39aa-4a8c-b92a-9ff8a6a2fa6b|GET /v2/apps/7f310103-39aa-4a8c-
b92a-
9ff8a6a2fa6b|0|rt=1460691002394 suser=bob suid=a00i2026-55io-
3983-
555o-40e611410aec request=/v2/apps/7f310103-39aa-4a8c-b92a-9
ff8a6a2fa6b
requestMethod=GET src=127.0.0.1 dst=192.0.2.1
cs1Label=userAuthenticationMechanism cs1=oauth-access-token
cs2Label=vcapRequestId

cs2=49f21579-9eb5-4bdf-6e49-e77d2de647a2::9f8841e6-e04a-498b-b3ff-d59cfe7cb7ea
cs3Label=result cs3=clientError cs4Label=httpStatusCode cs4=404

UAA Logging

UAA logs security events to a file, which can be accessed at /var/vcap/sys/log/uaa/uaa.log on the UAA virtual machine (VM). Since, these logs undergo automatic rotation, admistrators needs to configure a syslog drain, for purpose of forwarding system logs to log management service, and following events are logged:

- Authorization and Password Events
- SCIM Administration Events
- Token Events
- Client Administration Events
- UAA Administration Events

Dashboard single-sign-on logging

https://docs.cloudfoundry.org/services/dashboard-sso.html

Single Sign-On (SSO), assists users in the process of authenticating services, resources with a third-party service dashboards, utilizing the SP;s credentials. Service dashboards are web interfaces that assist users to have constant interaction, either with a few or entire features, which the services provide. Main functionality is to deliver streamlined user experience, and restricting recurring logins, across multiple accounts spread across managed services. It is to be noted and designed that, user's credentials aren't directly streamlined to the server, asOAuth protocol, already manages authentication. Enabling SSO for his purpose, CC needs a UAA client, empowered with necessary permissions for creation, deletion of clients for service brokers, those sending requests, client configuration can be performed by including listed snippet in cf-release manifest:

```
properties:
uaa:
clients:
Cc-service-dashboards:
secret: cc-broker-secret
scope: openid, cloud_controller_service_permissions.read
authorities: clients.read, clients.write, clients.admin
Authorized-grant-types: authorization_code, client_credentials
```

Responsibilities

Dashboard client field is a hash, which holds three fields: id is unique identifier for the Oath client, which will be generated for service dashboard on the token server (UAA), which will be utilized by dashboard for authenticating with token serve. In case of a particular client ID, allotted CF will return an error while registering or updating broker secret is the shared secret individual dashboard that will be used to authenticate with the token server (UAA) .redirect Uri is used by token server as an added security precaution. UAA won't be able to offer a token; in an event of callback URL declared by the service dashboard doesn't match the domain name in redirect_uri. And it is task of Token server to conduct matching test in domain name, to ensure any paths will match, example being service dashboard request.

Dashboard URL

It is compulsory for service broker to return a URL for the dashboard_url field in response to a provision request, it is the role of CC clients to expose this URL to users.dashboard_url can be found in the response from Cloud Controller to create a service instance, enumerate service instances, space summary, and other endpoints. Then, users are free to access service dashboard, with URL provided by dashboard_url

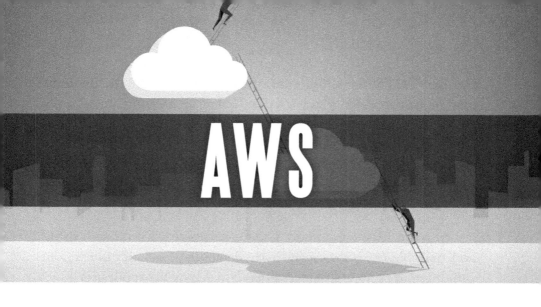

Amazon Web Services (AWS) cloud platform was conceptualized in 2006, in the aim of offering different services like compute, storage, database, applications to the customers on a pay per use model, the origins of which has been derived from the age old practice of providing utility services like water and power to the end consumers on a metered basis, and charged based on the actual consumption for businesses of all sorts and all sizes to install their own compute facility to conduct their own transactions, using internet .Currently almost all compute needs like database, storage, compute, applications and database are offered on the shared services model, from which consumers can chose from according to their own requirements, customize and use for the desired purposes. And AWS offers one of the best customization amongst its peers. The scalability factor helps the business grow, without investing on the traditional hardware, and can subscribe to any of the cloud service providers for host the applications and services. And such services are charged on consumption basis, which varies from different platform and service providers. These services can be subscribed by having a simple desktop and high speed internet connection and subscription to the respective service providers, credit cards are also accepted. For beginners AWS offers, free trails. Below described are the different services that are offered and described below are the different services

Elastic Compute Cloud EC2

http://docs.aws.amazon.com/AWSEC2/latest/UserGuide/concepts.
html

Amazon Elastic Compute Cloud (Amazon EC2) offers scalable and resizable compute capacity. By deploying EC2, administrators can different types of instances offered to deploy the applications and offer business services. There is no need to purchase any additional hardware, or software, may be some hardware need up gradation. By deploying EC2, the needed server instances can be launched and can be subscribe to additional instances on the fly. One can launch single to multiple instances within seconds, with simple subscription, and all that is needed is standard desktop, browser and high speed broadband. Once created and configured, users can start using the same for whatever purposes needed and the instances can be started and terminated any time. Instances are charged based on hours of usage and billed according to the client's needs. Within the instance the user can create instances, configure security and networking, and manage storage. Amazon EC2 permits scalability, and instances can be scaled up and scaled down as per the needs, and offers the following:

Virtual computing environments, known as *instances*

Preconfigured templates for your instances, known as *Amazon Machine Images (AMIs)*, that package the bits you need for your server (including the operating system and additional software)

Various configurations of CPU, memory, storage, and networking capacity for your instances, known as *instance types*

Secure login information for your instances using *key pairs* (AWS stores the public key, and you store the private key in a secure place)

Storage volumes for temporary data that's deleted when you stop or terminate your instance, known as *instance store volumes*

Persistent storage volumes for your data using Amazon Elastic Block Store (Amazon EBS), known as *Amazon EBS volumes*

Multiple physical locations for your resources, such as instances and Amazon EBS volumes, known as *regions* and *Availability Zones*

A firewall that enables you to specify the protocols, ports, and source IP ranges that can reach your instances using *security groups*

Static IPv4 addresses for dynamic cloud computing, known as *Elastic IP addresses*

Metadata, known as *tags*, that you can create and assign to your Amazon EC2 resources

Virtual networks you can create that are logically isolated from the rest of the AWS cloud, and that you can optionally connect to your own network, known as *virtual private clouds* (VPCs)

http://docs.aws.amazon.com/AWSEC2/latest/UserGuide/get-set-up-for-amazon-ec2.html

Listed below the process of creating instances

Sign Up for AWS
Create an IAM User
Create a Key Pair
Create a Virtual Private Cloud (VPC)
Create a Security Group

http://docs.aws.amazon.com/AWSEC2/latest/UserGuide/instance-types.html

EC2 offers s wide range of instance types optimized to suit different requirements. Instance type denotes a combination of CPU, memory, storage, and networking capacity, from which one can, chose the appropriate one for deployment. A single instance type has in it, single or multiple instance sizes thus permitting scalability and the common instance types are T2,

http://docs.aws.amazon.com/AWSEC2/latest/UserGuide/instance-types.html

Instance types

In the event of launching the instances, details like instance type, Instance size, instance region. The target environment and the target hardware, needs to be entered. Administrators need to indicate, the instance type, the target host Preconfigured installations are also available. In the event of launching the instances, when you launch an instance, the *instance type* that you specify determines the hardware of the host computer used for your instance. Each instance type is capable of offering different compute, memory, and storage capabilities are grouped in instance families based on these capabilities. During the configuration administrator can chose from these choices. Beside, In the event of launching the instances, details like instance type Instance size, and the instance region. The target environment and the target hardware, needs to be entered. Administrators need to indicate, the instance type, the target host Preconfigured installations are also available. EC2 dedicates some resources of the host computer, such as CPU, memory, and instance storage, to a particular instance. Amazon EC2 shares other resources of the host computer, such as the network and the disk subsystem, among instances. If each instance on a host computer tries to use as much of one of these shared resources as possible, each receives an equal share of that resource. However, when a resource is under-utilized, an instance can consume a higher share of that resource while it's available Selection of instances can be based on application, database or storage needs and each instance is guarantees certain levels of predictability, on the certain amount of CPU capacity, regardless of its underlying hardware.

Single instance offers higher or lower minimum performance from a shared resource. For instance, instance types with high I/O performance have a larger allocation of shared resources. Allocating a larger share of shared resources also reduces the variance of I/O performance. A good amount of applications require, moderate I/O performance may be sufficient and for standard purposes the following instances will be sufficient – t2.nano | t2.micro | t2.small | t2.medium | t2.large | t2.xlarge | t2.2xlarge | m4.large | m4.xlarge | m4.2xlarge | m4.4xlarge | m4.10xlarge | m4.16xlarge | m3.medium | m3.large | m3.xlarge | m3.2xlarge

Common configuration scenarios

http://docs.aws.amazon.com/AWSEC2/latest/UserGuide/Configure Instance.html

Single instance offers higher or lower minimum performance from a shared resource. For instance, instance types with high I/O performance have greater allocation of shared resources. Allocating a larger share of shared resources leads to reduction of the s the variance of I/O performance. Generally, a moderate I/O performance is essential for applications to work. By default, Amazon Linux instances are delivered, with pre-configured with an ec2-user account, but based on the requirements and environments, there could be need that can arise that, more accounts needs to be included. The default time configuration for Amazon Linux instances uses Network Time Protocol to set the system time on an instance. The default time zone is UTC.. In a circumstance of the environment having individual domain name, registered, the administrators can change the hostname of an instance to identify itself as part of that domain.

You can also change the system prompt to show a more meaningful name without changing the hostname. In the event of an instance being launched, in EC2, administrators have the option of passing user data to the instance that can be used to perform common configuration tasks and even run scripts after the instance starts and the configuration lets pass two types of user data to Amazon EC2, cloud-init directives, and shell script

EC2 instances and AMIs

http://docs.aws.amazon.com/AWSEC2/latest/UserGuide/ec2-instances-and-amis.html

An *Amazon Machine Image (AMI)* is a template that contains a software configuration (for example, an operating system, an application server, and applications) and by deploying these, users will be able to launch multiple instances, which is a copy of the AMI running as a virtual server in the cloud. Simultaneous launching of multiple instances is possible.

Instances and AMI 1

Source http://docs.aws.amazon.com/AWSEC2/latest/UserGuide/ec2-instances-and-amis.html

Users can launch different types of instances from a single AMI. And is mandatory to mention the instance type, instance size, instance region, the host computer AWS offers multiple choices of instances, with varying capabilities, a user can chose, with Each instance type offers different compute and memory capabilities. Developer has the choice of choosing from different types Based on the amount of memory and computing power that is needed for the application or software that is scheduled to run on the instance. Once you launch the instance, user has the complete control of the instance, and user can interact with the instance in the same manner that would be done with the traditional servers, the user possess full control of the instances and the instance can be used for any manner that the user wants to use, for example hosting website, testing applications. And user can start and stop instances any time.

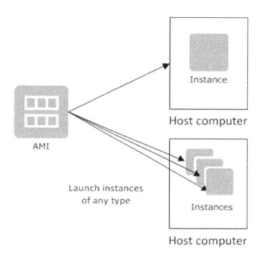

Amazon Web Services (AWS) publishes many Amazon Machine Images (AMIs) that contain common software configurations for public use. Also freelancers develop AMIs for different purposes, and some of them are also customized ones, Even an user can create own AMIs which enables to quickly launch individual instances. and deploy applications, All AMIs are categorized as either *backed by Amazon EBS*, which means that the root device for an instance launched from the AMI is an Amazon EBS volume, or *backed by instance store*, which means that the root device for an instance launched from the AMI is an instance store volume created from a template stored in Amazon, besides All AMIs are categorized as either *backed by Amazon EBS*, which means that the root device for an instance launched from the AMI is an Amazon EBS volume, or *backed by instance store*, which means that the root device for an instance launched from the AMI is an instance store volume created from a template stored in Amazon S3.

Amazon EC instance store

http://docs.aws.amazon.com/AWSEC2/latest/UserGuide/Instance
Storage.html

An *instance store* is exclusive storage block that is utilized for storing data, for fraction of time, and it is temporary in nature and this storage is located in disk that are directly connected to the servers or storage devices, which are physically attached to the host computer. Instance store is ideal for temporary storage of information that changes frequently, such as buffers, caches, scratch data, and other temporary content, or for data that is replicated across a fleet of instances, such as a load-balanced pool of web servers. This provide block level storage instances, An instance store consists of one or more instance store volumes exposed as block devices. The size of an instance store as well as the number of devices available varies by instance type. While an instance store is dedicated to a particular instance, the disk subsystem is shared among instances on a host computer. The virtual devices for instance store volumes are Instance types that support one instance store volume. Instance types that support two instance store volumes have ephemeral0 and ephemeral1, and so on. The virtual devices for NVMe instance store volumes are /dev/nvme[0-7]n1. Instance types that support one NVMe instance store volume have /dev/nvme0n1. Instance types that support two NVMe instance store volume have /dev/nvme0n1 and /dev/nvme1n1, and so on. This instance type determines the size of the instance store available and the type of hardware that can be deployed for the instance store volumes. Instance store volumes gets associated along with the instance's hourly cost and users must specifically indicate the instance store volumes that is to be deployed for hosting, when an instance is launched, instance (except for NVMe instance store volumes, which are available by default), and then format and mount them before using them, and users can't create an instance store, and made available, after the launch of instance. Certain w instance types use NVMe or SATA based solid state drives (SSD) to deliver very high random I/O performance and this configuration suits the needs of design where low latency and the data not to be persisted, post termination of instances, Few instance types use NVMe or SATA based solid state drives (SSD) to deliver very high random I/O performance, which especially can satisfy the requirement of storage with very low latency, but and there is no requirement of persistence in the event of instances getting terminated and listed below are instance types and associated volumes

Auto scaling

https://aws.amazon.com/autoscaling/?nc2=h_m1

Auto scaling is the fundamental for EC2 compute service, and main functionality is to assist in maintaining services availability, should be read as application availability, besides, helping administrators to maintain application availability, lets users to dynamically scale up or scale down, the compute capacity, which can be carried out automatically, according to the parameters that has been set. Users can deploy auto scaling for fleet management of EC2 instances, in order to monitor the health and the availability status of individual instances, to make sure, that the desired instances are up and running at any point of time. One can also configure the auto scaling for dynamic scaling, which leads to increasing the number of instances during the peak time, and release few instances, during off-peak loads, and this is done in order to maintain, performance and decrease capacity during lulls to reduce costs, auto scaling can be configured for environments, in which applications that have stable demand patterns or that experience hourly, daily, or weekly variability in usage. Application auto scaling, to automatically scale resources for majority AWS services. It doesn't matter, user runs a single instance, or thousands, auto scaling can be used to detect faulty instances and replace in the same on the fly, when configured, auto scaling will help in monitoring the applications, detect if unhealthy applications, and repair instances on the fly, and that too without downtime, with nil or minimal user intervention, which guarantees the compute capacity been made available

Monitoring the health of running instances

Auto Scaling guarantees, application are being able to receive traffic and that the instances themselves are functioning properly, this property helps in detects a failed health check, it can replace the instance automatically.

Automatic replacement of faulty instances

when faulty instance fails a health check, Auto Scaling automatically terminates it and replaces it with a new one, which means that it is performed automatically and without human intervention, and users are not required to for instance replacement

Balancing capacity across Availability Zones

Auto Scaling automatically balances EC2 instances across zones when multiple zones are configured, and always launches new instances so that they are balanced between zones as evenly as possible across the environment

Simple storage service – S3

http://docs.aws.amazon.com/AmazonS3/latest/dev/Introduction. html#overview

Amazon S3 has a simple web services interface that can be deployed to store and retrieve any amount of data, from anywhere any time, it offers persistent storage and capable of unlimited storage and can be accessed by simple browser users can create buckets, store and retrieve your objects, and manage permissions. Security features like authentication, key pairs can be created for data safety and integrity. ACLs and configuration files can be created and deployed.

S3 supports MFA. Data in stored in buckets, where multiple privilege rules can be created for storing, accessing and retrieving data. S3 is a bulk storage option from AWS. It can be accessed from a standard compute device and a browser and it is also suitable for deploying for industrial data. Benefits of S3:

Create Buckets – Create and name a bucket that stores data. Buckets are the fundamental container in Amazon S3 for data storage.

Store data in Buckets – Store an infinite amount of data in a bucket. Upload as many objects as you like into an Amazon S3 bucket. Each object can contain up to 5 TB of data. Each object is stored and retrieved using a unique developer-assigned key.

Download data – Download your data or enable others to do so. Download your data any time you like or allow others to do the same.

Permissions – Grant or deny access to others who want to upload or download data into your Amazon S3 bucket. Grant upload and download permissions to three types of users. Authentication mechanisms can help keep data secure from unauthorized access.

Standard interfaces – Use standards-based REST and SOAP interfaces designed to work with any Internet-development toolkit.

Buckets

Bucket is a container for objects stored in Amazon S3. Every object is contained in a bucket. It primarily serves the storage location for large volumes of data. for organizing name space, identify the account responsible for storage and data transfer charges, besides they play a role in access control, and they serve as the unit of aggregation for usage reporting. Users can configure, them to be created in specific regions, and users are provided privileges to create buckets of their choice and in any region of S3 creates an unique ID for each instance which is tagged and that is used as the object identifier, Objects are the fundamental entities stored in Amazon S3. Objects consist of object data and metadata. The data portion is transparent to Amazon S3. The metadata is a set of name-value pairs that describe the object, which, include some default metadata, such as the date last modified, and standard HTTP metadata, such as Content-Type. Administrators have the privilege to specify custom metadata at the time the object is stored. An object is uniquely identified within a bucket by a key (name) and a version ID. A key is the unique identifier for an object within a bucket. Every object in a bucket has exactly one key. S3 can be used to host static website

Working with S3 objects

http://docs.aws.amazon.com/AmazonS3/latest/dev/UsingObjects.html

S3 is a simple key, value store designed to store unlimited number of objects and these objects are stored in single or multiple buckets, and the object comprises of:

Key – The name that a user assigns to an object and it is used to retrieve the object.

Version ID – is a unique identifier, within the bucket and helps to associate instances to the objects, and within a bucket, a key and version ID uniquely identify an object. The version ID is a string that Amazon S3 generates when you add an object to a bucket.

Value – The content that is being stored. An object value can be any sequence of bytes. Objects can range in size from zero to 5 TB.

Metadata – A set of name-value pairs using which users can store information regarding the object. Users are given the privileges to assign metadata, referred to as user-defined metadata, to the objects in Amazon S3. Amazon S3 also assigns system-metadata to these objects, which it uses for managing objects. Sub resources – Amazon S3 adopts sub-resource method to store object-specific additional information. As sub resources are subordinates to objects, they are always associated with some other entity such as an object or a bucket.

Access Control Information – S3 supports resource based access control, such as an Access Control List (ACL) and bucket policies, and user-based access control, besides getting privileges to control access to the objects you store in Amazon S3.

S3 Storage classes

http://docs.aws.amazon.com/AmazonS3/latest/dev/storage-class-intro.html

S3 offers the following storage classes for the objects which one would wish to store and the selection needs to be made based on use case scenario and performance access requirements. All of these storage classes offer high durability:

STANDARD – This storage class suits the needs of for performance-sensitive use cases and frequently accessed data and it is the default storage class, and in the event of not indicating any specific storage class, during the time of upload, AWS automatically assumes it as a standard data and classified as Standard class

STANDARD_IA – This storage class (IA,is meant for in-frequent access, that is optimized for high latency and which does not required frequent and long life data storage cycle access and During the initial stages, users may upload objects using standard storage class and then use the bucket lifecycle configuration rule to transition objects. Typically it is chosen for the requirement, that calls for storage needs and for larger objects greater than 128 Kilobytes that you want to keep for at least 30 days, Glacier can be adopted for requirement of data that needs to be accessed not a frequent basis, and it is one of the best method for data large volumes of data archival and retrieval. Archived objects are not available for real-time access. And administrators must first restore the objects before you can access them.

However the management of the storage classes is performed class through Amazon S3. Administrators cannot specify GLACIER as the storage class at the time that you create an object. Users can GLACIER objects by first uploading objects using STANDARD, RRS, or STANDARD_IA as the storage class, post which administrators create transition these objects to the GLACIER storage class using lifecycle management Administrators should first restore the GLACIER objects before users can access them (STANDARD, RRS, and STANDARD_IA objects are available for anytime access). All the preceding storage classes are designed to sustain the concurrent loss of data in two facilities (for details, see the following availability and durability table).

Besides Amazon S3 also offers the following storage class which would allow to save costs by maintaining fewer redundant copies of your data.

REDUCED_REDUNDANCY – The Reduced Redundancy Storage (RRS) storage class is designed for noncritical, reproducible data stored at lower levels of redundancy than the STANDARD storage class, which reduces storage costs. For instance, le, if you upload an image and use STANDARD storage class for it, a user may compute a thumbnail and save it as an object of the RRS storage class.

The durability level) corresponds to an average annual expected loss of 0.01% of objects. For example, if a user store 10,000 objects using the RRS option, one can on an average expect to take financial hit and in an average to the tune of single object per year (0.01% of 10,000 objects).

Working with S3 buckets

http://docs.aws.amazon.com/AmazonS3/latest/dev/UsingBucket.html

Amazon S3 is designed as Cloud class storage, where massive amount of data can be stored and it sis cloud storage for internet, and it offers best solution for videos, photos and documents and in order to so, first a bucket needs to be created. One need to first choose an AWS region, and then upload data, and the first step is to create a bucket in one of the AWS regions, post which the buckets may be used for storage and retrieval purpose. Offers best option for storing industrial scale data, videos, and research and defense organizations commonly use this.S3 provides APIs for managing the objects.APIs are galore, with S3 for instance, user can create a bucket and upload objects using the Amazon S3 API, besides deploying for send requests to S3. Amazon S3 bucket names are globally unique, regardless of the AWS Region irrespective of the regions, so one can create the bucket in any region. A name is must. Buckets can be created in any region one needs to be deployed, and the same needs to be specified during configuration stage, and it would be economically viable, if one chooses, closest to his geography, AWS has continental presence, in order to optimize the latency and reduce costs, or even adhere to the local regulator compliances. By default, a user can create up to 100 buckets in each of live r AWS accounts, and if addionanal buckets are required the same can be done by submitting a request and it is mandatory provide name and AWS Region where you want the bucket created

Elastic block store EBS

http://docs.aws.amazon.com/AWSEC2/latest/UserGuide/Amazon EBS.html

EBS satisfies the requirement of quick access to data is warranted and which warrants long term persistence.EBS can be deployed in case of the primary storage for file systems, databases, or for any applications that require fine granular updates and access to raw, unformatted, block-level storage EBS is well suited for both database-style applications that rely on random reads and writes, and to throughput-intensive applications that perform long, continuous reads and writes. When data encryption is needed, EBS instances can be launched in the encrypted mode. These service offers, simple encryption option for EBS volumes, without even having to deploy, to build, manage, and secure independent systems and independent key management system. When user deploys an encrypted EBS volume and attach it to a supported instance type, data stored at rest on the volume, disk I/O, and snapshots created from the volume are all encrypted. The encryption occurs on the servers that host EC2 instances, thus offering g encryption of data-in-transit from EC2 instances to EBS storage. EBS encryption adopts AWS Key Management Service (KMS) master keys when creating encrypted volumes and any snapshots created from private encrypted volumes. In the case of first time creating encrypted the volumes, master key is created automatically. And this key is assigned .for the purpose of encryption, lest Customer Master Key (CMK) that user creates for separately using the AWS Key Management Service and creation of individual CMK and individual CMKs offer higher levels of flexibility which includes the ability to create, rotate, disable, define access controls, and audit the encryption keys used to protect the data. Users are provided with privileges to attach multiple volumes to the same instance within the limits specified by individual AWS account and by default EBS volumes are offered based on the subscription.

Features of EBS

http://docs.aws.amazon.com/AWSEC2/latest/UserGuide/Amazon EBS.html#w2ab1c25c29c15

With Provisioned IOPS SSD (io1) volumes, one can provision a specific level of I/O performance. Io1 volumes support up to 20,000 IOPS and 320 MB/s of throughput, which permits' administrators to predict the traffic and transaction volumes, besides, Throughput Optimized HDD (st1) volumes offer low–cost magnetic storage that defines performance in terms of throughput rather than IOPS. With throughput of up to 500 MiB/s, this volume type is a good fit for large, sequential workloads such as Amazon EMR, ETL, data warehouses, and log processing. Users can create EBS General Purpose SSD (gp2), Provisioned IOPS SSD (io1), Throughput Optimized HDD (st1), and Cold HDD (sc1) volumes up to 16 TiB in size and mount such volumes as devices in EC2 instances, simultaneously, one can mount multiple volumes on the same instance, but each volume can be attached to only one instance at a time. Besides, users can dynamically change the configuration of a volume attached to an instance. And with General Purpose SSD (gp2) volumes, users can expect base performance of 3 IOPS/GiB, with the ability to burst to 3,000 IOPS for extended periods of time. Gp2 volumes are ideal for a broad range of use cases such as boot volumes, small and medium-size databases, and development and test environments. Gp2 volumes support up to 10,000 IOPS and 160 MB/s of throughput. Using Provisioned IOPS SSD (io1) volumes, users can provision a specific level of I/O performance. Io1 volumes support up to 20,000 IOPS and 320 MB/s of throughput, which permits administrators to design predictably scalable design, which can support tens of thousands of IOPS per EC2 instance Even though, Throughput Optimized HDD (st1) volumes presents low-cost magnetic storage that defines performance in terms of throughput rather than IOPS. With throughput of up to 500 MiB/s, this volume type is suitable for large, sequential workloads such as Amazon EMR, ETL, data warehouses, and log processing; Cold HDD (sc1) volumes present low-cost magnetic storage that defines performance in terms of throughput rather than IOPS. With throughput of up to 250 MiB/s, sc1 is offers suitable solution for large, sequential, cold-data workloads. sc1 option provides inexpensive block storage, if the requirement is in-frequent data access, besides optimizing on cost.Fundamentlly EBS presents raw, unformatted block devices developers shall utilize this and create file system on top of the existing volumes or simply put to use for storing data and even application data. File systems can be created on top of such volumes and put to use for any purpose, just like a hard drive Copying snapshots though simple process, due precautions needs to be followed because it involves movement of data across devices, and internet links. One, can copy snapshots to other regions and then restore them to new volumes there, making it easier to leverage multiple AWS regions for geographical expansion, data center migration, and disaster recovery.

Elastic map reduce

http://docs.aws.amazon.com/emr/latest/ManagementGuide/emr-what-is-emr.html

the first step by using a Pig program

Process a second input data set by using a Hive program

Write an output data set, the input is data stored as files in your chosen underlying file system, such as Amazon S3 or HDFS. This data passes from one step to the next in the processing sequence. The final step writes the output data to a specified location, such as an Amazon S3 bucket.

Steps are run in the following sequence: .

The state of all steps is set to PENDING.

When the first step in the sequence starts, its state changes to RUNNING. The other steps remain in the PENDING state.

After the first step completes, its state changes to COMPLETED.

The next step in the sequence starts, and its state changes to RUNNING. When it completes, its state changes to COMPLETED.

This pattern repeats for each step until they all complete and processing ends. EMR is a managed cluster solution which simplifies the process of executing large data frameworks like Hadoop, Apache on AWS to process and analyze vast sets of data, open-source projects, such as Apache Hive and Apache Pig. Users can process vast data for analytics purposes and business intelligence workloads. Also, users has the freedom to deploy AMR to transform and move large amounts of data into and out of other AWS data stores and databases, such as Amazon Simple Storage Service (Amazon S3) and Amazon Dynamo.

Clusters and nodes

Central component of Amazon EMR is the *cluster*. A cluster is a collection of EC2 instances, and each cluster instance is termed as node, and individual node has role within the cluster, as is termed as node type, and EMR can be deployed to install multiple different software components on each node type, giving each node offering each node a role in a distributed application like Apache Hadoop. Master node: a node which manages the cluster by running software components which coordinate the distribution of data and tasks among other nodes—collectively referred to as slave nodes—for the purpose of processing. The master node tracks the status of tasks and monitors the health of the cluster.

☐ Core node: a slave node that has software components which run tasks and store data in the Hadoop Distributed File System (HDFS) on that executes the cluster.

Submitting work to the cluster

EMR provides with, multiple choices to be specified as the work needs to be executed

Supply the entire definition of the work to be done in the Map and Reduce functions. Which is generally performed for clusters that process a set amount of data and then terminate when processing is complete?

Create a long-running cluster and use the Amazon EMR console, the Amazon EMR API, or the AWS CLI to submit steps, which may contain one or more Hadoop jobs

Create a cluster with a Hadoop application, such as Hive or Pig, installed and use the interface provided by the application to submit queries, either scripted or interactively.

Processing data

In the event of launching cluster, one needs to select the framework and applications that are needed for installing the data processing needs requirements. There are two ways to process data in your Amazon EMR cluster: by submitting jobs or queries directly to the applications that are installed on your cluster or by running *steps* in the cluster.

Submitting Jobs Directly to Applications

Users are provided with the facility to submit jobs and interact directly with the software that is installed in the enterprises EMR cluster and to perform this, one need to create a link master node over a secure connection and access the interfaces and tools that are available for the software that runs directly on organizations cluster, besides EMR permits to directly submit jobs and directly interact with the software components that has been installed in the EMR cluster and in order to accomplish, user needs to first create master node over a secure connection and access the interfaces and tools that are available for the software that runs directly on your cluster. he following is an example process using four steps:

Submit an input data set for processing

Process the output of

Cluster configuration

http://docs.aws.amazon.com/emr/latest/ManagementGuide/emr-plan.html

The following guidelines will help in creating suitable configurations

What region to run a cluster in, where and how to store data, and how to output results.

Whether a cluster is long-running or transient, and what software it runs. See Configure a Cluster to be transient or Long-Running and Configure Cluster Software.

The hardware and networking options that optimize cost, performance, and availability for your application. See Configure Cluster Hardware and Networking.

How to restrict access to cluster resources and data. See Configure Access to the Cluster.

How to set up clusters so you can manage them more easily, and monitor activity, performance, and health. See Configure Cluster Logging and Debugging and Tag Clusters.

How to integrate with other software and services. See Drivers and Third-Party Application Integration

Configuration of hardware, cluster and networking

http://docs.aws.amazon.com/emr/latest/ManagementGuide/emr-plan-instances.html

Due care needs to be taken while creation of EMR clusters, how to configure EC2 instances, the networking options in EC2, the size of the instance, and d location.EC2 instances in an EMR cluster are organized into *node types*. There are three node types in an Amazon EMR cluster: the *master node*, the *core node*, and *task nodes*. Each node performs pre-defined roles that are defined by the distributed applications which would be installed in the cluster for instance of Hadoop Map Reduce or Spark job, Where, components on core and task nodes process the data, transfer the output to Amazon S3 or HDFS, and provide status metadata back to the master node. In the case of a single node cluster, all components that runs on the master node.

Master node

The master node manages the cluster and typically runs master components of distributed applications. For example, the master node runs the YARN Resource Manager Service to manage resources for applications, as well as the HDFS NameNode service. Besides, it assists in tracking the status of the jobs submitted to the cluster, and monitors the health of the instance groups. Besides performing the task of tracks the status of jobs submitted to the cluster. SSH can be deployed tTo monitor the progress of a cluster, Users are permitted to SSH into the master node as the Hadoop user and either look at the Hadoop log files directly or access the user interface that Hadoop or Spark publishes to a web server running on the master node.

Core nodes

Core nodes are managed by the master node. Core nodes run the Data Node daemon to coordinate data storage as part of the Hadoop Distributed File System (HDFS).Which, also execute the Task Tracker daemon and perform other parallel computation tasks on data that installed applications require. For instance, a core node runs YARN Node Manager daemons, Hadoop Map Reduce tasks, and Spark executors. Like the master node, at least one core node is required per cluster. Multiple core nodes can be created, and also multiple EC2 instances in the instance group. But, there can exist a single one core instance group or instance fleet. With instance groups and users can add and remove EC2 instances while the cluster is running or set up automatic scaling.

Uniform instance groups

Uniform instance groups provide a easy configuration. Each Amazon EMR cluster shall contain up to 50 instance groups: one master instance group that contains one EC2 instance, a core instance group that contains one or more EC2 instances, and up to 48 optional task instance groups. a single core and task instance group can contain any number of EC2 instances, and the scalability feature permits each instance group to be scaled in the way of adding and removing EC2 instances manually, or users can configure up automatic scaling.

http://docs.aws.amazon.com/emr/latest/ManagementGuide/emr-plan-access-iam.html

EMR supports IAM policies. IAM is a web service which facilitates AWS customers to manage users and their permissions. Users can deploy IAM to create user based policies and attach them to users. Policies that are one, when configured allow access and also determine what actions a user can perform with EMR and other resources. For instance, a use can be permitted to view EMR clusters in an AWS account but not create or delete them, users can be given rights to tag the EMR clusters and then use the tags for applying fine grained privileges to users on independent clusters, or a group of clusters that share the same tag. For instance, administrators can permit user to add one more tag, the existing EMR clusters and then use the tags to apply for permissions. to the users on individual clusters,

Relational database services RDS

https://aws.amazon.com/rds/details/

Amazon Relational Database RDS is a managed relational database service which offers developers six familiar database engines to select from, including Amazon Aurora, MySQL, MariaDB, Oracle, Microsoft SQL Server, and PostgreSQL. This implies, one can use AWS with EBS, users continue using the code, applications, and tools that one is already familiar with, and continue using the same platform and systems, RDS handles regular database tasks like provisioning, patching, backup, recovery, failure detection, and repair. RDS simplifies user experience, facilitates easy replication, to improve availability and reliability for production workloads. With the unique feature Mult-AZ deployment choice, users can seamlessly execute mission-critical workloads with high availability and built-in automated fail-over from enterprises primary database to a synchronously replicated secondary database. Configuring Read Replicas, one can achieve higher levels of scalability, and higher levels of scale out, which could in most cases, be beyond the capacity of a single database deployment for read-heavy database workloads. Comes with a Lower Administrative Burden and simple interfaces to configure and adopt. One can utilize the feature rich management console, CLIs, and built in APIs, to make calls to access the capabilities of a production-ready relational database in minutes. database instances are pre-configured with parameters and settings appropriate for the engine and classes from which one will selectman launch instances and connect to the application, within minutes and it delivered with built in tools which supports customization, and configuration building, and supports automatic software patching

Amazon RDS General Purpose Storage is an SSD-backed storage option delivers a consistent baseline of 3 IOPS per provisioned GB and offers s the ability to burst up to 3,000 IOPS, and this storage can be deployed for a wide range of database workloads

Amazon RDS Provisioned IOPS Storage

Designed to deliver, fast, predictable and consistent I/O performance and it is a SSD backed storage option. Users can create instances, specifying the required IOPS rate, which can be specified while creating, delivers a consistent throughput, and users can mention the IOPS rate, even when the database instance is created, and the same will be provisioned for the lifetime of the database instance. This storage type is optimized for I/O-intensive transactional (OLTP) database workloads. Users have the option of provisioning 30,000 IOPS per database instance, although your actual realized IOPS may vary based on your database workload, instance type, and database engine choice. Scalability

Dynamic scaling - Higher levels of scalability where one can scale the compute and memory resources powering your deployment up or down, up to a maximum of 32 vCPUs and 244 GiB of RAM. Compute scaling operations typically complete in a few minutes.

RDS reserved instances

https://aws.amazon.com/rds/reserved-instances/

Users can select amongst 3 payment options, as reserved instances. Provided with the Upfront option, users pay for the entire Reserved Instance with one upfront payment and this option comes with huge discounts, compared to on-demand pricing, and with partial upfront plan, the payment mode is a low one time upfront payment, The No Upfront option does not require any upfront payment and provides a discounted hourly rate for the duration of the term. All Reserved Instance types are available for Aurora, MySQL, MariaDB, PostgreSQL, Oracle and SQL Server database engines.

Features

Amazon offers reserved instances, 3 payment options - All Upfront, Partial Upfront, and No Upfront. Subscribing for reserved instances, can lead to savings up to 69% over On-Demand rates when used in steady state. This category of instances is simple to use and need no change in the manner how RDS is used. And when AWS generates the invoice all such parameters, will be automatically incorporated, and the necessary financial benefits will be worked out and passed on to the subscribers. All Upfront and Partial Upfront Reserved Instances can be purchased for one or three year terms, while, No Upfront Reserved Instances are only available for one year term. Reserved Instances are available in all the AWS regions Reserved Instances are available for all supported DB Engines.

Payment options

No Upfront RIs – No Upfront RIs offer a significant discount (typically about 30%) compared to On-Demand prices. Users are not required to pay any upfront fees, but need to make commitments for subscribing for the reserved instances, over the period of reserved instance term, and this is termed as annual term

Partial Upfront RIs- this plan offers, higher discounts, than the upfront options, and payment is made only for the

Partial Upfront RIs offer a higher discount than No Upfront RIs (typically about 60% for a 3 year term). You pay for a portion of the Reserved Instance upfront, and then pay for the remainder over the course of the one or three year term. This option balances the RI payments between upfront and hourly.

All Upfront RIs – All Upfront RIs offer the highest discount of all of the RI payment options (typically about 63% for a 3 year term) and payment has to be made, full term, one or three, based on the contract, with a single upfront fees, and receive the best hourly prices

Instance types

https://aws.amazon.com/rds/instance-types/

Offers range of instance types, which has been a selection of instance types optimized to fit different relational database use cases. Instance types comprise varying combinations of CPU, memory, storage, and networking capacity which gives the users, give you the flexibility to choose the appropriate mix of resources that could best suit the database. A single instance type includes one or more instance sizes, thus giving the users for increasing the resources when required, and subscribes for; instances that is actually needed for deploying target workloads Offers range of instance types, which has been a selection of instance types optimized to fit different relational database use cases. Instance types comprise varying combinations of CPU, memory, storage, and networking capacity which gives the users, give you the flexibility to choose the appropriate mix of resources that could best suit the database. A single instance type includes one or more instance sizes, thus giving the users for increasing the resources when required, and subscribe for, instances and instance offered are

db.m4.large	2	8	Yes	Moderate
db.m4.xlarge	4	16	Yes	High
db.m4.2xlarge	8	32	Yes	High
db.m4.4xlarge	16	64	Yes	High
db.m4.10xlarge	40	160	Yes	10 Gigabit

Standard – Previous Generation

db.m3.medium	1	3.75	–	Moderate
db.m3.large	2	7.5	–	Moderate
db.m3.xlarge	4	15	Yes	High
db.m3.2xlarge	8	30	Yes	High

Memory Optimized – Current Generation

db.r3.large	2	15	–	Moderate
db.r3.xlarge	4	30.5	Yes	Moderate
db.r3.2xlarge	8	61	Yes	High
db.r3.4xlarge	16	122	Yes	High
db.r3.8xlarge	32	244	–	10 Gigabit

Burstable Performance – Current Generation

db.t2.micro	1	1	–	Low

db.t2.small	1	2	–	Low
db.t2.medium	2	4	–	Moderate
db.t2.large	2	8	–	

Glacier

https://aws.amazon.com/glacier/

Glacier is an extremely a low cost, durable and highly available, storage service, especially designed for data archival, and long term data backups, and long term backup solution for any kind of business. It is so cheap AWS offers glacier at the starting price of $0.004 per gigabyte per month, which is drastic saving compared to traditional storage Amazon guarantees 99.99% availability and at the stating price of $0.004 per gigabyte per month, which is significantly cheaper than the cheapest traditional devices and AWS offers three options for access to archives, from a few minutes to several hours. And listed below are the properties

Economy of scale

A single instance is offered at $0.004 per gigabyte per month, and glacier can be used archive very large data sets, and it can be used for large archival requirements, few application areas are medical research, and defense.

Highly secure

Supports data transfer over SSL, while encrypting automatically encrypting data at rest. Also, IAM can also be deployed, to provide access controls and IAM can be accessed and configured through browser.

Durable

Glacier offers a highly durable storage infrastructure designed for long-term backup and archive and the data is striped across multiple devices and multiple locations, in order to achieve redundancy.

Scalability

This storage offers unlimited capacity, and virtually, AWS doesn't set any upper limit, for storing, AWS has installed Glacier, all across globe, and a user can chose the location, near his datacenter, which will help customers to have high latency. Offers a highly durable storage infrastructure designed for long-term backup and archive, and the data is redundantly stored across multiple facilities and multiple devices in each facility.

Uploading and retrieving

Upload and retrieval operations are carried out using AWS SDKs, or the underlying Glacier APIs Glacier is supported by the AWS SDKs for Java, .NET, PHP, and Python (Boto). The SDK libraries wrap the underlying Amazon Glacier APIs, simplifying your programming tasks. These SDKs provide libraries that map to an underlying REST API and enable you to easily construct requests and process responses.

Archiving data

AWS Management Console can be used to create vaults, configure vault-level access permissions, and setup SNS notifications for data retrieval is an easy-to-use web interface that provides the capability to create vaults, configure vault-level access permissions, and setup SNS notifications for data retrieval The console also presents a storage usage summary for each vault as well as the last refresh time for the vault inventory, There are three methods to deploy S3 lifecycle rules for archival, One can configure rules to constantly archive the frequently accessed S 3 objects depending on the age of the objectives 90 days or older, besides archiving on predefine durations like quarter end. Besides, users can create set up archival rules on versioned buckets to retain previous object versions for roll-back at a lower cost. Also, the data can be transferred to S3 and immediately archive to Glacier with a zero-day transition rule, and leverage the object keys in Amazon S3 for real-time listing.

<u>Dynamo DB</u>

http://docs.aws.amazon.com/amazondynamodb/latest/developerguide/Introduction.html

Dynamo is a fully managed NoSQL database service which offers s fast and predictable performance with seamless scalability. It helps in easing out the administrative overheads operating and scaling a distributed database, leaving behind the concerns of hardware configurations, and provisioning, patch management or provisioning. This service fits into the environment, where the requirements are like users can create database tables that which store and retrieve any amount of data, and serve any level of request traffic. Users shall scale up or scale down the tables' throughput capacity without downtime or performance degradation, and use the AWS Management Console to monitor resource utilization and performance metrics. Dynamo lets users to delete expired items from tables automatically, which will aid in to helping to reduce storage usage and the cost of storing data that is no longer relevant, Dynamo automatically distribute the data and traffic for all the tables over a sufficient number of servers to handle The r throughput and storage requirements, while maintaining consistent and fast performance Entire data is stored on solid state disks (SSDs) and automatically replicated across multiple Availability Zones in an AWS region, providing built-in high availability and data durability.

http://docs.aws.amazon.com/amazondynamodb/latest/developerguide/HowItWorks.CoreComponents.html

Core components

Tables, items, and attributes constitute the core components with which that users operate work with a *table* is a collection of *items*, and each item is a collection of *attributes*. Dynamo uses primary keys to uniquely identify each item in a table and secondary indexes to support more querying flexibility. Users can configure, can use Dynamo Streams to capture data modification events in Dynamo tables.

Tables

Items – Each table contains multiple items. An *item* is a group of attributes that is uniquely identifiable among all of the other items In Dynamo; there is no limit to the number of items you can store in a table. Items – Each table contains multiple items. An *item* is a group of attributes that is uniquely identifiable among all of the other items. In a *People* table, each item represents a person. For a *Cars* table, each item represents one vehicle. Items in DynamoDB are similar in many ways to rows, records, or tuples in other database systems. In DynamoDB, there is no limit to the number of items you can store in a table.

Attributes

Each item is composed of one or more attributes. An *attribute* is a fundamental data element, something that does not need to be broken down any further. For example, an item in a *People* table contains attributes called *PersonID, LastName, FirstName,* and so on. For a *Department* table, an item might have attributes such as *DepartmentID, Name,Manager,* and so on. Attributes in DynamoDB are similar in many ways to fields or columns in other database systems. of the others in the table. In the *People* table, the primary key consists of one attribute (*PersonID*). Besides the primary key, the *People* table is schema less, which implies that there is no prior requirement, of attributes, or the data types need to be defined earlier and every item can be assigned their own attributes Most of the attributes are *scalar*, which implies that there can have only one value. Strings and numbers are common examples of scalars. Besides, some of the items have a nested attribute (*Address*). Dynamo supports nested attributes up to 32 levels deep, In the *People* table, the primary key consists of one attribute (*PersonID*). Besides than the primary key, the *People* table is schema less, which denotes that neither the attributes nor their data types need to be defined earlier d. Each item can have its own distinct attributes. Majority of the attributes are *scalar*, which indicates there can be only one value. Strings and numbers are common examples of scalar and a few the items have a nested attribute (*Address*). Dynamo support nested attributes

Elastic block store EBS

http://docs.aws.amazon.com/AWSEC2/latest/UserGuide/Amazon EBS.html

EBS) offers block level storage volumes, for deploying EC2 instances, which are highly available and reliable, instances, which can be attached on any running instance that is in the same Availability Zone. EBS volumes that are attached to an EC2 instance are exposed as storage volumes that persist independently from the life of the instance. EBS can be deployed on the environments of swift data access and long term persistence and EBS volumes fit the requirement storing of file systems databases for set of applications, which needs to have. Fine granular updates and access to raw, unformatted, block-level storage. Amazon EBS is well suited to both database-style applications that rely on random reads and writes, and to throughput-intensive applications that perform long, continuous reads and writes and for encryption users can launch EBS volumes as encrypted volumes and this encryption comes, without the requirement of designing, building and manage and secure the in-house key management system. And when an user you create an encrypted EBS volume and attach it to a supported instance type, data stored at t rest on the volume, disk I/O, and snapshots created from the volume are all encrypted. The encryption occurs on the servers that host EC2 instances, providing encryption of data-in-transit from EC2 instances to EBS storage.EBS encryption adopts s AWS Key Management Service (AWS KMS) master keys when creating encrypted volumes and any snapshots created from user deployed encrypted volumes and simultaneously and users can create an encrypted EBS volume in a region, a default master key is created for the first time automatically. This key is deployed for EBS encryption unless user opts for select a Customer Master Key (CMK) that user created separately using the AWS Key Management Service. Having independent CMK gives the advantage of higher flexibility to create, rotate, disable, define access controls, and audit the encryption keys used to protect your data.

Features of EBS

http://docs.aws.amazon.com/AWSEC2/latest/UserGuide/Amazon
EBS.html#w2ab1c25c29c15

Users can create EBS General Purpose SSD (gp2), Provisioned IOPS SSD (io1), Throughput Optimized HDD (st1), and Cold HDD (sc1) volumes up to 16 TiB in size and can mount these volumes as devices on company's EC2minstances,besides User can mounting multiple volumes on the same instance, however, each volume can be attached to only one instance at a time and one can also dynamically alter the configuration of the volumes attaché to an instance, using CLIm GUI, and scripts With General Purpose SSD (gp2) volumes, deployed, users can foresee base performance of 3 IOPS/GiB, with the ability to burst to 3,000 IOPS for extended periods of time. Gp2 volumes are ideal for a broad range of use cases such as boot volumes, small and medium-size databases, and development and test environments. Gp2 volumes support up to 10,000 IOPS and 160 MB/s of throughput. With Provisioned IOPS SSD (io1) volumes, users can provision a specific level of I/O performance. Io1 volumes support up to 20,000 IOPS and 320 MB/s of throughput, which allows predicting the best or maximum of to tens of thousands of IOPS per EC2 instance, when scaling occurs. Throughput Optimized HDD (st1) volumes offer low-cost magnetic storage that determines performance in terms of throughput rather than IOPS. With throughput of up to 500 MiB/s, this volume type is a good option for large, sequential workloads such as Amazon EMR, ETL, data warehouses, and log processing, Cold HDD (sc1) offers low-cost magnetic storage that defines performance in terms of throughput rather than IOPS. With throughput of up to 250 MiB/s, sc1 it ideally fits for meeting the requirements of large, sequential, cold-data workloads, and if users need infrequent access to the data, and save on costs, sc1 provides inexpensive block storage. EBS act, as raw, unformatted block devices, where file systems can be created on top of the volumes, create a block device and configure them for any purposes, one wants to use, than one the traditional hard disk is being used, and can apply encryption to secure these volumes, and create a secure hard drive, to put to use for wide range of needs. Besides users can use encrypted EBS volumes to meet a wide range of data-at-rest encryption requirements for regulated/audited data and applications. EBS volumes can be are created in a specific Availability Zone, and can then be attached to any instances in that same Availability Zone. In order to expose these volumes external to the AZ, user can create Zone, you can create a snapshot and restore that snapshot to a new volume anywhere in that region and once AZ has been created, users can copy snapshots to other regions and then restore them to new volumes there, making it easier to leverage multiple AWS regions for geographical expansion, data center migration, and disaster recovery.

http://docs.aws.amazon.com/AWSEC2/latest/UserGuide/Instance
Storage.html

Instance store offers temporary block-level storage for user's instance. And this is located on which is physically attached to the host computer Instance store is suited for the storing information, that changes often, for ex, buffers, caches, scratch data, and other temporary content, or for data that is replicated across instances in different regions in the such as load-balanced pool of web servers. An instance store constitutes of one or more instance store volumes exposed as block devices. The size of an instance store as well as the number of devices available varies by instance type, but an instance store is dedicated to a particular instance; the disk subsystem is shared among instances on a host computer. The virtual devices for instance store volumes are ephemeral [0-23]. Instance types that support one instance store volume have ephemeral0. Instance types that support two instance store volumes is assigned tags like phemeral0 and ephemeral1. Instance Store Lifetime With help of GUI, users can mention instance store volumes for an instance only, in the event of launching the same and EBS doesn't permit detachment of instance store volume from one instance and attach it to a different instance. The data in an instance store persists only during the lifetime of its associated instance and if the server re-boots automatically or intentionally turned off, the instances persist, but the data in the instance store gets deleted, and under the following cases

The underlying disk drive fails
The instance stops
The instance terminates

Hence users should not depend on instance store for valuable long term information, but consider installing more reliable options like Amazon S3, Amazon EBS, or Amazon EFS.In the event of self-terminating, or occurs due to any technical reasons, every block of storage in the instance store is reset, in such a case full configuration steps needs to be carried out. And in case of instance termination, even a single block level storage is reset, in which case the data can't be accessed though the instance store of another instance In situation of an user creating an AMI from an instance, the data on its instance store volumes aren't preserved and isn't present on the instance store volumes of the instances that users wishes to launch from the AMI.

Instance store and volumes

http://docs.aws.amazon.com/AWSEC2/latest/UserGuide/Instance Storage.html

Instance type determines the size of the instance store available and the type of hardware used for the instance store volumes and the same in added as a part of hourly cost. One has to explitiy specify instance store volumes that needs to used during the instance launch, with the exception of NVMe instance store volumes that are available by default, and format and mount them before using them. The instances store volumes create and launch the same, even after launching them. Few instance types which uses use NVMe or SATA based solid state drives (SSD) to deliver very high random I/O performance and this is considered a good choice when users are looking for storage with low latency and in the same time, the data not to be configured for persistence and few of the instance types are

c1.xlarge	4 x 420 GB (1,680 GB)	HDD
c3.large	2 x 16 GB (32 GB)	SSD
c3.xlarge	2 x 40 GB (80 GB)	SSD
c3.2xlarge	2 x 80 GB (160 GB)	S
c1.xlarge	4 x 420 GB (1,680 GB)	HDD
c3.large	2 x 16 GB (32 GB)	SSD

m1.small
1 x 160 GB†
HDD

m1.medium
1 x 410 GB
HDD

Cloud front

http://docs.aws.amazon.com/AmazonCloudFront/latest/Developer
Guide/Introduction.html

Cloud Front is a web service that accelerates up distribution of users static and dynamic web content, in the likes of .html, .css, .php, and image files, to users and content is delivered using the exhaustive network Amazon datacenters termed as edge locations, and AWS has such locations across globe, And in the instance, a user requests for content which you are serving with Cloud front, the traffic is routed Is routed to the edge location which facilitates the lowest latency (time delay), such that contends are delivered with the best possible performance and in case of contents not in the edge, Cloud front retrieves it from an Amazon S3 bucket or an HTTP server (for example, a web server), which could have been identified as the source for the final version

How contents are delivered?

http://docs.aws.amazon.com/AmazonCloudFront/latest/Developer
Guide/HowCloudFrontWorks.html

Cloud Front is a web service which assists in accelerating distribution of static and dynamic web content, such as .html, .css, .php, and image files, to subscribes, delivers users contents content through a worldwide network of data centers which is termed as edge locations. In the event of users requesting content, which passes through cloud front, the request is redirected to the edge location, which offers least possible latency, in such a manner that, content is delivered with the best possible performance When a user requests content that you're serving with Cloud Front, the user is routed to the edge location that provides the lowest latency (time delay), so that. Cloud front serves the image using the a specific URL, one can effortlessly reach the same, and view images, which is done seamlessly, unaware that the process of the request was routed from one network to another—through the complex collection of interconnected networks that comprise the internet—until the image was found, and which gives the user the chance, to navigate the particular URL and view the image, Cloud Front accelerates process of accelerating content distribution, in the manner of routing user's requests to edge locations, which is the best source from where contents can be distributed effectively. Cloud front edge locations, is generally that is considered to offering the lowest latency. This significantly reduces the number of networks that your users' requests that should pass through, which improves performance. Users get lower latency—the time it takes to load the first byte of the file—and higher data transfer rates, also this service helps getting higher reliability and availability because copies of the files, which is also termed as objects are now hosted in multiple edge locations around the globe Users also get increased reliability and availability since e copies of the files (also known as *objects)* are now held in different locations

Amazon Virtual private Cloud VPC

http://docs.aws.amazon.com/AmazonVPC/latest/GettingStarted Guide/ExerciseOverview.html

Virtual private cloud (VPC) is a virtual network that closely mimic a traditional network that an organization deploy in-house, alongside of enjoying the benefits of scalable features of AWS. The starting point, users shall a VPC with IPv4 CIDR block, a subnet with an IPv4 CIDR block, and launch a public-facing instance into selected subnet, and the instance would be operational capable of communicating with internet, besides being able to access internal instances from local desktop using SSH, if Linux is installed or through remote desktop client in case of a desktop in Windows environment and this configuration can be deployed for designing public-facing web server; for example, to host a blog the following steps are to be followed for configuration. Create a non-default VPC with a single public subnet. Subnets helps in consolidating instances, that could be defined by individual security and operational requirements, besides, public subnet is one which has access to the Internet through an Internet gateway. Creating security groups for the instances, this would aid in regulating the traffic only through specific ports, and launch EC2 instances, into the subnet. Associate an Elastic IP address with designated user's instance, through which one can gain instant access to internet

Steps to create a VPC, (technical definition hence no rephrasing possible)

Creates a VPC with a /16 IPv4 CIDR block with 65,536 private IP addresses and attach to an internet gateway to VPC, which Creates a size /24 IPv4 subnet (a range of 256 private IP addresses) in the VPC. Creates a custom route table, and associates it with your subnet, so that traffic can flow between the subnet and the Internet gateway users make use of the Amazon VPC wizard in the Amazon VPC console to create a VPCand the steps are:

Creates a VPC with a /16 IPv4 CIDR block (a network with 65,536 private IP addresses)..

Attaches an Internet gateway to the VPCCreates a size /24 IPv4 subnet (a range of 256 private IP addresses) in the VPC.

Creates a custom route table, and associates it with your subnet, so that traffic can flow between the subnet and the Internet gateway

Process of content delivery 1

http://docs.aws.amazon.com/AmazonCloudFront/latest/Developer Guide/HowCloudFrontWorks.html

Described above is the process that cloud front follows for delivering services and this is what occurs when users requests objects Once you configure Cloud Front to deliver your content, here's what happens when users request your objects:

A user accesses specific website or application and submit requests for one or more objects, such as an image file and an HTML file.

DNS routes the request to the Cloud Front edge location, which is one is perfectly placed to serve the user's request, which often turns out to be the nearest Cloud Front edge location in terms of latency, and routes the request to that edge location.

Once the requests reaches Cloud front, first the cache is checked for requested file, if the file is been located, Cloud Front returns them to the user.

And in the event of the file not being traced, the following is performed

Cloud Front compares the request with the specifications in company's distribution and forwards the request for the files to the applicable origin server for the corresponding file type—for example, to users Amazon S3 bucket for image files and to intranet HTTP server for the HTML files.

The origin servers send the files back to the Cloud Front edge location.

As soon as the first byte arrives from the origin, Cloud Front begins to forward the files to the user. Cloud Front also adds the files to the cache in the edge location for the next time someone requests those files

Virtual private cloud VPC

http://docs.aws.amazon.com/AmazonVPC/latest/UserGuide/VPC_Introduction.html

VPC facilitates launching of AWS resources into private virtual network, which resembles, traditional network that can be seen operating in as in-house datacenter, but added with the full advantages of AWS infrastructure and offering full range of its services, VPC is the networking layer for EC2, and it virtual network dedicated to individual user accounts. It offers logical separation for the resources and operates independently. Users can launch the instances and host the services like EC2 instances. Users can launch AWS resources, such as Amazon EC2 instances, into respective user accounts using VPC. Users have complete control over their instances, can configure VPC; can select its IP address range, create subnets, and configure route tables, network gateways, and security settings. Users can launch any aws services, and can use this for any purposes, like developing application, testing software. One can create multiple subnets, within their contracted limits, also in offer is multiple IP ranges and individual IP addresses, and can create unlimited subnets. For security, one utilize a range of features such as use multiple layers of security, including security groups and network access control lists (ACL).AWS also supports third party security utilities

By launching the instances into a VPC instead of EC2-Classic, users can avail the following benefits

Assign static private IPv4 addresses to your instances that persist across starts and stops

Optionally associate an IPv6 CIDR block to your VPC and assign IPv6 addresses to your instances

Assign multiple IP addresses to your instances

Define network interfaces, and attach one or more network interfaces to your instances

Change security group membership for your instances while they're running

Control the outbound traffic from your instances (egress filtering) in addition to controlling the inbound traffic to them (ingress filtering)

Add an additional layer of access control to your instances in the form of network access control lists (ACL)

Run your instances on single-tenant hardware

Users can control as how the instances that has to be launched into a VPC access resources outside the VPC. And default VPC includes an Internet gateway, and each default subnet is a public subnet. Each instance that is being launched into the default zone. Each instance that you launch into a subnet possesses a private IPv4 address and a public IPv4 address. These instances shall communicate with the Internet using e Internet gateway. An Internet gateway which helps the instances to to connect to the Internet through the Amazon EC2 network edge, and default, By default, each instance that you launch into a no default subnet has a private IPv4 address, but no public IPv4 address, unless you specifically assign one at launch, or you modify the subnet's public IP address attribute. These instances can communicate with each other, but can't access the Internet.

Identity access management

http://docs.aws.amazon.com/IAM/latest/UserGuide/introduction.html

Granular permissions

Administrators are grant different set of permissions to different set of user, to access different set of resources, as a user, you can permit few users full access and full control any of AWS services. And for example, you can selectively grant privileges, ex. read-only access to just some S3 buckets, or permission to administer just some EC2 instances, or to access your billing information but nothing else

secure access to AWS resources for applications which runs on Amazon EC2

IAM can be configured to create a secure environment that can offer secure which run on EC2 instances the credentials that they need in order to access other AWS resources, like S3 buckets and RDS or Dynamo databases.

Multi-factor authentication- MFA

Users can chose to deploy two factor authentication to individual accounts, besides to individual users, for securing the data and applications, this is an additional security feature, Users can add two-factor authentication to the account and to individual users for extra security. During configuration, administrator should configure, access control, access key, password and encryption keys, and code from specially configured has to be provided needs s to be supplied

Identity federation

IAM permits the use of credentials who already have the credetentials, in some other environments, to get a temporary access control to another environment, viz corporate network

PCI DSS Compliant

IAM supports the processing, storage, and transmission of credit card data by a merchant or service provider, and has been validated as being compliant with Payment Card Industry (PCI) Data Security Standard (DSS).

Consistent

IAM achieves high availability by replicating data across multiple servers within Amazon facilities across the world. In the event of request to change some data is successful, the change is committed and safely stored and replication has to happen, across IAM, which can take some time However, the change must be replicated across IAM, which can take some time Which include creating or updating users, groups, roles, or policies and in such case, it is recommended that changes not recommend that you do not include such IAM changes in the critical, high-availability code paths of your application, but is is advisable that changes are carried out, and users in a separate, initialization sequence, users can run less frequently and the success of operation, depends on cross checking, that changes has been propagated before production workflows depend on them, Amazon doesn't charge for IAM, while users will be charged only for use of other AWS products by IAM users. AWS Security Token Service is an included as part if IAM isn't charge Users are charged only for the use of other AWS services that are accessed by your AWS STS temporary security credentials.

Security features outside of IAM

http://docs.aws.amazon.com/IAM/latest/UserGuide/introduction_security-outside-iam.html

One can adopt, IAM to control access to tasks which could be carried out using the AWS Management Console, the AWS Command Line Tools, or service APIs using the AWS SDKs. A few products have some other means secure their resources. Some use cases are listed

Amazon EC2

In Amazon Elastic Compute Cloud you log into an instance with a key pair (for Linux instances) or using a user name and password (for Microsoft Windows instances).

Amazon RDS

In Amazon Relational Database Service you log into the database engine with a user name and password that are tied to that database.

Amazon Workspaces

In Amazon Workspaces, users sign in to a desktop with a user name and password.

Amazon WorkDocs

In Amazon WorkDocs, users get access to shared documents by signing in with a user name and password.

The above access control techniques are not part of IAM. Deploying IAAM, allows users to control the manner the products are administered, like creating or terminating of instances, configuring new Amazon Workspaces desktops, and likewise. That is, IAM helps to control the tasks which are being executed by making requests to Amazon Web Services, and through which, it assists in it helps in controlling access to the AWS Management Console. However, IAM does not offer much assistance, for tasks like signing in to an operating system (Amazon EC2), database (Amazon RDS), desktop (Amazon Workspaces), or collaboration site (Amazon WorkDocs). And in this case it is highly important to read the document related to the security options

OPENSHIFT

https://docs.openshift.com/enterprise/3.0/architecture/index.html

OpenShift v3 is a layered system system which has been architected to designed to expose underlying Docker and Kubernetes concepts in a highly detailed fashion, focusing on simple composition of applications by developers, for example installation of Ruby and push code and MYSql, and as compared to earlier versions.

Layers

Docker offers the abstraction for packaging and creating Linux-based, lightweight containers. Kubernetes supports the cluster management and orchestrates Docker containers on multiple hosts. Open shift adds Source code management, builds, and deployments for developers, Administering and alerting and promoting images to scale as they flow through the system Performs the task of managing application at scale besides Has provisions for configuring and tracking for an organization, that employees large number of developers. Open Shift has been designed to be powered by a micro services–based architecture of smaller, decoupled units that work together; it can be made to run on top or alongside Kuberbets clusters, containing information about objects stored inetcd, a reliable clustered key-value store. Those services are broken down by function. It is capable of running on top or alongside, Kubernets clusters, which contains data about the objects stored inetcd, a reliable clustered key-value store. Those services are broken down by function:

- REST APIs, which expose each of the core objects.
- Controllers, which read those APIs, apply changes to other objects, and report status or write back to the object.

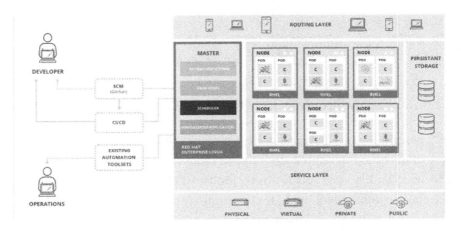

OpenShift Architecture Overview 1

Controllers can initiate calls to the REST API in order to alter the state of the system. Controllers give orders to invoke the REST API to read the user's desired state, and attempt to bring the other parts of the system into sync. To cite, a situation, when a user requests a build they create a "build" object. The build controller recognizes that a new build has been created, and runs a process on the cluster to perform that build. When the build has been completed the controller updates the build object, again invoking relevant the REST API and the gets to view the status, which in all probability indicates completion user sees that their build is complete. The controller pattern means that much of the functionality in Open Shift is extensible. The manner the builds are run and launched can be customized independently of how images are managed, or how deployments happen. In reality, controllers are controllers are performing the "business logic" of the system, taking user actions and transforming them into reality Open shift, by the way of customization, provides a chance to The running controllers to be replaced with own users logic By customizing those controllers or replacing them with your own logic, different behaviors can be implemented. And from administrative stand point, from a system administration perspective, this also means the API can be deployed to script common administrative actions on a repeating schedule. OpenShift makes the ability to customize the cluster in this way a first-class behavior..

https://docs.openshift.com/enterprise/3.0/architecture/infrastructure_components/kubernetes_infrastructure.html

Master components

API server- The function of The Kubernetes API server is to validate, configure the data pods, services, replication controllers, besides assigning pods to nodes and synchronizes pod information with service configuration

etcd – servers as storage area for persisting master data components watch etcd for any changes and bring back to the desired state, this component can be configured for high availability, typically deployed with 2n+1 peer services.

The controller manager server monitors s etcd for changes to replication controller objects and then deploys s the API to enforce the desired state.

Pacemaker –

Forms the core technology of the High Availability Add-on for Red Hat Enterprise Linux, Facilitating g consensus, fencing, and service management which shall be executed on all master hosts to make sure, that all active-passive components have at least one instance running, and can be executed on all master hosts to ensure that all active-passive components have one instance running.

Virtual IP

API server- The function of The Kubernetes API server is to validate, configure the data pods, services, replication controllers, besides assigning pods to nodes and synchronizes pod information with service configuration

etcd – servers as storage area for persisting master data components watch etcd for any changes and bring back to the desired state, this component can be configured for high availability, typically deployed with 2n+1 peer services.

The controller manager server monitors s etcd for changes to replication controller objects and then deploys s the API to enforce the desired state.

Pacemaker

Pacemaker is the core technology of the High Availability Add-on for Red Hat Enterprise Linux, Facilitating g consensus, fencing, and service management amd can be executed on all master hosts to ensure that all active-passive components have one instance running. It can be run on all master hosts to ensure that all active-passive components have one instance running.

Virtual IP

It is Optional to be adopted, used when configuring highly-available masters.

The virtual IP (VIP) is the single point of contact, but not a single point of failure, for all OpenShift clients that:

- cannot be configured with all master service endpoints, or
- Un-aware how to neither load balance across multiple masters nor retry failed master service connections.

There is one VIP and it is managed by Pacemaker

Highly Available Masters

While in a single master configuration, the availability of running applications remains if the master or any of its services fail., failure of master services reduces the ability of the system to respond to application failures or creation of new applications. You can optionally configure your masters for high availability to ensure that the cluster has no single point of failure. In a single master configuration, availability of applications, persists, even the master of any services fail, but in case of failure to the master services, impacts the functionality of system to respond to application failures or creation of new applications, administrators has the privileges to create configurations for ensuring high availability for clusters to ensure availability

Image registry

https://docs.openshift.com/enterprise/3.0/architecture/infrastructure_components/image_registry.html

OpenShift can make use of any running server that has implemented the Docker registry API as a source of images, including the canonical Docker Hub, private registries run by third parties, and the integrated OpenShift registry. Open Shift presents an integrated Docker registry that enhances the capability to provision new image repositories on the fly, which gives users, by default reserve a slot for deploying the builds to push the resulting images, simultaneously letting users to automatically have a designated location, for builds to push the final images. In the event of new image being pushed into the integrated registry, it sends a notification to, the registry notifying OpenShift about the new image, sending all information, about it, which migh include namespace, name, and image metadata Different pieces of OpenShift react to new images, creating new builds and deployments.

Integrated registry

This platform offers an integrated Docker registry which enhances s the ability to provision new image repositories on the fly, simultaneously giving permissions, besides permitting users by default, create storage configurations for their builds to push the final images. In the event of a new image gets pushed to the integrated registry, the registry in turn notifies OpenShift about new image pushed to integrated registry, after simultaneously passing all information about the transaction, and image metadata. Different pieces of OpenShift react to new images, creating new builds and deployments. OpenShift is capable of can communicating with registries in order to to access private image repositories with the use of credentials provided by the use, which gives Open shift the liberty to push and pull images to and from private repositories

Image registry

https://docs.openshift.com/enterprise/3.0/architecture/infrastructure_components/image_registry.html

OpenShift can utilize any server implementing the Docker registry API as a source of images, including the canonical Docker Hub, private registries run by third parties, and the integrated OpenShift registry. OpenShift can utilize any server implementing the Docker registry API as a source of images, including the canonical Docker Hub, private registries run by third parties, and the integrated OpenShift registry, offers an integrated Docke registry that possess ability to provision new image repository on fly. Comes with built in capabilities to capabilities that permits for provisioning images on fly. Which permits users register a location for their builds which permits users by default? have location for the builds and deployments

Authentication

OpenShift has capabilities through it can communicate with registries to access private image repositories using credentials supplied by the user which means, . OpenShift is capable to push and pull images to and from private repositories.

Containers and images

https://docs.openshift.com/enterprise/3.0/architecture/core_concepts/containers_and_images.html

Containers can be described as the basic unit of open shift application. The basic units of OpenShift applications are termed as containers Generally, Linux container technologies are acknowledged as lightweight mechanisms for isolating running processes, meaning that they will have restrictive interactions only with their designated sources. This platform supports executing Multiple application instances can be running in containers on a single host with complete transparency Ideally, each container is designed o host single service (also called a "micro-service"), such as a web server or a database, though containers can be used for arbitrary workloads. By default, The Linux kernel has been incorporating capabilities for container technologies for long and that is the strength of Linux. The management interface is simple to use, company has developed More recently the Docker project has developed a easy-to-use interface for Linux containers on a host. OpenShift and Kubernetes add the ability to orchestrate Docker containers across multi-host installations

Docker Images

Docker containers are based on Docker images. A Docker image is a binary that has in it all of the requirements for running a single Docker container, besides metadata describing its needs and capabilities and is akin to packing technology. Docker containers have access to resources to which they have been defined in the image, unless users are assigned addional accessprovileges, during the creation. By deploying the same image in multiple containers across multiple hosts and load balancing between them, OpenShift can provide redundancy and horizontal scaling for a service packaged into an image. Docker can be deployed directly to build images, image builders can utilize the images, which can be directly injected, however, Open shift also provides builders capabilities, than can be helpful in creating an image, by including users code or configurations, into existing images, As applications evolve over time, it is recommended to create and continue to represent different versions of the same image.

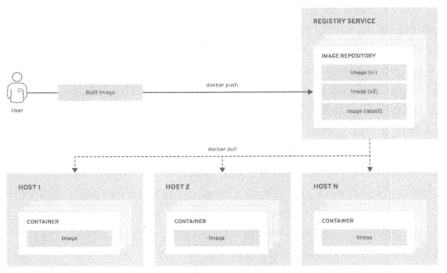

Relationship between containers, images 1

Each different image is rare tagged with unique name, associating with a hash sequence. Which is lengthy, and contains combination of hexadecimal s and typically 12 characters in length, and another format which is followed as applying tags viz v1, v2.1, GA, replacing version numbers? Registry can be defined as master collection, where one or multiple images are stored; it is simply a repository for Images. Besides, each image repository contains one or more tagged images Docker have its own registry – Docker Hub. Docker can also work with environment, where third party registries are registered. Red Hat provides a Docker registry at registry.access.redhat.com for subscribers. OpenShift can also supply its own internal registry for managing custom Docker images.

Labels

https://docs.openshift.com/enterprise/3.0/architecture/core_concepts/pods_and_services.html

Labels are deployed to organize, group, or select API objects. Instance, pods are "tagged" with labels, and then services use label selectors to identify the pods they proxy, which enables services to reference groups of pods, also treating pods with potentially different Docker containers as related entities. Majority of objects shall include labels in their metadata, such that, it can be deployed for grouping group arbitrarily-related objects.

Services

Kubernetes can also double up as internal load balance, that it identifies a set of replicated pods in order to proxy the connections it receives to them. Backing pods can be added to or removed from a service arbitrarily while the service remains consistently available, allowing anything which t depends on the service to refer to it at a consistent internal address. Services are assigned an IP address and port pair which, when accessed, proxy to an appropriate backing pod, besides a service uses a label selector to find all the containers running that provide a certain network service on a certain port. Labels are created to organize, group, or select API objects. For instance, pods are "tagged" with labels, and then services use label selectors for purpose of identifying if they are proxies, which makes it simpler for services to reference groups of pods, even treating pods with potentially different Docker containers as related entities. Most objects can include labels in their metadata, such that labels can be configured to group arbitrarily-related objects; and th example all of the pods, services, replication controllers, and deployment configurations of a particular application can be grouped.

https://docs.openshift.com/enterprise/3.0/architecture/core_concepts/deployments.html

Replication controllers

Role of the replication controller is to make sure,at any point of time, a certain number of pods are running always and accenttally if those are deleted, the replica controller takes up the task automatically, similarly if there are extra pods running, controller deletes the excess to match the number,
The definition of a replication controller consists mainly of:

1. The counter of replicas desired (which can be adjusted at runtime).
2. A pod definition for creating a replicated pod.
3. A selector for identifying managed pods.

Deployment and deployment configurations

Sectors represent a collection of labels that all of the pods which are being administered by the replication controller should have, hence that specific set of labels are joined to the pods such that, that set of labels is included in the pod definition that the replication controller instantiates This selector is used by the replication controller to determine how many instances of the pod are already running in order to adjust as needed. The function of auto-scaling and load balancing does not come under the ambit of replication controller, which is primarily based on load or traffic since the it isn't the part of replication controllers job to imitate auto scaling Replication controllers are a core Kubernetes object, Replication Controller. The Kubernetes documentation has more details on replication controllers.

Building on replication controllers, OpenShift adds expanded support for the software development and deployment lifecycle with the concept of deployments In the process of building replication controllers, OpenShift adds expanded support for the software development and deployment lifecycle with the concept of deployments and most simple scenario is creation and replication of new controllers and allows it to initiate pods. OpenShift deployments exhibits the ability offers transition from an existing deployment of an image to a new one and also define hooks to be run before or after creating the replication controller. The OpenShift Deployment Configuration object defines the following details of a deployment:

1. The elements of a Replication Controller definition.
2. Triggers for creating a new deployment automatically.
3. The strategy for transitioning between deployments.
4. Life cycle hooks.

In the event of deployment is triggered, either manual or automatic, deployed pod manages the deployment (including scaling down the old replication controller, scaling up the new one, and running hooks). Each time a deployment is triggered, whether manually or automatically, a deployed pod manages the deployment (including scaling down the old replication controller, scaling up the new one, and running hooks). Pods remain active for indefinite period of time, even though it has successfully completed the task which is designed to retain its logs of the deployment the deployment pod remains for an indefinite amount of time after it completes the deployment in order to retain its logs of the deployment. Where a deployment is superseded by another, the previous replication controller is retained to enable easy rollback if needed.

Deployments and Deployment Configurations

By Building on replication controllers, OpenShift adds expanded support for the software development and deployment lifecycle with the concept of deployments creates a new replication controller and lets it start up pods, besides supporting the ability to transition from an existing deployment of an image to a new one and also define hooks to be run before or after creating the replication controller and OpenShift Deployment Configuration object defines the following details of a deployment:

1. The elements of a Replication Controller definition.
2. Triggers for creating a new deployment automatically.
3. The strategy for transitioning between deployments.
4. Life cycle hooks.

In an event of deployment being triggered, either manually or automatically a deployer pod manages the deployment which doesn't scaling down the old replication controller, scaling up the new one, and running hooks), besides, deployment pod is retained for indefinite period of time well the deployment is over, so as to retain logs of deployment.

<u>Templates</u>

In an event of deployment being triggered, either manually or automatically a deployer pod manages the deployment which doesn't scaling down the old replication controller, scaling up the new one, and running hooks), besides, deployment pod is retained for indefinite period of time well the deployment is over, so as to retain logs of deployment.

Networking

https://docs.openshift.com/enterprise/3.0/architecture/additional concepts/networking.html

Kubernetes guarantees that pods are able to network with each other, and allocates each pod an IP address from an internal network. Which ensures, all containers within the pod behave as they on the same host? Assigning g each pod its own IP address means that pods can be treated like physical hosts or virtual machines in terms of port allocation, networking, naming, service discovery, load balancing, application configuration, and migration and it is not needed to create links between pods, but is recommended to have a pod have a pod communicating directly using IP.but to create a service that in turn communicates within services. If the environment hosts multiple services like frontend and backend services for use with multiple pods, in order for the frontend pods to communicate with the backend services, environment variables are created for user names, service IP, and more And in case of service deletion, new IP address can be created and d assigned to service which requires the frontend pods to be recreated in for the purpose of picking up the updated values for the service IP environment variable. Besides it is necessary that the backend service has to be created before any of the frontend pods to ensure that the service IP is generated correctly and the same can be offered to the frontend pods as an environment variable. Precisely for this reason, OpenShift is delivered with a built-in DNS helping services to so that the services can be reached by the service DNS as well as the service IP/port. OpenShift supports split DNS and by executing SkyDNS on the master that answers DNS queries for services. The master listens to port 53 by default.

Persistent storage

https://docs.openshift.com/container-platform/3.5/architecture/additional_concepts/storage.html

Managing storage is different from managing compute, needs specific knowledge, container platform utilizes Kubernetes persistent volume (PV) framework to let administrators provision persistent storage for a cluster. By deploying adopting persistent volume claims (PVCs), developers can create request for PV resources even having to understand details of underlying storage infrastructure. VCs are project specific which are created to use of developers as a method to use PV. PV resources aren't tagged to any single project instead they can be shared across entire OpenShift container platform cluster and claimed from any project. Once PV has been bounded to a PVCu it is impossible to be binded be bound to additional PVCs. This has the effect of scoping a bound PV to a single namespace (that of the binding project). PVs are described as Persistent Volume API object, which h represents a piece of existing networked storage in the cluster which can be provisioned by the administrator and it is yet another resource in the cluster. PVs are volume plug-ins like Volumes however posses a lifecycle independent of any individual pod which utilizes s the PV. PV objects capture the details of the implementation of the storage, be that NFS, iscsi, or a cloud-provider-specific storage system. PVCs are defined by a PersistentVolumeClaim API object, which represents a request for storage by a developer It is similar to a pod in that pods consume node resources and PVCs consume PV resources. pods can request specific levels of resources (e.g., CPU and memory), while PVCs can request specific storage capacity and access modes (e.g, they can be mounted once read/write or many times read-only).

https://docs.openshift.com/container-platform/3.5/architecture/core_concepts/containers_and_images.html#containers

Containers

Fundamental units OpenShift Container Platform applications are termed as containers, which are utilized for isolating, a running process, that limits interaction, between designated resources. Typically, applications instances are executed, which are capable of being executed on containers on a single host without, while cutting off visibility into each others' processes, files, and networks. Typically, each container delivers, single service, also referred as micro-service, viz web server or database, with liberty of containers being used hosting arbitrary workloads. For long, Linux kernels are being incorporated, as part of container capabilities. It also comes with, user-friendly management interface for Linux containers on a host. OpenShift Container Platform and Kubernetes add necessary capabilities, to orchestrate Dockers-formatted containers across multi-host installations. Though user's, don't interact with Dockers CLI or service, while utilizing, OpenShift Container Platform, understand its features, terminology is important to get acquainted with, their roles in OpenShift Container Platform, methods of how applications function within containers. Docker RPM's are delivered along with, RHEL 7, Centos, Fedora, enabling users to experiment, independently from OpenShift Container Platform.

Init Containers

Init containers are simply, Technology Preview feature, which aren't supported within RH production service level agreements (SLAs),which may not be completed of its full functionality, which RH recommends to be utilize in production. Such features facilitate, early access to features, which permits, users to test functionalities, simultaneously, offering feedback, during development. Individual pods, has capabilities to host init containers in addition to application containers .Containers, permits users to reorganize, deploy scripts, binding codes. nit containers are different from regular ones, where init, perennially runs to complete, it is necessary, that adminstratoror's, must ensure successful completion of init containers, before subsequent is initiated. Images Containers in OpenShift Container Platform are based on Docker-formatted container images. Images, are binary, which incorporates all pre-requisites, needed for executing unitary container, besides metadata, which describes its requirements, capabilities. Technically, images can be considered packaging technology. Containers are permitted to access resources that has been defined in the image, unless, explicit permissions are granted to containers when it is created. By deploying, same image in multiple containers across multiple hosts, load balancing between them, OpenShift offers the needed redundancy, horizontal scaling for service packaged into an image. It is recommended, to utilize Dockers CLI directly, for purpose of building images, however, OpenShift Container Platform also providers developers, builder images, which helps in creation of fresh images, by including customized codes, configuration to existing images. As, application development life-cycle spans, periods, a single image name, can practically refer to multiple versions of the "same" image. And for the same above mentioned reason, a single image name can actually refer to many different versions of the "same" image .Different images, are identified by unique hash, which is long hexadecimal number, which generally shortened to 12 characteristics. Container Registries container registry is a service, designed for storage, retrieval of Dockers-formatted container images. Registry contains are treated as collection of single or multiple image repositories .Individual image repository contains one or more tagged images. Dockers offer, proprietary registry, Dockers Hub. OpenShift permits, use of private or third-party registries. RH offers registry at registry access. By deploying, similar image in multiple containers across multiple hosts and load balancing between them, OpenShift Container Platform, delivers redundancy, horizontal scaling for services that are packaged into images. CLI, GUIs are facilities provided, for building images. OpenShift Container Platform too, offers builder images, which accelerates process of creating fresh images, by adding user's code, configuration to existing images, and since applications evolve over time, single image name, can be co-related to multiple versions, of existing image. Individual images, are identified with, its hash, typically along hexadecimal number. Containers in OpenShift Container Platform, is based on Docker-formatted container images. An image is a binary, which contains all necessary requirements for operating, an unitary containers, besides metadata describing its needs, capabilities which are needed for executing unitary container, and also, metadata,which explains requirements, capabilities, has to be treated as, packaging technology. Core property of container, is that it has access to resources, enlisted in image, and by configuring resource access which has been defined within image, unless one explicitly grants access, during creation.

By deploying, similar image in multiple containers across multiple hosts and load balancing between them, OpenShift Container Platform, delivers redundancy, horizontal scaling for services that are packaged into images. CLI, GUIs are facilities provided, for building images. OpenShift Container Platform too, offers builder images, which accelerates process of creating fresh images, by adding user's code, configuration to existing images, and since applications evolve over time, single image name, can be co-related to multiple versions, of existing image. Individual images, are identified with, its hash, typically along hexadecimal number. Containers in OpenShift Container Platform, is based on Docker-formatted container images. An image is a binary, which contains all necessary requirements for operating, an unitary containers, besides metadata describing its needs, capabilities which are needed for executing unitary container, and also, metadata, which explains requirements, capabilities, has to be treated as, packaging technology. Core property of container, is that it has access to resources, enlisted in image, and by configuring resource access which has been defined within image, unless one explicit grants access, during creation. . By deploying, similar image in multiple containers across multiple hosts and load balancing between them, OpenShift Container Platform, delivers redundancy, horizontal scaling for services that are packaged into images. CLI, GUIs are facilities provided, for building images.

OpenShift Container Platform too, offers builder images, which accelerates process of creating fresh images, by adding user's code, configuration to existing images, and since applications evolve over time, single image name, can be co-related to multiple versions, of existing image. Individual images, are identified with, its hash, typically along hexadecimal number.

https://docs.openshift.com/container-platform/3.5/architecture/additional_concepts/scm.html

This platform utilizes the benefits of already existing system SCM which is existence o source control management (SCM) systems hosted either internally (such as an in-house Git server) or externally, recently released versions offer support to supports Git solutions

- SCM integration is tightly coupled with builds, the two points are
- Creating a BuildConfig using a repository, that permits s building the application inside of OpenShift Container Platform.
- Users can create a BuildConfig manually u or permit or let OpenShift Container Platform create it automatically by inspecting your repository.
- Triggering a build upon repository changes

www.ingramcontent.com/pod-product-compliance
Lightning Source LLC
Chambersburg PA
CBHW051224050326
40689CB00007B/796